Dedication

To my daughter, Lesley,
and my son, Glenn.
Vilma Barr

To my wife, Judy,
and my sons, Josh and Matt,
and to my loyal clients.
Charles E. Broudy

Library of Congress Cataloging in Publication Data

Barr, Vilma.
  Designing to Sell, A Complete Guide to Retail
  Store Planning and Design / Vilma Barr and Charles E. Broudy.
  – 2nd ed.
      p.   cm.
  Includes biographical references and index.
  ISBN 0-07-003888-0
  1. Stores. Retail – Planning. Stores. Retail – Design and
  Construction.
  I. Broudy, Charles E. II. Title.

HF5429.B318   1990
725'.21–dc 20
                              90-13293
                                 CIP

For information about our audio products, write us at:
Newbridge Book Clubs, 3000 Cindel Drive, Delran, NJ 08370

Copyright ©1990 by McGraw-Hill, Inc. All rights reserved. Printed in the United States of America. Except as permitted under the United States Copyright Act of 1976, no part of this publication may be reproduced or distributed in any form or by any means, or stored in a data base of retrieval sytem, without the prior written permission of the publisher.

1234567890   FGR/FGR   9543210

ISBN 0-07-003888-0

The editor for this book was Joel Stein, and the design was by Two Twelve Associates, Inc. New York City, David Gibson, project manager, and Terrie Dunkelberger and Julie Marable, project designers. Production supervision was by Business/Professional Editorial Services, Inc. The book was set in New Baskerville and Univers. It was created electronically by Two Twelve Associates using PageMaker® 3.2 on the Apple® Macintosh.™

Printed and bound by Arcata Graphics Company.

For more information about other McGraw-Hill materials, call 1-800-2-MCGRAW in the United States. In other countries, call your nearest McGraw-Hill office.

Previous page and cover:
Episode, San Francisco (Charles E. Broudy & Associates)

Designing to Sell

A Complete Guide to Retail Store Planning and Design

Second Edition

Vilma Barr
Charles E. Broudy, FAIA

McGraw-Hill, Inc.

New York	Lisbon	Paris
St. Louis	London	San Juan
San Francisco	Madrid	São Paulo
Aukland	Mexico City	Singapore
Bogotá	Milan	Sydney
Caracas	Montreal	Tokyo
Hamburg	New Delhi	Toronto
	Oklahoma City	

Acknowledgments

The authors want to express their appreciation to the many individuals and organizations who have helped us to produce the Second Edition of *Designing to Sell*: the design firms and merchandising organizations that contributed data and project illustrations; the staff members of Charles E. Broudy & Associates, and Alexandra Hershdorfer of Business/Professional Editorial Services, for their text support and editorial assistance; Irwin Bernstein, of Drum Communications, for invaluable production coordination; Terrie Dunkelberger, the book's gifted designer, and David Gibson, who created the book's special format, both of Two Twelve Associates; and to Joel Stein, senior editor of Architecture and Civil Engineering books for McGraw-Hill, Inc., for his encouragement and continued support.

Vilma Barr and
Charles E. Broudy, FAIA

Contents

	Acknowledgments	iv
	Introduction	vi
Chapter 1	How to Develop A Program	1
Chapter 2	Shaping the Store's Interior	9
Chapter 3	Basic Store Layouts	23
Chapter 4	Exterior Store Design	37
Chapter 5	Colors, Materials and Finishes	51
Chapter 6	Lighting	65
Chapter 7	Signs and Graphics	81
Chapter 8	Displaying Merchandise	95
Chapter 9	Systems	107
	HVAC Systems and Their Application, *by Ken Meline, PE*	108
	Support Systems	112
	Security Systems	116
Chapter 10	Construction	119
	Legal Considerations for Retail Store Design: Roles, Responsibilities, and Procedures *by Charles R. Heuer, Esq., AIA*	129
Chapter 11	Shopping Centers and Malls	139
Chapter 12	Trends in Merchandising Facilities	155
Chapter 13	The Future of Retailing	171
	Gap Stores Amplify the Merchandising Message *by Millard S. Drexler, The Gap, Inc.*	172
	The Winners and the Losers, *by Harris Gordon, Deloitte & Touche*	174
	Sheppard Line Subway To Be Glitzy Malls *by Christopher Hume, The Toronto Star*	176
	Bergdorf's Magic Formula Crosses Fifth Avenue *by Ira Neimark, Bergdorf Goodman*	177
	Pea In the Pod Pampers Customers With Style, *by Dana and Marcello Rosen, Pea in the Pod*	178
	Revlon Breaks the 25-Inch Barrier *by Hernando Sanchez, Revlon, Inc.*	180
	The Keeper of the Image *by Cynthia Cohen Turk, MARKETPLACE 2000*	182
	The Rouse Company: dimensions in Competitive Positioning *by Larry Wolf and Susan Haight, The Rouse Company*	184
Chapter 14	Retail Graphic Standards	185
	Photo Credits	193
	Bibliography	195
	Glossary	196
	Index	199
	About The Authors	202

Introduction

In the five years between the publication of the First Edition of *Designing to Sell*, and this Second Edition, the retailing industry has undergone enormous changes. As Ira Neimark, chairman and CEO of Bergdorf Goodman, said in an interview for this book in early 1990, "There have been more changes in retailing over the past 18 months than have occurred over the past 40 years."

Specialty stores have replaced department stores as the industry's pacesetters. Retailing has become a global enterprise; foreign ownerships of U.S. stores has been balanced by U.S. retailing organizations expanding overseas, often with a local joint venture partner. Manufacturers want control over channels of distribution to the customer, and are opening chain units in suburban malls as well as downtown areas. Renovation of shopping centers and malls has replaced new construction as the number of choice sites availble for development shrinks. Traditional retailers have formidable competition from strong new retail contenders: megamalls, megastores, off-price centers, discount centers, and others.

Industry leaders agree that the design of a store and its merchandise presentation is more important than ever before. Merchants are keenly aware of image; they pay more attention now to shaping their store's presention in the media and creating a unique shopping environment as part of the overall differentiation strategy. Closely coordinated are advertising, graphics–from shopping bags to bus enclosures, direct mail, the store front, windows, and the ambience of the store itself. Merchandisers are betting heavily on clearly communicating their point-of-view to their target market to capture, retain, and grow their market share.

We have observed an overall increase in the number of design professionals producing solid, innovative retail projects, and we have included examples of what we consider some of the best recent work from the U.S. and overseas. Nearly all of the more than 100 photos in this edition are new, and reflect the fresh thinking and imaginative handling of space integrated with merchandising philosophy. We have expanded the "Shopping Centers and Malls" chapter, and have added two new chapters, "New Trends in Retailing," and "Retail Graphic Standards." This edition also includes color text pages.

Producers and retailers have placed customer shopping and buying patterns high on their research agendas: they are listening to, watching, and analyzing where consumers shop, where they do not shop, what they buy, and what and why they do not buy. Retailers are following consumers into the Toronto subways and Chicago's Merchandise Mart with plans for shops, dining, and entertainment complexes.

Retailing is the focus of our market-driven economy. Store design in this decade will reflect the verve and creativity of this dynamic industry.

Vilma Barr

Charles E. Broudy, FAIA

How To Develop A Program

1

A program is a useful and necessary tool. It is used to define the needs of the client, the constraints around which the design will be developed, and the budget to make the design feasible. It can be as simple as a one-page checklist or as complex as a multiple-page document of questions and answers, depending on the scope of the project. The program becomes a reference for the designer and the client throughout the design process.

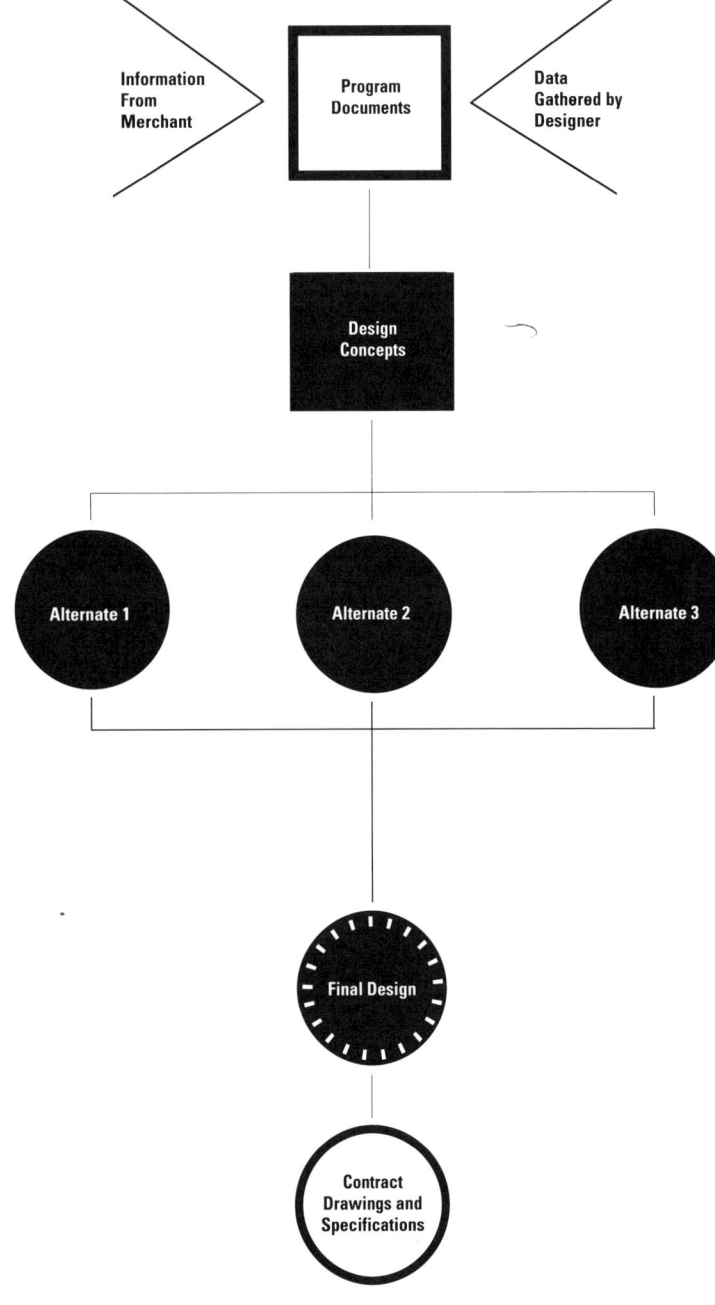

It is the designer's job to ask the relevant questions that provide the data base for the design development phase.

Gather the client's merchandising thoughts, for these translate into the program's backbone. The program is the basis for verbal communication throughout the project.

1 How To Develop A Program

Pre-programming Menu

As design professionals develop the program and later the plan for a retail store, they play three roles: to create as a designer; to think as a merchant; and to act as a customer. The designer's proposed solutions can be evaluated in relationship to these basic merchandising concepts.

What brings the customer into the store?
Quality

Need

Value

Price

Impulse

What attracts the customer to enter the store?
Architectural design

Window design

Signage

The store interior

The store's "image"

How do customers perceive the store environment?
Relationship to the exterior

Need to "feel" the store is:
- not menacing
- not confusing
- not threatening
- comfortable with the design
- friendly

A place to explore

What moves customers through the store?
Destination point within the store

Floor plan (the store's layout)

Signage

Displays

Environmental factors
- lighting
- sound

What motivates customers To buy?
Perceived value

Design

Price

Ambience

Merchandise presentation

How can the selling environment reinforce the visual image of the merchandise?
The right background
- lighting
- colors
- materials

The right format
- Create settings that emulate the actual end use, for hard or soft goods
- Give merchandise "a point of view" that is in context with the overall design mood

What are the responsibilities of the store architect?
Orchestrates the project, from programming to final punch list

What does the store architect have to consider during the project?
Corporate culture

Image

The merchandise

Budgets

Codes

Schedules

The objectives of store design
The recognition factor: A store needs to stand out, regardless of its size—large or small.

Strategic differentiation
- To counter sameness of merchandise
- To give the store a recognizable personality

Program Checklist

Program Data

Project Name

Location

Size

Number of floors

Questions	Basic Project Information	Descriptions and Comments

1 Overall considerations

Exterior Environment

What is the nature of the surrounding neighborhood? Define the adjacent commercial area: shopping center or block; strip or freestanding stores.

How will existing colors, textures, architectural styles, and graphics affect the store's design?

Is traffic primarily vehicular or pedestrian?

Other

Characteristics of the Merchandise

What will be sold in the store?

Clothing: men's, women's, children's

Accessories: belts, scarves, hats, hosiery, jewelry

Shoes

Home furnishings: furniture, carpeting, lamps and lighting, wall decor

Other

What will be the range of styles?

Basic, classic

Trendy, promotional

Seasonal

Impulse, or big ticket

Full markup or discount

Other

How To Develop A Program

	Question	Basic Project Information	Descriptions and Comments
	What is the merchandise breakdown?		
	Percent each will account for total sales		
	Sales per square foot for each category		
	Stock turns per year		
	Other		
Customer Profile	Age		
	Geographical distribution		
	Income level		
	Size range		
	Other		
2	**Characteristics of the store**		
Type of Service	Full service		
	Self-service		
	Combination		
Plan of Space	Linear		
	Open		
	Enclosed		
	Random		
	U-shape		
	Other		
Siting Considerations	Proximity of merchandise to front, perimeter, or rear of store		
	Location of cash wrap to merchandise		
	How merchandise will be viewed by customers		
	Other		

4

Question	Basic Project Information	Descriptions and Comments

3 Merchandising

Quantity	Number of	Styles	Colors
Seasonal Considerations	Weather		
	Holidays		
	Calendar considerations (back-to-school, cruisewear, etc.)		
Item Pricing	Hang tags		
	Stickers		
Sign Considerations	Type needed for floor and counter use		
	Use of name brands as an important attraction		
	Other		

4 Merchandising specifics

Wall displays, accessible by sales personnel	
Wall displays, above 80 inches	
Island displays	
Secure displays, under glass	
Manufacturers' displays	
Other	

5 Stock

Concealed in floor displays	
Stored in drawers or behind doors	
Stockroom and backup areas	
Remote storage	
Other	

1 How To Develop A Program

Six Basic Planning Diagrams

After completion of the Program Checklist, the designer then begins to visualize options for the store's concept.

Each of the six basic planning diagrams shown here is an early schematic which illustrates categories of information that have to be considered as part of the programming process.

They are sketchy, conceptual visual tools.

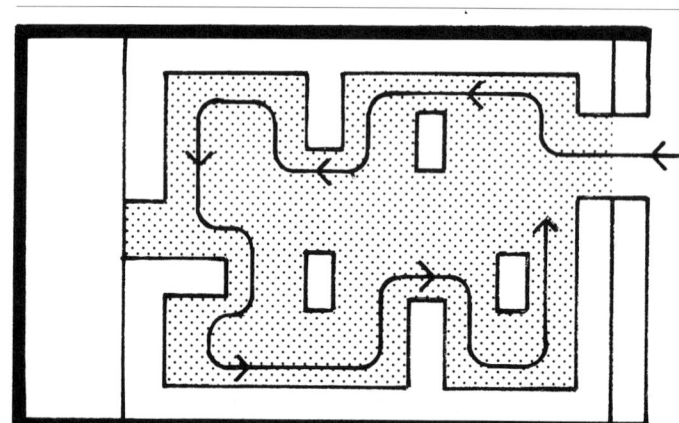

Interior Traffic Flow Characteristics
Traffic flow is based on the psychology of shoppers' movements inside a store and the pathways they follow to the various sections. The most common patterns are:
- entrance to exit
- front to back
- side to side
- diagonal

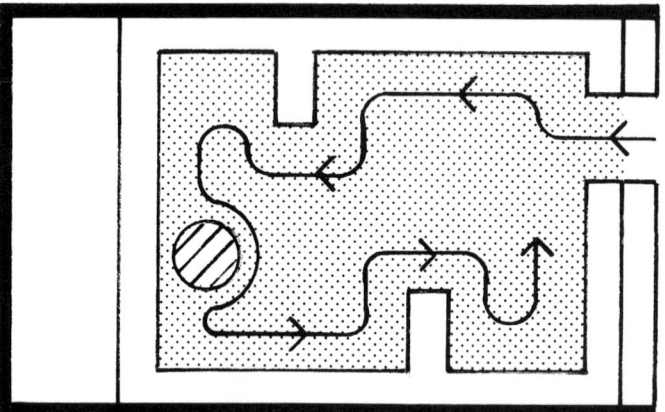

Merchandise Siting
Customers respond to placement or location of products within the store. Shoppers gravitate toward staple items, and most merchants place them at the rear of the store. This technique will draw the traffic from the front to the back of the store, exposing them to additional merchandise and displays and increasing impulse purchasing.

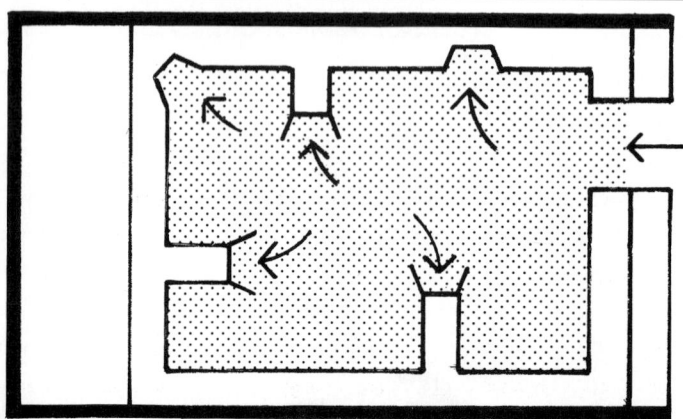

Visual Display
High-impact displays draw in-store traffic to merchandise sections of the sales floor. Displays can be free-standing, or ceiling or wall mounted. They can be composed of mannequins, props, massed arrangements of merchandise, or electronic displays, used singly or in combination.

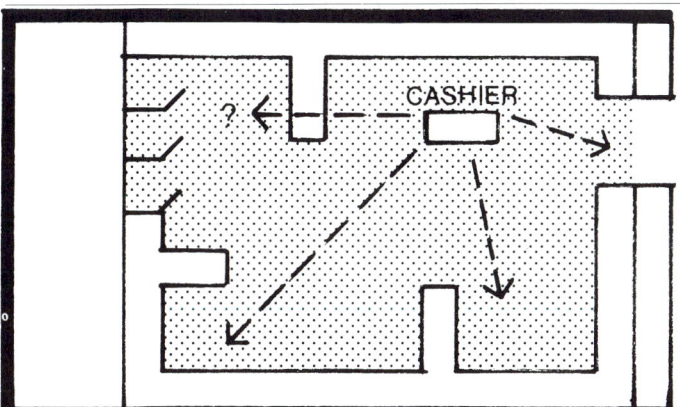

Security
Visual surveillance of the sales floor from a central point plays an important part in the store owner's theft-deterring program. Remember to allow for mirrors or cameras to compensate for tall displays or partitions. Electronic article surveillance (EAS) systems require electronic pedestals, usually at store exits.

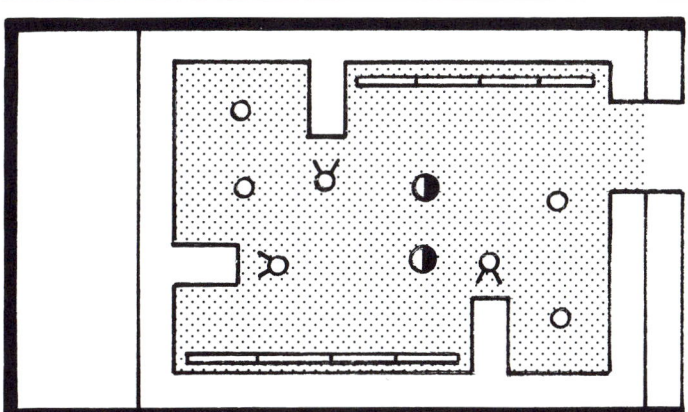

Lighting
The quality of the lighting can make or break both the store's design and merchandise presentation. Many retailers consider lighting to be the most important decorative tool at their disposal. Since lighting represents a major operating expense, it should be flattering to merchandise and customers and value-engineered (most efficient to operate over the life of the fixture).

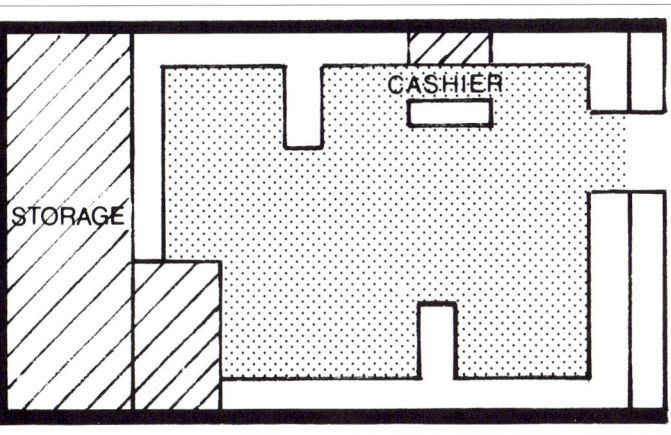

Storage, receiving, back-of-the-house requirements
These support space requirements include: how merchandise is received from vendors and sent to customers; how merchandise is brought into the department; how much stock will be on the selling floor and how much will be concealed; staff functions; and operations and building functions.

Other considerations

Electronic:
- Computerized record and stock-keeping equipment
- Cash registers
- Charge account equipment

Local codes:
- Sprinkler system
- Fireproof materials
- Watts/square foot requirements or other energy usage limitations

Time frame:
- Opening date
- Building code and other agency approvals
- Advance ordering of equipment and supplies.

1 How To Develop A Program

Developing and Guiding the Scheme
Designing a retail store is like creating a stage set. Shopping is an experience in which people act out their innermost hopes, dreams, aspirations, and desires. A shopping excursion can be a personal minidrama for customers; their imaginations are going full tilt while they are in the store, visualizing how attractive they will be in a new skirt, how a new chair will look in the living room, or how much a gift will be appreciated.

Store design combines as much fantasy as economics.

- **"Pie-in-the-sky" solutions are possible.** There are no absolutes in retailing.

- **Present unusual, imaginative design ideas.** Take a gamble and show the retail client a brand new concept.

Presenting design options
Taste, timing, and razor-sharp judgment produce successful retail store design.
    Create multiple alternative drawings, each well-founded in concept. Each alternative should address the fundamentals, the subjects of the program's queries.

Present three to five schematic alternatives to the client, and ask for reactions. Here is what you might expect:

- The client will challenge you to defend your design. You will be asked to explain your theory and concepts on the various proposed solutions, referencing the program topics.

- As you explain your schemes, adjust your position and understanding of the problems, and the client will do the same. This is an exercise in mental attitude, not a contest of will or ego.

- Practice "active listening" by restating the client's comments. Use phrases like "What I think I heard you say was"... and "Let me summarize what you said about"...

- Clients want to feel that they are getting valuable business judgment from you, as well as creative design. They should feel that they have participated in an equitable give-and-take negotiating session..

- Before the first design review concludes, make sure that you feel that the subject has been stretched to its limits, and that together you and your client can attain the ultimate quality solution. Building goodwill early in the decision-making process makes the designer's job easier later on.

Incorporating changes
Learn to "think on your feet" at design reviews. Bend, mold, and modify your designs while the client is present. Certainly, some ideas will need quiet and solitary concentration to develop. But have the confidence to offer solutions on the spot with the assurance that they can work.
    Professional merchants and retail managers face situations every day when they make go or no-go decisions on opportunities with the potential for increasing profit–a new merchandise offering, a chance to participate in a vendor-sponsored promotion, a new ad campaign, or a new store design. For merchants, the optimal store design is one which takes its place on a continuum of sales-stimulating, profit-building techniques. Designers are part of the merchant's team; the drive to create a memorable space should be on the same level with their desire to boost their client's profit structure.
    At the meeting to review the refined schemes, summarize the decisions made at the first meeting. Minimize roadblocks that will stall the acceptance of a final scheme.

Shaping the Store's Interior

2

The benchmark of a successful retail store design is how effectively the environment and the merchandise are integrated. It starts at the front door and stops at the bottom line.

Merchants are asking designers to create spaces that tempt shoppers to spend money more freely. Store designers are in the business of seduction as well as design.

The new Boyd's men's store in downtown Philadelphia occupies a former funeral home. Merchandise display elements fit smoothly into the elegance and tradition of the original space.

Design: Charles E. Broudy & Associates

② Shaping the Store's Interior

The three most important factors in organizing a retail store's interior plan are:

- merchandise
- customers
- sales staff

A shopper entering a store can well be compared to an actor stepping onto a stage. The store itself is the theater; the stage is the selling floor; the items of merchandise are the props. Customers are the main players, and the sales staff is the supporting cast. Lighting, colors, materials, finishes, and displays add to the ambience of the setting. The senses are primed for an experience. The customer is also the audience, seeking an exciting shopping experience.

With an investment in the merchandise and the physical plant, merchants are both producers and directors. Instead of praise from *The New York Times* theater critic, their measure of public acceptance is the cash register reporting on the effectiveness of the store design on sales. It is the store designer's mission to shape the store just as a set designer creates the backdrop for a theatrical vehicle.

Macy's is more than a great store. It's great theatre.

Lights, drama, action! At Macy's the show is the store. There is glamor  and excitement at every turn. A soaring main floor. Shop after shop of super-charged style. Celebrities. Events. Tiny cafes and restaurants to see and be seen in. A magical store for kids. The nostalgia and romance of the Corner Shop Antique Gallery. The Cellar.  Plus, so much more! So if you're in town for some star-studded excitement, make your first stop Macy's. It's more than a store. It's Broadway's longest running hit.

macy's
Remember me to Herald Square

1   Macy's bills itself as Broadway's longest running hit in this full page ad that ran in the theater program for the Brooklyn Academy of Music.

10

2
A model helps to express the relationship between the merchandise and the store design.

The bench mark of success in store design is how effectively the environment and the merchandise are integrated. The measurement of such success begins at the front door and stops at the bottom line.

Gordon Segal, co-founder and president of the Crate & Barrel chain of household products and accessories stores, is a strong proponent of the store-as-theater concept.

"We have always thought of shopping as theater. People have to feel the drama and excitement of being in the store. We use special lighting and fabric backdrops, upbeat music, and live plants, brilliant copper or massed glass.

"We create the atmosphere of a fully-staged Broadway play.

"There should be no doubt in the minds of our associates about who are the players and who is the audience. When the cash register rings, it's applause!"

Star-quality retail interiors help turn lookers into buyers.

Not everyone who walks through a store's entrance has a specific purchase in mind. Many forces contribute to the positive interaction between the customer and the product: accurate pricing, pleasant salespeople, creative displays, clever point-of-purchase techniques, eye-stopping signs.

But without solidly-conceived interior architecture and a sales-stimulating plan, they become disparate elements, unfocused and uncoordinated.

The store's design is the largest single in-store investment that the merchant will make to stimulate sales and contribute to the profitability of the merchandise. According to Bernard S. Vinick, FASID, chairman of Vinick Associates, Hartford, remodeling a store should bring a 20-to-30-percent increase in sales that should be maintained. "Just by changing a storefront, sales can increase 30 percent," he said.

2

Solidly-conceived architecture and a sales-stimulating plan form the backbone of successful store interiors. A model of the Sackler Gallery Museum Shop at the Smithsonian Institution helped to communicate the design concept.

Design: Charles E. Broudy & Associates.

2 Shaping the Store's Interior

The business of merchandising

▸ Bringing in the business is the high-road to success in retailing. And business means turnover. The more times a merchant can turn the stock in a year, the higher the return on the merchandise. A store can make a profit of $1000 on a watch, $3000 on a piece of furniture, or 50 cents on a magazine. The more times this gross margin amount is repeated, the higher the gross profit. Big ticket items turn over less quickly than lower-price goods or impulse items.

▸ Stores today have fewer salespeople and wider merchandise assortments. Except for a few salons and specialty stores such as Nordstrom and Barneys New York, salespeople who still practice the fine art of retail selling are hard to find. At the same time, the number of product lines that fill retailers' shelves and selling floors has proliferated. Many stores have become self-service and semi-self-service.

Big-ticket items like furniture and entertainment units still require informed sales personnel who can tactfully approach a shopper and then reliably explain the product's benefits. But, for the most part, merchandise has to sell itself: it has to sing out from the walls, platforms, or floor on its own and make the shopper interested enough to consider buying it.

The trend to fewer salespeople and less stock began in the late 1960s. As the inflation rate rose, the cost of inventory increased, and merchants reduced the amount of back-up stock they carried. More merchandise is now out in front, on the sales floor; less is out of the customer's sight. Yet, they still have to make the store look full. Skimpy displays turn shoppers off. In ready-to-wear stores, frontal merchandise display units are an effective way of stretching floor inventory and visually maximizing the impact of the items.

Design for the Merchandise
Retail store designers must visualize the space with its most important element–the merchandise–in place. Otherwise, the process becomes an exercise in creating shelves and rods. They will also be running the risk of eliciting the most sacrilegious of all store design client critiques: "The store looked great before we put the merchandise in it!"

A prominent midwest architect revealed in an interview: "Our architectural purpose is to sell merchandise." And he advised designers: "Make the design promote the merchandise. Don't do anything to move the eye away from the merchandise."

Get into the retail mood
The merchant-designer team gives the store interior its visual personality, whether it is a new store or a remodeling project. Retailers are shortening the time between remodeling schedules; they now find that they must remodel every five years to keep looking fresh. In the fast-paced fashion business, a dowdy store defeats the sales appeal of timely merchandise and reduces the customer's perception of its value.

Top designers agree that retailers are selling expectations. "When people walk into stores, they are looking for surroundings that reinforce their aspirations

3
The merchandise stands out in crisp relief

3

The design program for this 1,000-square-foot Electronics Boutique prototype store in Cross Gates Mall, Albany, N. Y., a chain retailer of computer software, had two basic criteria: an image targeted to the merchandise and the market; and a design that would be easily adapted to different store sizes and shapes. To take advantage of the strong visual appeal of the packaging, the designers blended gray for floors, walls, ceiling, and display fixtures so that the merchandise stands out in crisp relief. At the front of the store, the curve of the cashwrap station is repeated overhead by blue neon. An angled aluminum ceiling grid adds sparkle and dimension.

*Design:
Planned Expansion Group, White Plains, New York.*

13

The Gap, London

Create a framework around the merchandise

The Elements of a Store Interior

1	Non-skid carpet treads recessed in wood	10	Directional accent lighting
2	Stairway with landings to permit easy access to lower levels	11	Low brightness fluorescent lighting lens for ambient lighting
3	Open vista encourages shoppers to use stairway to lower level	12	Drywall dropped lighting trough and beam highlights ceiling
4	Natural wood floor adds warmth to the color and materials scheme, a counter point to white fixtures and trim	13	Lights, sprinklers, and grilles are integrated into the ceiling layout
5	See-through glass railing provides unobstructed view between levels	14	The armoire is a multi-purpose cabinet for merchandise presentation: hanging, shelving, face-outs, and display
6	Two- and three-way movable merchandise display fixtures		
7	Merchandise display table		
8	Wall lighting to supplement accent lighting and ambient lighting		
9	Slatwall for display flexibility		

*Design:
Charles E. Broudy
& Associates*

② **Shaping the Store's Interior**

4

The store design reinforces the customers' image of themselves

and the particular image they have of themselves," said J. T. Nakaoka, head of a Los Angeles architectural firm that created the interiors for Bergdorf Goodman's new $21 million men's store across Fifth Avenue from its main store.

"We're not in the design business; we're in the seduction business," commented veteran retail architect Kenneth Walker, president of Walker Group/CNI, New York.

Before a line is drawn for a new store design, the merchant and the designer have to project themselves inside the store and act as the customer would. Many subtle unseen elements play on the senses to motivate the shopper to buy. From an honest answer to "What would make me buy *here*?" often comes the project's mission statement and central design theme.

Designers should analyze what makes them go into a store. What kind of message do you get when you approach a store? Does the store say, "Stay out unless you want to spend a lot of money," or, "I'm tasteful and conservative, solid and stable," or does it shout, "Discount and self-service!" How do you feel when you get inside? Elegant? Thrifty? Inspired?

A department in a department store has to project the image of the designer or manufacturer as well as the department store. This was a preliminary design for NYC Bloomingdales.

*Design:
Charles E. Broudy & Associates*

16

5
A real stage for the merchandise

Where would you prefer to purchase a new soap dish? Bloomingdale's? The neighborhood c. 1940 hardware store? One of the 2,000 Wal-Mart outlets?

Designing for the sales staff
As part of the data gathering phase, it is a smart idea to closely observe the movements and patterns of the sales staff on the job. How they serve customers, write sales receipts, electronically enter transactions, handle stock, wrap and bag merchandise, and interact with other employees should be evaluated to become part of a functional retail environment.

The designer has to be familiar with what salespeople will and will not do to stock the department and get merchandise for customers. How far will they reach up or bend down on a day-in, day-out basis? What physical and psychological factors does the designer have to be aware of? Will the hardware to be specified for storage units function smoothly so as to reduce stress and fatigue?

Changing the pace
The most productive retail interiors are like musical compositions, offering expertly-conceived changes of pace and pleasant surprises. Customers are literally a moving target; the skillful designer will orchestrate them from the front to the back of the store, and from side to side (the "pin ball-machine effect").

By varying such elements as the lighting, materials, signs, and the rhythm of the displays, the designer can create spatial excitement, an integrated, identifying signature for the store. *The designer is projecting the merchant's image—the important point-of-view—that will identify the store with the merchandise to establish an important competitive edge.* Many stores in the same

The concept of the retail store as a theater is given literal meaning in the 1,700-square-foot Hahn Shoes store in The Galleria at Tysons II, Mclean, Va. Using a background of draped, hand-painted canvas, merchandise is presented as if suspended in mid-air.

Design: The Architecture Group, Baton Rouge, La.; Sammy L. Vincent, AIA, project designer.

5

2 Shaping the Store's Interior

6
Strong geometric forms can create the theme

The interplay of circles, curves, and horizontal lines were translated in wood with sharply defined contrast strips for the men's shoe department at Raleighs, Washington, D. C. Sets of carpet-covered risers and the stepped-back ceiling restate the strong geometric theme.

Design: Robert Young Associates, Inc., Alexandria, Va.; Fred George, V.P. Design.

6

7
Techniques for successful store interiors include changes of pace and pleasant surprises

7
block, in the same shopping center, carry identical or similar merchandise. The successful in-store image will become part of the client firm's promotional umbrella, assuming a place along with advertising, special events, and publicity to generate sales volume, year-round.

Shaping the store
Retail spaces come in all sizes and shapes.

Impossible spaces invite designers to expand their creative horizons and often turn out to be the most exciting. Experienced store designers would rather work in tough areas like a narrow space, a triangle, or a space that wraps around a corner than a space with four identical corners and a flat ceiling.

For this Hemisphere store in San Francisco, such architectural elements as columns, curved and straight cornices, arched display niches, and a change in the ceiling and floor levels visually direct customers from one area to another. The clear, sharp modern classic setting reflects the image of the apparel.

Design: Charles E. Broudy & Associates

19

② Shaping the Store's Interior

8 *Hermès on Union Square*

Choosing a thematic structure is an important decision. It can be determined by geometric shape, the merchandise itself, or by visual presentation.

▸ Treat areas like ceilings and walls above the typical sight line. These surfaces can be utilized to handle merchandise or displays so that every inch of space works to support merchandise presentation.

▸ Remember cubic footage, and take advantage of it.

▸ In a space with a high ceiling, beams or baffles can be dropped to highlight a display island or define a traffic pattern, and subliminally create a space.

▸ If standard display cases or fixtures are not available, create a special design.

8 **The 4,000-sq.-ft. Hermès store is one of the most prestigious shops that face onto San Francisco's Union Square. The project required coordination with the client's offices in New York and Paris.**

Design:
Project architect: Rena Dumas Architecture Interieure, Paris; Rena Dumas-Hermès;
Coordinating architect: Whisler-Patri, San Francisco; Kevin E. Dill, project director.

9
Keep the design level high and the maintenance low

Specify products that do not show finger marks or scratches, or that require frequent cleaning and polishing. The white plastic laminate used for this custom armoire for The Gap stores is both easy to clean and an effective showcase for merchandise.

*Design:
Charles E. Broudy & Associates*

9

2 Shaping the Store's Interior

▶ Use quality materials when they enhance the merchandise, but do not put costly materials in places where they will have no positive impact on either the customer or the merchandise.

▶ Flexibility and adaptability are at the core of successful retail plans. Display stands, racks, counters, gondolas, and everything else that does not impinge on the structural stability of the building will probably be moved. Spaces that can withstand such modifications and still maintain their design integrity are characterized by an integrated product environment with a unifying, well-detailed architectural theme.

Operational considerations

Retail traffic takes its toll on furnishings and finishes, as does the moving and shifting of merchandise and display elements. Merchants do not want to replace items because they have become shabby before the end of their projected useful life. If the acceptable life cycle for carpeting is six years, it should not be worn out in three years. If showcases are an eight-year item, the veneer should not be peeling off in four years.

Products that show finger marks or scratches or that require frequent polishing or hand scrubbing should be avoided unless the store has a large maintenance budget and can afford this type of intensive care. Otherwise, every item specified should be carefully scrutinized from a minimal-maintenance viewpoint.

Another important store-shaping factor is security. Protecting both the merchandise and the premises are of constant concern to retailers. Mechanical and electronic systems can be customized to help control theft and deter vandalism. Guards posted at entrances, and in larger stores, plainclothes detectives circulating through the facility, help to apprehend shoplifters. Designers should keep in mind that clear sightlines permit store personnel to visually patrol the sales floor and identify suspicious activity to thwart attempted shoplifiting or a burglary. A platform can be constructed for the cash wrap station to give employees a higher vantage point. (See the Security section of Chapter 9, Systems.)

Another operational area in which designers need to educate themselves is the "back of the house." This includes:

▶ Marking, receiving, and shipping of merchandise, and the supporting paperwork systems

▶ Departmental wrapping and salescheck processing

▶ Office space

▶ Cafeteria and lunchroom

▶ Locker room

These items can be described in a separate programming form and their spatial requirements incorporated early into the master plan.

Basic Store Layouts

3

How can the store's floor plan stimulate sales? By the proper direction of the traffic flow, incorporating the psychology of shoppers' movements and patterns made within a retail store. Avoid creating a maze. Consider the "pinball" effect so that the plan will drive traffic from the front to the back of the store, and will subconsciously bump shoppers from side to side.

Materials symbols

Carpeting

Showcases and display

Ceramic and marble tile

Wood flooring

Windows and glass

Metal

KNOW CHARACTERISTICS OF EACH.

3 Basic Store Layouts

There are two basic planning guidelines that designers should keep in mind when they reach the floor layout phase:

• Use 100 percent of the space allocated in the lease.

• Do not sacrifice function for esthetics. Successful plans combine both to the fullest.

The six basic plans illustrated here are not the only potential solutions that can be developed for the owner's consideration, but they form the foundation on which variations can be created.

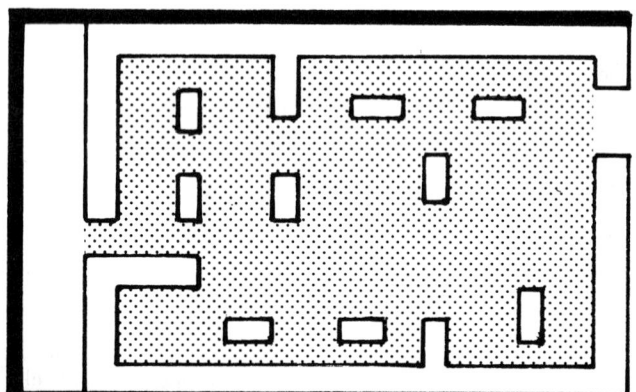

Straight plan
This is an economical plan and can be adapted to any type of store, from gift shops to apparel stores, from drug stores to shoe stores. It uses walls and projections to create niches and smaller spaces. The straight plan lends itself well to pulling customers to the back of the store. To define transition from one section of the store to another, displays can be placed to help lead shoppers. Elevate floor levels for a change of pace.

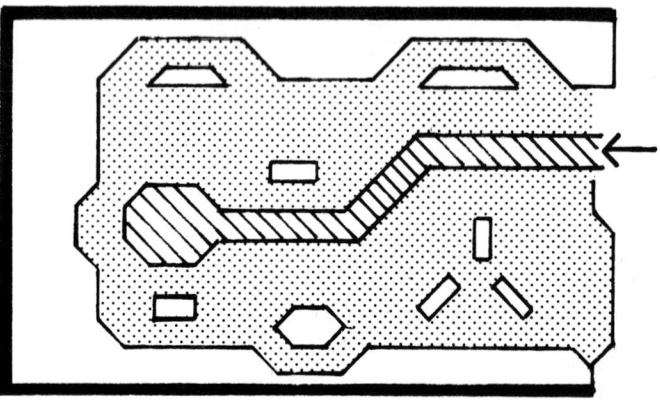

Pathway plan
Applicable to virtually any type of store, the pathway plan is particularly suited to stores over 5,000 square feet and on one level. A good architectural organizer, it pulls shoppers smoothly from the front to the rear without interruption by floor fixtures. The pathway plan, which can take a variety of shapes, is particularly applicable for apparel stores where shoppers do not want to feel that they have to fight their way to the back through a maze of merchandise. The floor and ceiling can be used to create directional elements off the path.

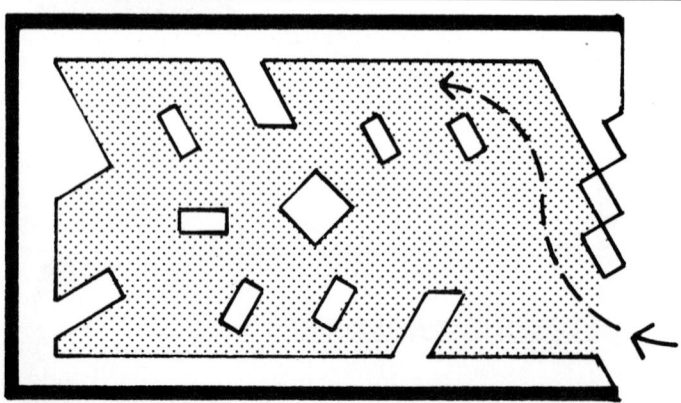

Diagonal plan
For self-service stores, a diagonal plan is optimal. It permits angular traffic flow and creates perimeter design interest and excitement in movement. Both soft goods or hard goods stores can take advantage of the diagonal plan. The cashier is in a central location, with sight lines to all areas.

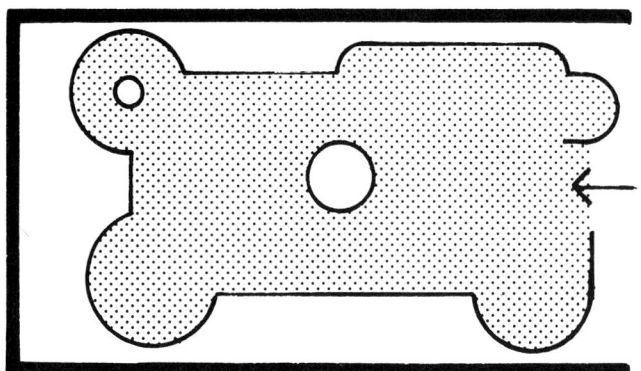

Curved plan

For boutiques, salons, or other types of stores carrying high-end merchandise, the curved plan creates an inviting, special environment for the customer. Construction costs are higher than for retail interiors designed on an angular or straight plan. The curved theme can be emphasized with walls, ceiling, and corners. To complete the look, specify circular floor fixtures.

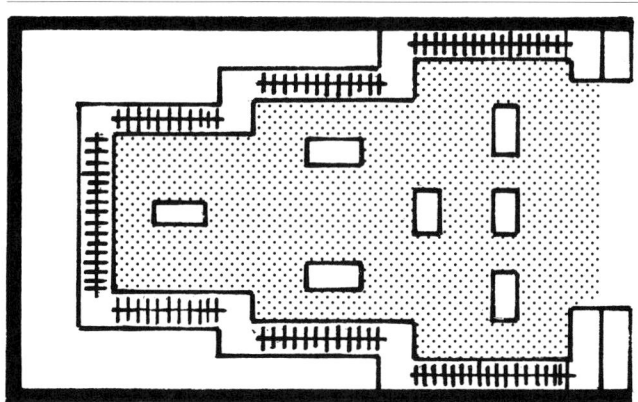

Varied plan

For products that require back-up stock to be immediately adjacent (shoes and men's shirts, for example), the varied plan is highly functional. Box or carton storage is created off the main sales floor with perimeter wall stocking. Typical of the varied plan is a "bellows" effect, a tapering of the space that focuses on a special purpose area in the rear. Service departments in stereo, jewelry, or hardware stores can be located in this narrow end.

Geometric plan

This is the most exotic of the six basic plans. The designer creates forms and shapes derived from showcases, racks, or gondolas, and can use wall angles to restate the shapes dominating the sales floor. It comfortably allows for fitting rooms without wasting square footage, making it especially suitable for apparel stores. It can nicely accommodate adjacent storage, making it an alternative to the varied plan for shoe stores and gift shops. Ceiling and floors can be lowered or raised to create zones and departments.

③ Basic Store Layouts

1
D. F. Sanders
Boston, Mass.
1,500 square feet
Straight plan

2
Contemporary housewares and gift store is in a century-old townhouse

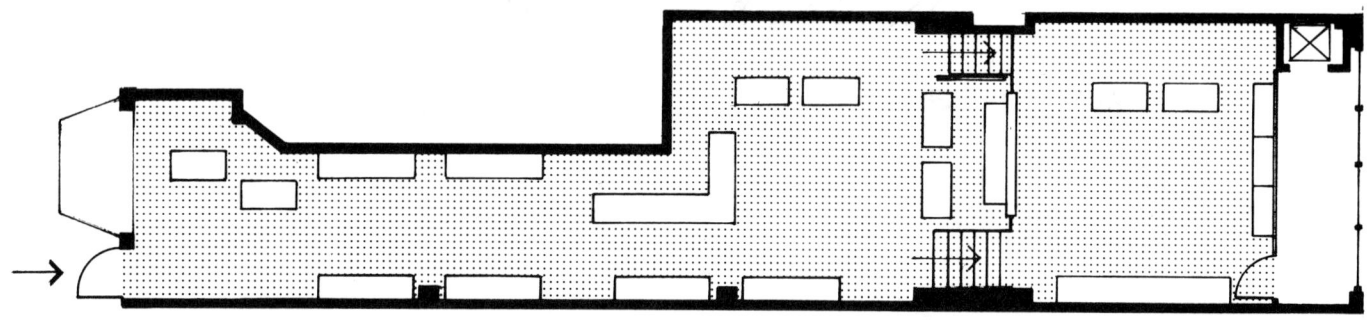

1

2

A Newbury Street address identifies a store as a purveyor of high-quality merchandise. For the designer, the location often means such constraints as an irregular long and narrow shape and a change in floor height. New York City-based D. F. Sanders chose to take over an existing retail space on the first floor of a 100-year old townhouse for its Boston branch. The straight plan was the choice here, to pull customers through the 10-foot-wide throat at the front (an elevator lobby is adjacent) to the 20-foot-wide back half of the store. The open-slat display units are actually steel pie tray holders used by commercial bakeries; Sanders' design director customized this industrial stock item with glass shelving and had them painted grey/green. This unifying color is used throughout the store, including the stain for the wood glass-topped showcases in the foreground.

Design:
Craig Jackson, D. F. Sanders;
Architecture:
Charles E. Broudy & Associates.

3
The Coffee Grinder
New York City
300 square feet
Straight plan

4
Sales volume doubled following the renovation

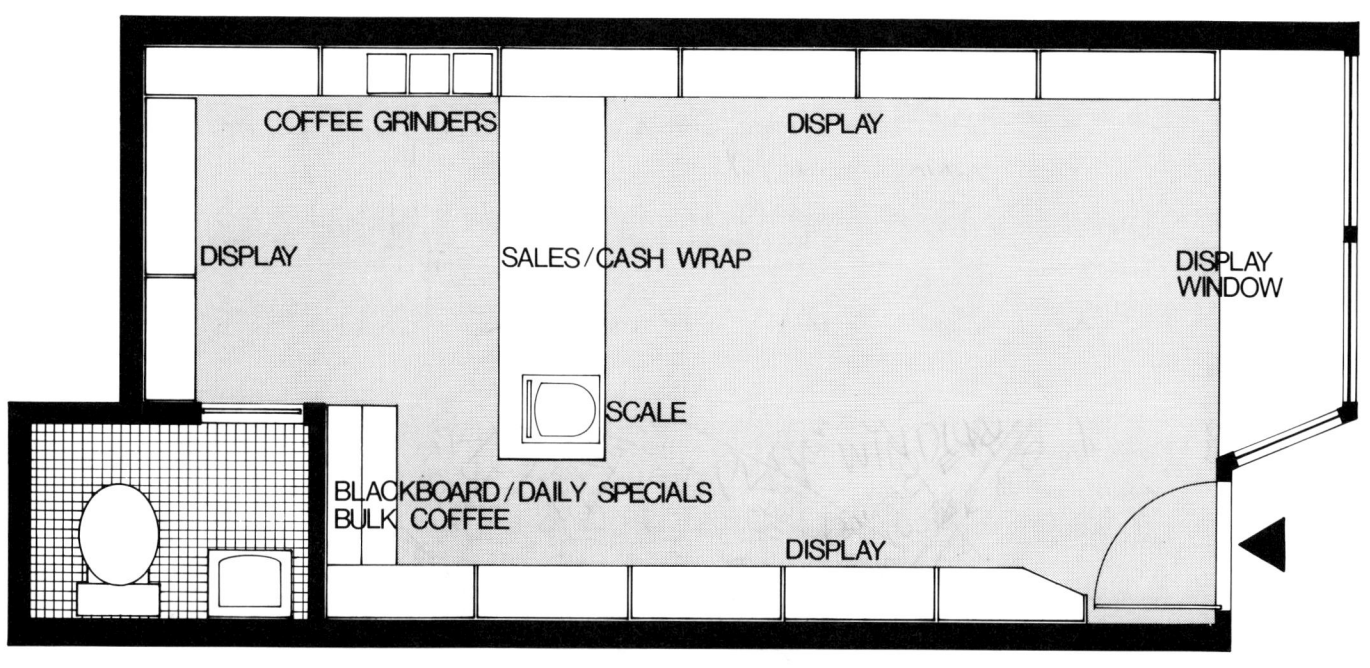

3

4

Before renovation, The Coffee Grinder was dark, crowded, and disorganized. The 10-year-old store had, however, a devoted clientele for its coffees, teas, spices, and gourmet and housewares items. The designers functionally and visually organized the floor space and storage spaces, and allowed the products to speak for themselves. By moving the counter from the front to the back of the store, customers can now see merchandise and product displays. A new canopy and logo gave the store a "street presence." Shoppers told the owner that they thought it was a brand new store, so little resemblance did the new space bear to the old. Volume doubled in the first month.

The Coffee Grinder was constructed in less than one month, on a budget of under $35,000.

Design:
Design & Planning/
Interiors, New City,
New York; Ellen S.
Fisher, ASID, principal
in charge.

27

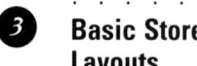

Basic Store Layouts

5
*J. Riggings
Axonometric view of 2,800 sq. ft. prototype store, Cincinnati
Varied plan*

6
Plan view showing store's three zones

7
A 50 percent increase in sales has been achieved

J. Riggings, a chain of over 200 mid-priced men's clothing stores, completed a re-imaging program to adjust to a changing marketplace. Appealing primarily to an under-40 buyer, a new prototype store in the Tri-County Mall, Cincinnati, is more contemporary and flexibile, and was designed to help customers coordinate their selections, leading to an increase in cross sales and multiple sales. The store has three distinct zones: the front zone for casual wear; the rear zone for suits; and a center transaction zone.

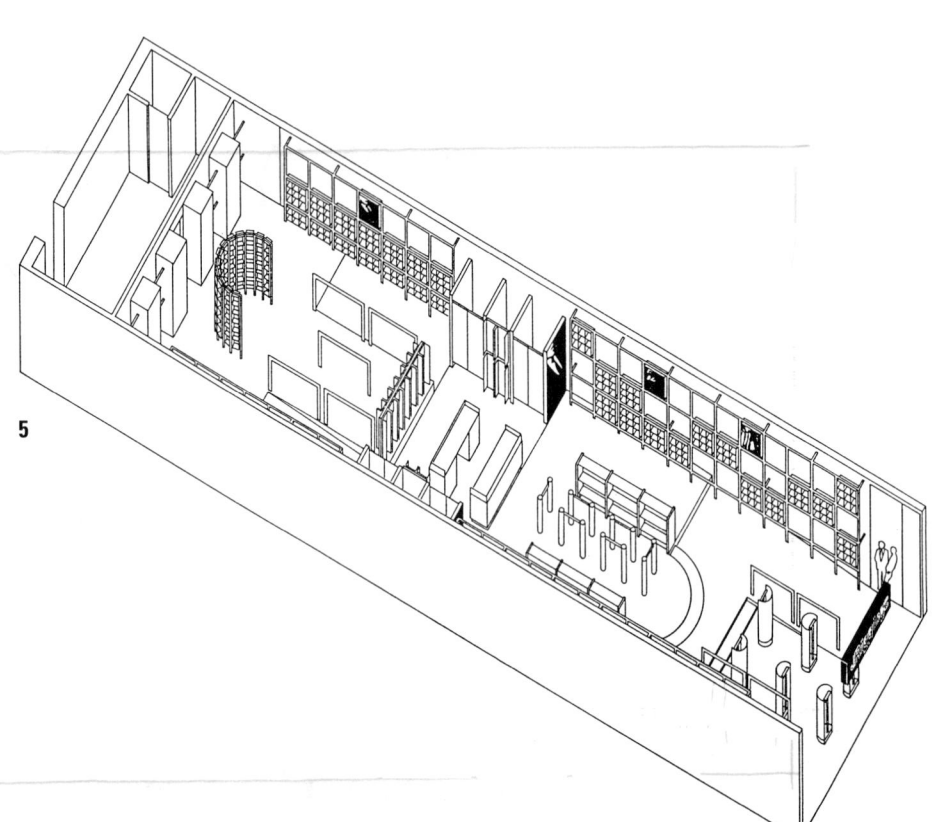

5

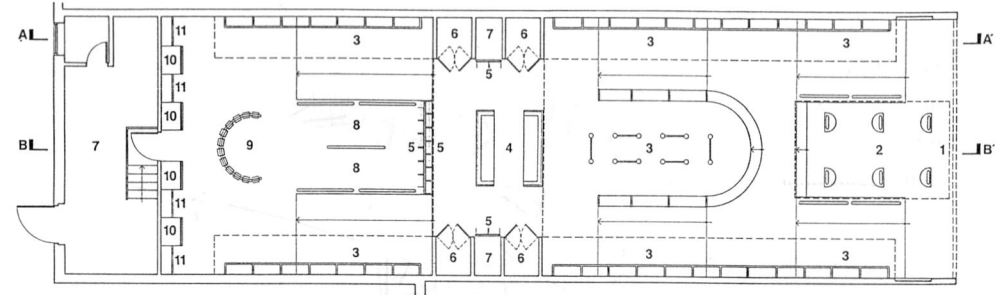

6

A flexible grid system for merchandise display flanks the entire store. The wood ceiling is defined by a dark green metal canopy at the entrance.

*Design:
Robert P. Gersin Associates, New York City; Ingrid Caruso, project director.*

7

28

8
*The Coach Store
South Street
Seaport Mall
New York City
1,500 square feet
Straight plan*

9
*The colonnade
was added to the
interior of the c. 1805
building*

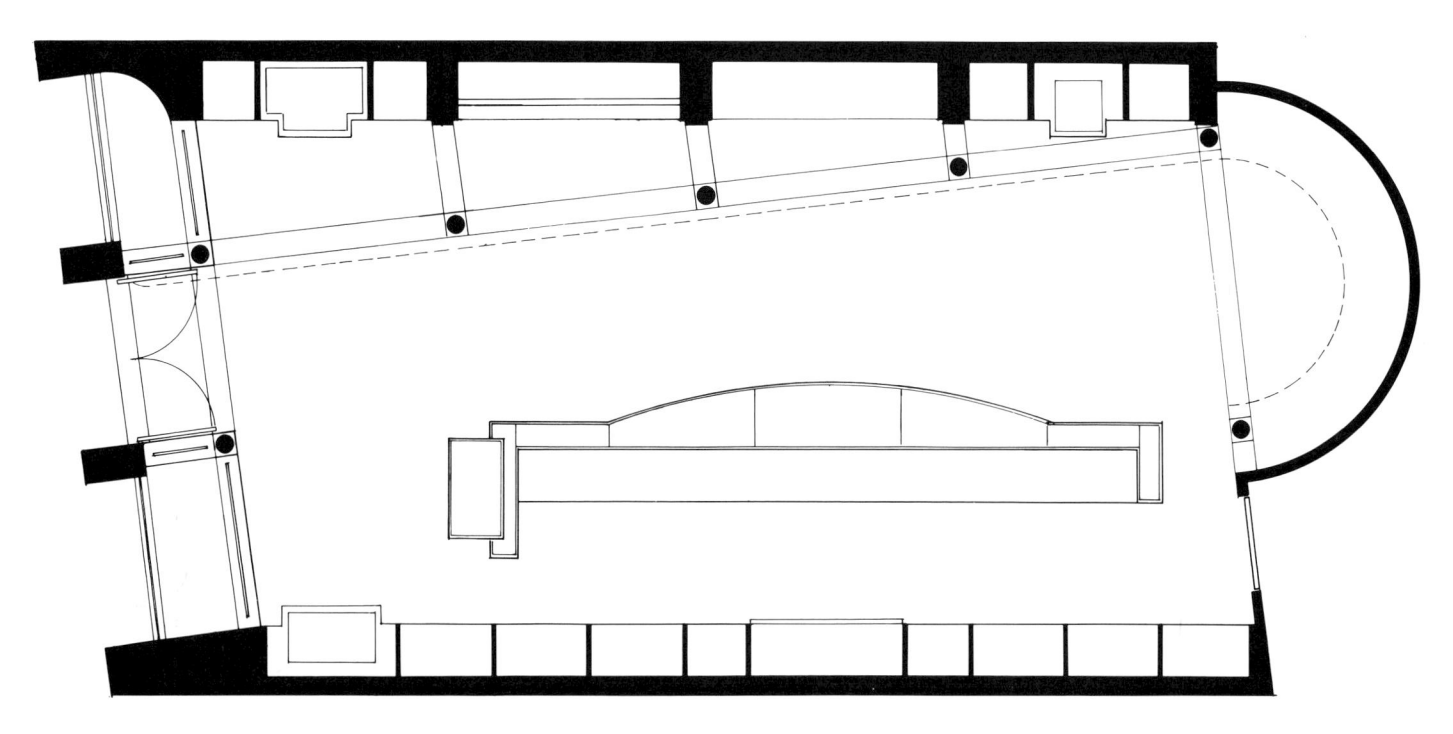

8

Coach Leatherware, New York City-based manufacturer of handbags and leather goods, operates 35 free standing stores in urban areas and shopping centers across the country. For its branch in the South Street Seaport Mall, a Rouse Company development that transformed mostly abandoned early nineteenth century warehouses and commercial buildings into a shopping and entertainment mall at the foot of Manhattan, the designers angled one wall and added the colonnade to create niches for merchandise display. A cove-lit curved rear display area leads the shopper through the store.

*Designer:
Rosenblum-Harb
Architects, New York
City.*

9

Nan Duskin

High Style

Nan Duskin, long synonomous in Philadelphia with women's designer clothing and accessories, moved from its original Walnut Street location to occupy space on the first and third levels of The Rittenhouse, a new 36-story mixed-use highrise on West Rittenhouse Square. The primary design constraint for the entry level, which sells accessories and cosmetics, was the close 12-foot column spacing occurring on the window side facing the Square. To reduce their bulk, the columns were sheathed in mirrors and outlined with black marble surrounds, the same material used for the floor. The columns anchor three curved-front, custom marble-based showcases which are highlighted with brass and under-counter illumination. Armoires against the perimeter exterior wall are of these same materials. A glass-enclosed elevator takes customers to the third floor apparel sales area and beauty salon.

Location:
Philadelphia

Size:
17,000 square feet

Designer:
Charles E. Broudy & Associates

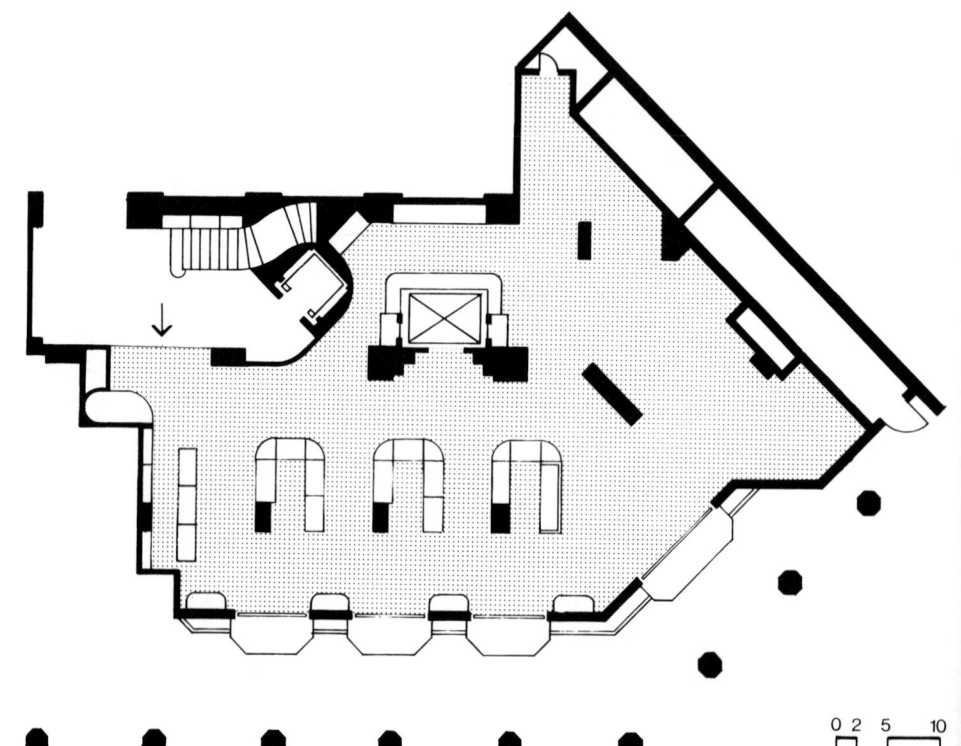

10
Varied plan

11
Mirrors disguise columns on the first floor

11

3 **Basic Store Layouts**

12
*First Issue
(Liz Claiborne)
Short Hills Mall,
New Jersey
3,400-square-foot
prototype store
Geometric and
diagonal plan*

13
*A sculptural theme is
played against a
monochromatic
background*

12

0 2 5 10

Against a soft neutral ground of warm tan and taupe, angled geometric shapes are the basis for an unconventional solution to the design of the first of a chain of retail stores operated by women's apparel maker, Liz Claiborne Inc. French stone and end grain wood are the basic materials for the sales floor and perimeter display and architectural elements. The counterplay of angles directs the shopper through the displays of upper-mid price women's career clothes and sportswear. Triangular stone platforms which are used for open storage of back-up inventory also hold tall live plants. The raised illuminated cove ceiling restates the plan, and helps direct the shopper to the rear of the store.

13

*Design:
Charles E. Broudy &
Associates.*

32

14
Artlines
Honolulu
700 square feet
Varied plan

15
The interior recreates the feeling of a bazaar

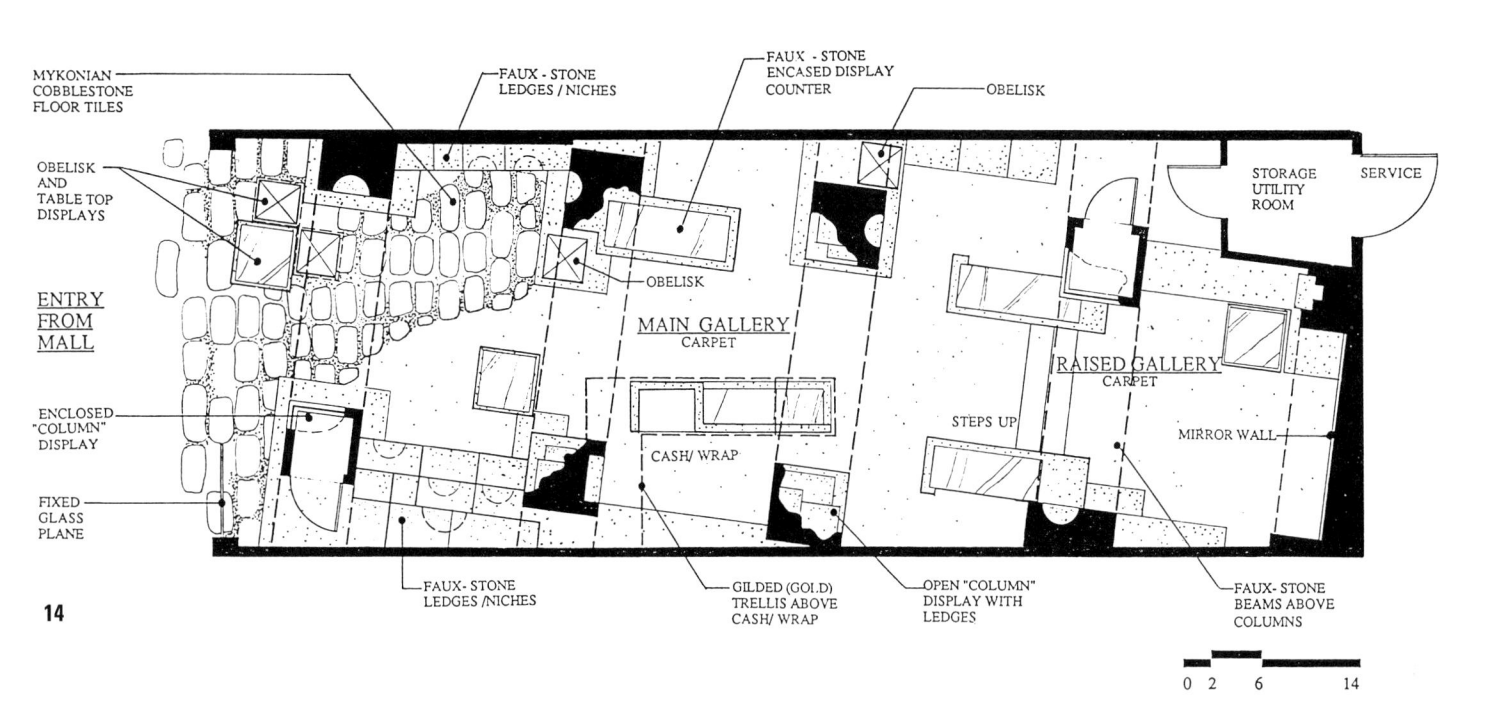

14

Located in the Ala Moana Shopping Center, Artlines handles antiques, gifts, and jewelry. The owners wanted to "create a place where myths and legends may find a home;" the constraints were time, money, and space. An old-world bazaar theme gives shoppers the feeling that they are discovering unique artifacts. The columns are aligned longitudinally, but skewed to diverge from the axes of the mall. Ledges, niches, and plinths allow for maximum display surfaces. A mirror at the rear extends the perception of the store's depth.

Artlines' construction cost was $75,000.

*Design:
AM Partners Inc., Honolulu; Gary K. Kawakami, AIA, partner in charge.*

15

33

③ Basic Store Layouts

16
*Sadow's
North Dartmouth,
Mass.
7,000 square feet
Geometric plan*

17
The owner wanted an environment somewhere between a residence and a spaceship

18
Axonometric

16

17

18

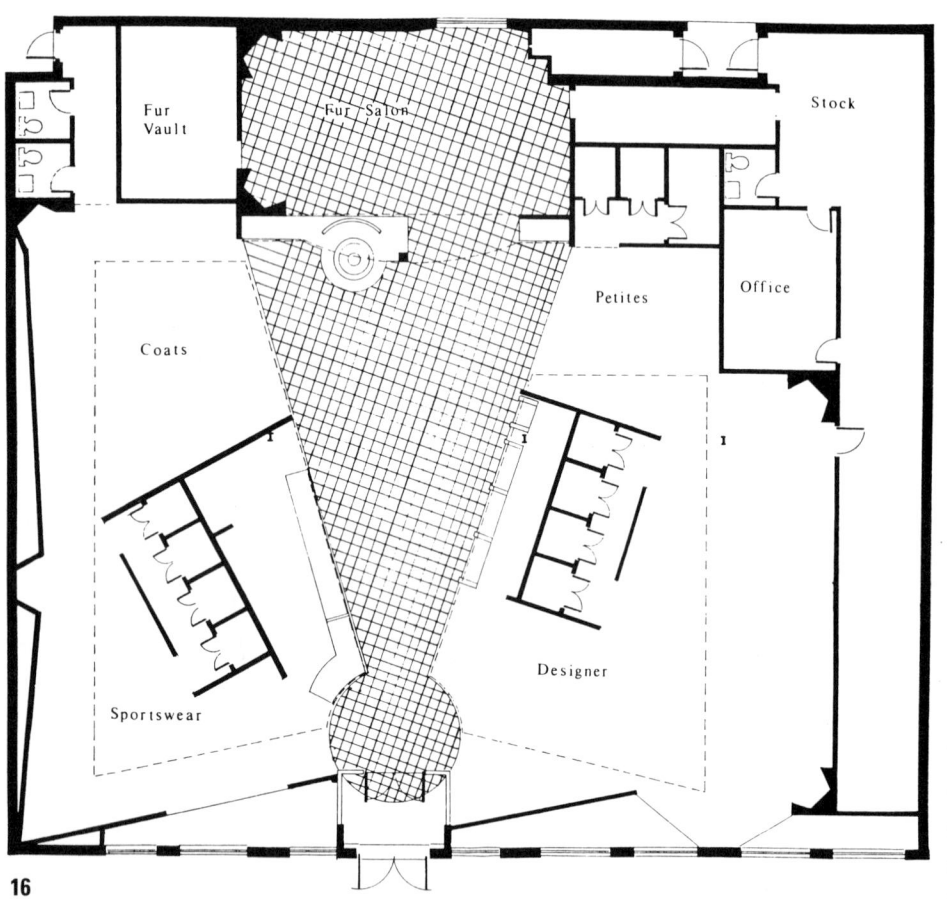

The design strategy for Sadow's women's apparel store in the Faunce Corner Crossing Shopping Center was based on three concepts: the manipulation of geometry to create powerful and exciting space; broad expanses of forms and surfaces; and contrast. Two major grids split apart at the entrance to create a keyhole-shaped "piazza." The zones to either side contain overscaled sales counters and dressing pavilions which are defined by suspended ceiling planes above which the metal roof structure is visible. Around the perimeter are 10'-foot-high display surfaces. A classic stone pineapple fountain at the fur salon entrance in the rear of the store is a focal point. Horizontal tube uplighting in graduated lengths repeats the wedge of the plan.

*Design:
Design West, Boston;
Elizabeth Armstrong,
partner in charge.*

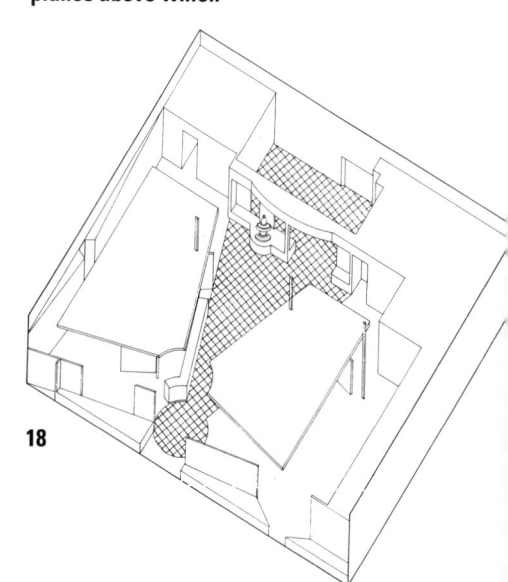

19
The Pfaltzgraff Store
Oak Court Mall
Memphis
3,600 square feet
Diagonal and pathway plan

20
Shoppers can see multiple angled displays.

Successful merchandising of tabletop items is highly dependent on visual coordination between place settings, flatware, and accessories. Pfaltzgraff, one of the country's leading makers of quality china and pottery, opened its first retail store to bring its products directly to the consumer in a setting of warmth and graciousness. The 35-foot-wide space provided sufficient width to handle the combination diagonal/pathway plan which directs shoppers to the angled wood display fixtures and additional merchandise displays on the perimeter wall. The ceiling line is important to the store's design. Arches and pediments top the freestanding fixtures and wall display units. Plants soften the vista below the dropped ceiling, and a contrasting illuminated cove lighting defines the center pathway.

Design:
Charles E. Broudy & Associates

20

19

0 2 5 10

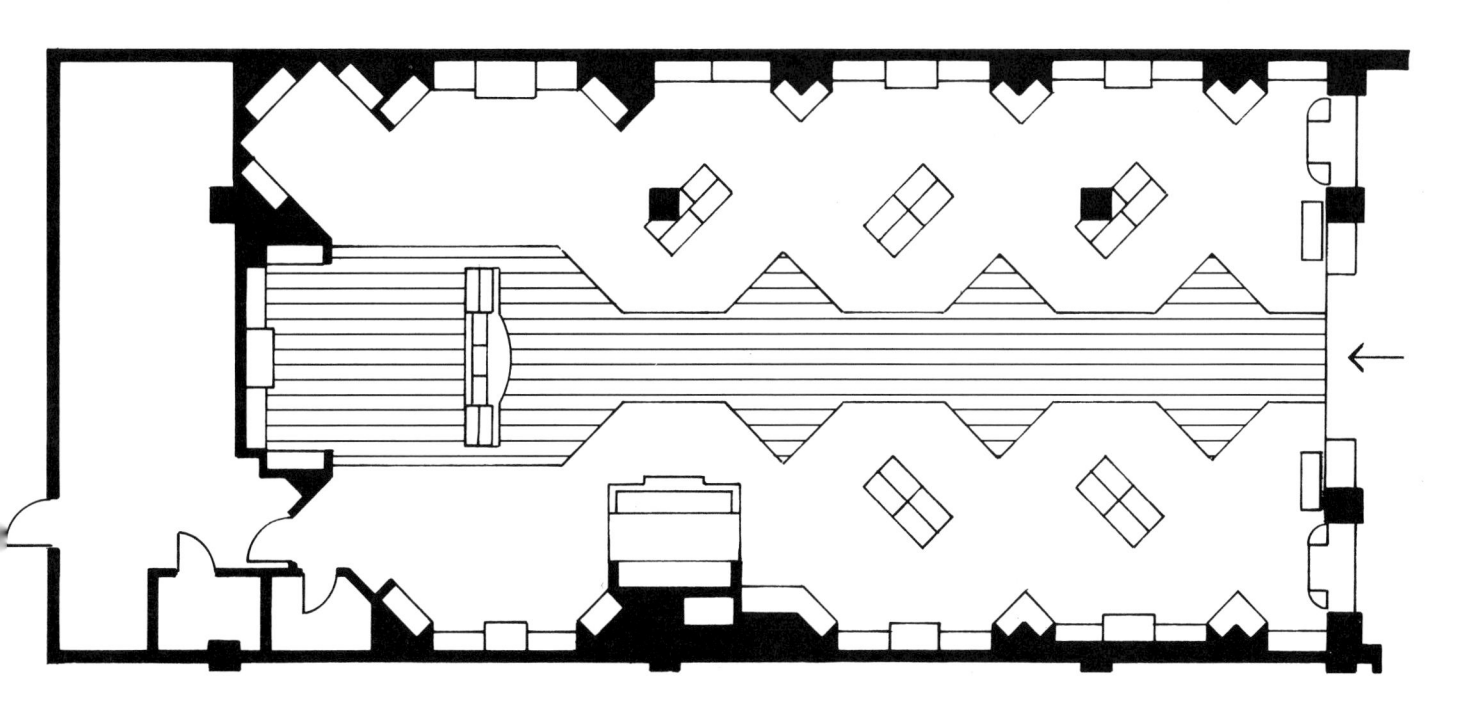

35

3 Basic Store Layouts

21
Episode
San Francisco
7,000 square feet
Curved plan

22
A sweeping and dramatic setting for a women's apparel store

21

0 2 5 10

22

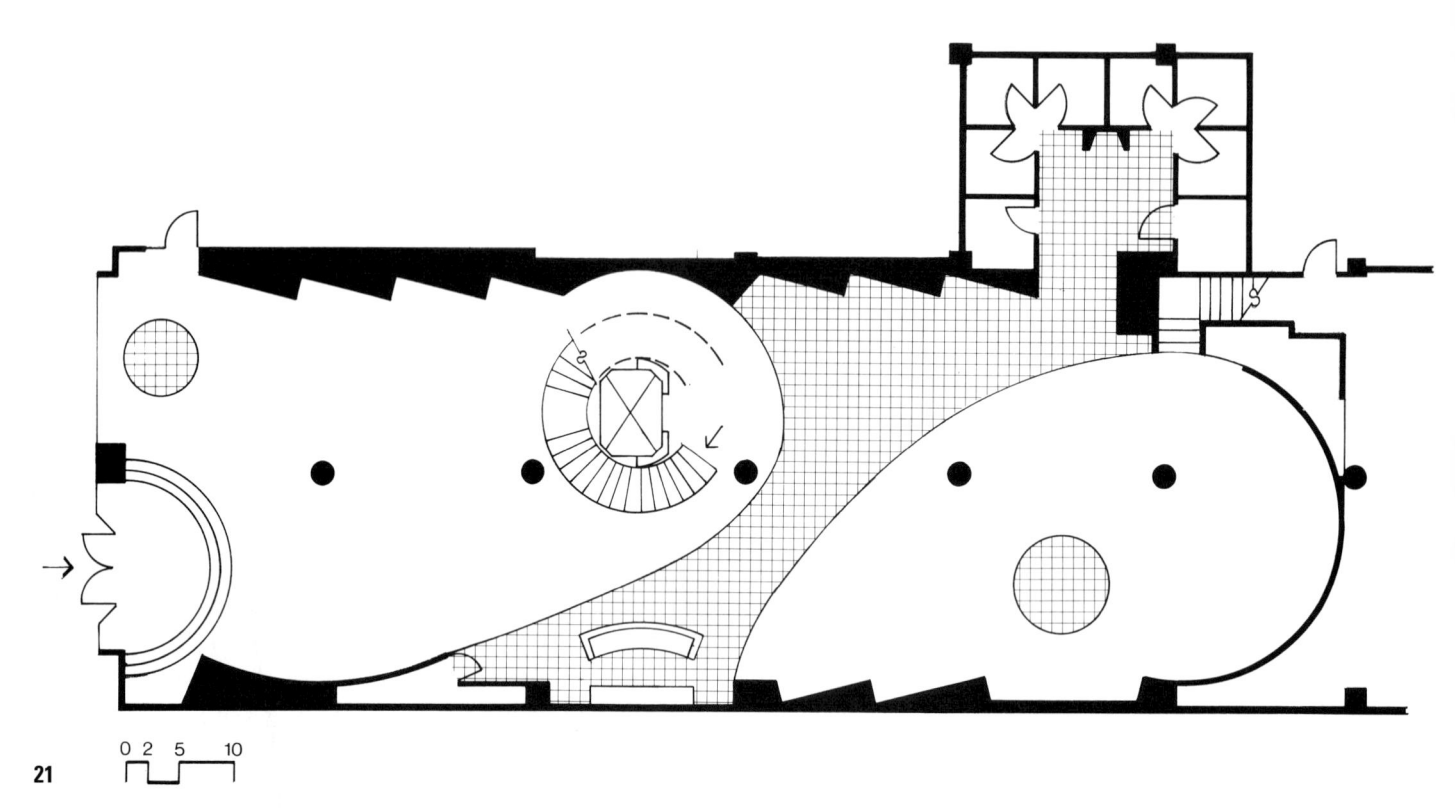

For this bi-level store on Post Street in downtown San Francisco, the curved staircase and elevator are major features of this sophisticated plan. Episode, an upper-mid price women's clothing chain, targets its store design strategy to both international and American shoppers. The cove-lit drop ceiling restates the curve of the planked wood flooring. Ionic columns add a classic note to the interior and are a unique and effective interpretation of the circular concept. On the second level, polished granite flooring separates the main selling areas. Two angled glass panels support a curved display shelf, which becomes a visual punctuation point.

Design:
Charles E. Broudy & Associates

36

Exterior Store Design

4

The elements of exterior store planning and design:

- Site selection, location, and access
- Size, shape, and parking
- Environmental considerations
- Materials for storefronts
- Windows
- Awnings and canopies
- Portals and doorways
- Vestibules
- Signs
- Lighting

Nordstrom's 328,000-square-foot store on Market Street near San Francisco's Union Square occupies the top five floors of the 10-level San Francisco Centre, a new vertical mall. It faces the cable car plaza used daily by 300,000 people. Developer was The Gordon Company, San Francisco.

Design: Whisler-Patri, San Francisco; Piero Patri, FAIA, principal in charge.

4 Exterior Store Design

The purpose of the store's exterior is *to sell*, through the use of materials, lighting, signs, and windows. This is true for stores that face the street, the highway, or an enclosed mall's promenade.

Merchants expect their store's front to help them to achieve a critical edge over competition by pre-selling customers before they walk in. The design of the exterior and windows communicates the store's image and is an important strategic differentiation element.

While a merchant may undertake a partial or full interior remodeling approximately every five years to look current, the exterior can look perfectly fine for a dozen years or more if the design theme does not become dated. A trendy exterior can be an option for a store carrying that type of merchandise, but a more prudent approach is to adopt a design that is based on simple, classic, and distinctive concepts.

A "Silent Salesperson"

The main objective of the storefront is to entice, funnel, or vacuum shoppers into the store. Merchants pay a healthy rent for frontage on a busy street, highway, or mall because of traffic–the location generates the kind of pedestrian or vehicular traffic for their type of store. *High traffic stimulates action, and profits.*

The storefront can be considered a sales-stimulating, long-lived advertisement, like a lively architectural billboard.

Site Selection, Location, and Access

Only occasionally do designers become involved with the site selection decisions for a bank, school, or office building. It is not unusual, however, for a merchant to ask the store designer to evaluate a site under consideration. Retailers, with their predilection for instinctive action, want to know: "*If you were the owner of the store, would you locate here?*"

Before answering, the designer should have the following information relating to the site:

▶ demographics

▶ marketing studies

▶ zoning ordinances

If the merchant and the designer are having a difficult time making up their minds about a site, what can sway their decision? Sometimes the answer is "industry gifts," enticements offered by the landlord to sign on a tenant. These are usually in the form of allowances for construction, ranging from 10 to 100 percent. At the upper end of the gift scale, the deal becomes virtually a turnkey operation: the landlord does all the construction, and the tenant moves in. If the landlord increases the allowance to make a less desirable location more appealing, or to fill up a slow-renting mall or center, the merchant is taking a chance by signing a lease.

Retail Site Categories

▶ **Destination store:** Shoppers will travel to the location of a particular store. A major department or specialty chain store is a destination store.

▶ **Destination area:** Refers to clusters of a related group of stores, like jeweler's row or antiques row, rather than one particular store.

▶ **Traffic generator:** Actively promoted shopping malls or downtown areas that draw foot or vehicular traffic.

▶ **Neighborhood center:** Strip centers or storefront shopping areas that draw from approximately a two mile radius. Many strip centers are being remodeled to concentrate on a particular type of merchandise, such as apparel or discount.

▶ **Community center:** Drawing from a 3- to 5-mile radius, these centers provide convenience goods and services. They should be located for access from major thoroughfares.

▶ **Regional center:** Draws from up to a 20-mile radius and contains one or more anchor destination stores.

1
A glittering facade that grabs shoppers

2
A successful storefront design draws traffic in an enclosed mall

2
The storefront is a lively multi-dimensional architectural billboard; its mission is to entice, funnel, or vacuum shoppers inside. For T. Deane, a large-size women's apparel store in Bridgewater Commons, N. J., a painted wood structure frames the open-back display windows and glass vestibule.

Design: Charles E. Broudy & Associates

1
The design of the new facade for the 201,000-square-foot Strawbridge & Clothier branch in the King of Prussia Shopping Center near Philadelphia included the addition of a glazed two-story rotunda and entry to provide a new image and identification. Alternative bands of framed transparent and translucent glazing create bold grids and permit views of the skylight and second-level restaurant. The prefabricated parapet cap was added to alter the appearance of the entire building.

Design: RTKL Associates, Inc., Baltimore; Thomas S. Gruber, principal in charge.

4 Exterior Store Design

Size, Shape, and Parking

A regularly-shaped space makes for a more efficient layout. The amount of frontage along a street or highway is critical. A parcel with a narrow frontage and a considerable quantity of rear acreage does not offer a positive presence for the store even if the demographics appear favorable. Contributing to presence are:

- Good vista
- Good vehicle access
- Good entrance
- Good architecture
- Good lighting
- Good signs

Provide as much parking as possible, on grade or in multilevel structures. The ratio of square feet of building to square feet of parking depends on the size of the store or shopping center, and the local zoning codes. While no designer wants to stand accused of blighting the landscape with acres of parking lots, the fact remains that America moves on wheels, and those wheels represent traffic to many retailers. Trees, planting, and landscaping techniques such as berms can relieve the flat expanse of a paved parking lot.

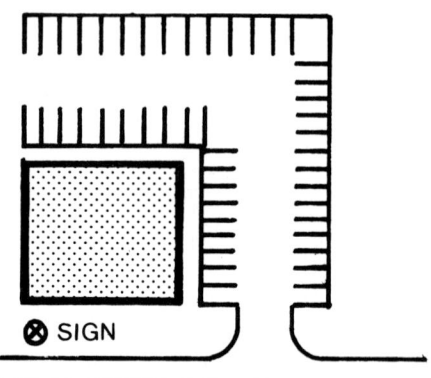

In an open site, the slope of the ground should not be extreme. Highway access to parking lot, sign tower, or building sign is important.

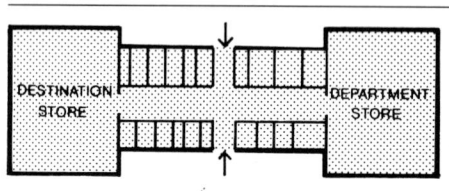

In an enclosed mall, a site near a department store or destination store is most desirable, as well as proximity to the mall entrance.

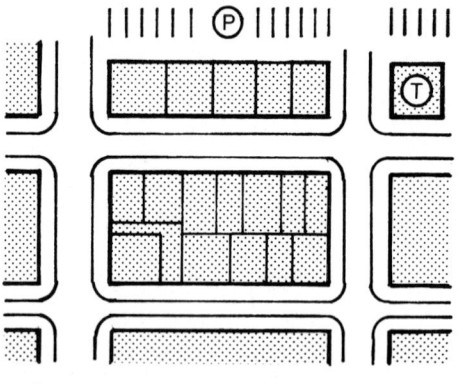

The potential mall tenant should know that neighboring stores will carry merchandise in a compatible price range. Other factors are public transportation (T), and parking (P).

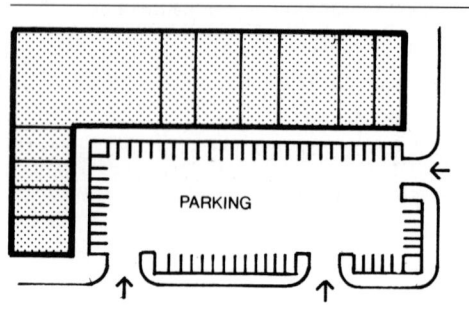

Primary considerations for a strip center are parking access, and visibility of signs. A canopy over the walkway is an important shopper convenience.

3
An expanded neighborhood center with two exposures

The 310,000-square-foot McMullen Creek Market in Charlotte, N. C., illustrates the landlord's control over a storefront in an open air shopping center. The brick, tile and metal materials, and the building configuration leave the store designer with limited expression.

Design: Dalton Moran Shook Architecture Inc., Charlotte, N. C.; Terry E. Dalton, AIA, principal in charge.

Environmental Considerations

Regional enclosed malls of 350,000 square feet and over (gross leasable area, or GLA), not including anchor stores, are often designed with two or more levels. Site costs are thereby reduced, as are walking distances. A parking structure reduces open-air parking and is a shopper convenience.

Environmental considerations include:

▸ topography

▸ drainage

▸ subsoil conditions

▸ zoning

▸ utilities

▸ presence of hazardous waste materials

▸ emissions controls

▸ environmental impact statement requirements

A qualified civil engineering or landscape architectural firm can be retained by the store planner to define requirements and handle technical aspects of planning and construction. Budgetary, esthetic objectives, and legal requirements will affect the final site plan.

• Earth moving should be kept to a minimum. A steeply sloping site can be adapted for retail use, but the costs for contouring the site should be well understood before proceeding.

3

41

4 Exterior Store Design

A classic of exterior store design

- Control of storm water runoff, through sedimentation and retention ponds, is part of the site program.

- Responsibility for extending the sewer, water lines, and power lines to the site should be dealt with early in the site evaluation process by the owner and the municipality.

- Some communities require extensive buffering between areas zoned for residential and those rated for commercial zoning. Community reviewers of the site plan will pay particular attention to how much and what kind of buffering space is proposed.

Approvals from agencies, public advisory groups, and neighborhood committees are needed for both new construction and remodeling. To meet various laws and statutes, the owner may have to file an extensively documented environmental impact statement dealing with water and air quality, traffic impact estimates, analysis of future water and power needs, the projected construction timetable, and other items. Concerns of planning commissions, arts councils, and historical committees must be addressed in written documentation and presentations.

The designer should develop a realistic schedule so that the merchant is clear from the beginning about the length of time the approval process will take. Shortcuts in the approval process often come back to haunt both the store operator and the designer.

Materials for Storefronts

Cost, appearance, and availabilitiy are the three basic guidelines for material selection. Almost any material can be used if the designer has the creative freedom and the budget. How the materials will be handled depends on the designer's creativity and ability to interpret and communicate the merchandising message. (See Table 4-1.) Constants include restrictions imposed by local ordinances or by design constraints imposed by the shopping center's standards. Stainless steel, for example, is not appropriate in warm, desert-like locales like Sante Fe, where adobe and terra cotta comprise much of the architectural fabric.

Other considerations are:

Regional weather. Natural stucco and stained wood are fine for Pacific coast, southwest, and southern states, but they will not give long service in the frost belt.

Neighborhood compatibility. If the planned exterior is not contextual with the neighborhood, the owner and the designer should have sound reasons for breaking the harmony. If the objective is a shock effect, be prepared for neighborhood backlash.

Time, cost. Using materials that are not native or local to the project, such as shipping Pennsylvania brick to Louisiana or Italian marble to Ohio, requires sufficient lead time and funds.

Maintenance. Wood is handsome and distinctive but needs regular maintenance. Brass and bronze are elegant but require regular polishing to keep their luster.

Windows

A store's display window is the first direct link the shopper has with the goods within the store. Like a movie poster or theater playbill, it provides a preview of the attractions inside.

Windows help focus the store's merchandise to its target market. The proportions and display techniques complement the merchandise and enhance the shopper's perceptions of its value. High-priced jewelry is particularly effective shown in small cube windows, precisely illuminated and artfully arranged. Limited market, popularly-priced electronic equipment such as calculators and stereos attract shoppers with closely-packed displays in bright, closed-back windows (broad

4
Louis Sullivan's masterful design for Chicago's Carson Pirie Scott & Co. is characterized by double bands of coiling thickets of iron ribbons that extend down State and Madison Streets, and then are massed together to form the monumental curved front entrance. The upper floors are a grid of Chicago-style windows.

42

Table 4-1		Materials for Storefronts	
Material		**Considerations**	**Best uses**
Wood		Gives warm, soft look. Natural finish will be destroyed by elements; needs constant maintenance. Some woods, such as oak, need multiple coats of shellac or varnish. Others, such as cedar shingles and redwood, weather naturally and require little upkeep.	Versatile; can be used to advantage in all design settings, contemporary as well as period.
Metals	Bronze, brass	Handsome, expensive. Needs maintenance to keep brightness and sheen.	Appropriate for jewelry or fine apparel stores that require a quality appearance.
	Aluminum	Coated (duranodic) comes in many colors and finishes, both satin and polished. Lightweight. Pliable.	Popular because of contemporary look and low maintenance.
	Stainless steel	Low-maintenance. Expensive. Long-lasting. Malleable.	Very good for urban installations. Cool and sleek effect.
	Baked or porcelain enamel steel	Available in bright colors. Long-lasting.	Good application if sharp contrasts are required.
Masonry	Natural stone, brick marble, granite	Selection will usually be regional because of availability and transportation costs. Fairly high cost, even with veneers. Very low maintenance. Historic preservation requires careful matching of materials.	These materials work well in environments where they pick up the theme of materials set by surrounding structures. Convey solidity, timelessness.
Stucco		Can be worked into interesting shapes. variety of textures available. Can go over concrete block. Manufactured with insulation backing or lightweight metal or wood framing. Not recommended for very cold climates.	Excellent for exteriors and interiors of stores in warm-weather climates. Pliability is a major asset.
Glass	Glass block	Combines solid facade with translucency.	Can be teamed with other materials in contemporary design plan.
	Transparent glass	Emphasizes interior store activity. May be security problem. Ultraviolet rays could damage merchandise. Gates may be necessary to protect glass for stores not in enclosed malls.	Best material for permitting views of merchandise and store interior.
	Opaque glass	Available in colors. Carrara (black) glass can be dramatic when installed as a facade.	Good for deco, modern, or contemporary designs.
	Translucent glass	Used for clerestory windows where light but not transparency is needed.	Effective if back-lit. Presents a warm glow in evening hours.
	Mirrors	Reflectance gives dimensional quality. Lightweight. Can be framed with metal for street fronts or malls.	Can be used in urban or natural settings but should reflect a dramatic or visually appealing view.
Plastic	Acrylics (clear and opaque); laminates	Very adaptable. Good for canopies. Sometimes permitted for storefronts in malls.	Works well for signage and canopies. For larger installations, get manufacturer's estimated life of product for your region.

4 Exterior Store Design

5
The open-back window: The store becomes the backdrop

6
Awnings as environmental advertising

appeal, large display).

Most display windows belong to one of two types:

- closed back, creating its own environment

- open back, where the store itself forms the backdrop

A cross between the two utilizes partial shutters or hanging banners behind the windows to partition the space between storefront display and selling floor.

Apparel merchants differ in the closed- vs. open-back preference. Some prefer the additional interior hanging or shelf display space that a closed-back window provides inside the store. Others believe the sight of the merchandise selection inside is a strong draw, well worth sacrificing a few linear feet of display space.

If the store has a visual merchandising or display director, their ideas and merchandise presentation techniques should be incorporated into the window design. Often lighting will determine the shape and design of the store's window and front. Lighting can be exposed, hidden, theatrical, or any combination of the three. The window should be dimensioned so that the installed lighting does not hit the top of a mannequin's head or a display object. Leave "aiming distance" from the light source to the display itself.

Portable platforms provide flexibility to mount settings at floor level or in tiers. Space allotted to the window should be sufficiently deep to accept effectively-lit platforms.

Enclosed mall stores often have no windows at all. Here, retail establishments open onto a controlled environment. Gondolas and other display units are placed a few feet inside the store. Tenants in upscale vertical urban malls like Trump Tower in New York maintain a traditional doors-and-windows approach; shops in midprice malls such as Horton Plaza in San Diego, and most suburban malls are a mixture of traditional and open front. In malls featuring popular-priced merchandise, most storefronts are open to attract the greatest number of shoppers.

The store designer can help the merchant establish visual standards for window display. Through a series of sketches, the designer can suggest groupings or positioning of items with appropriate lighting and props. Here, designers can use their imagination and show how to hang items, floor-mount them, or suspend them.

Awnings and Canopies

Awnings and canopies offer protection from the weather to customers, and protect merchandise in the windows from sun damage. They are also environmental advertising: by displaying the store's name, awnings and canopies also function as a sign and enhance the store's exterior identity.

Many materials can be utilized for awnings. In addition to the traditional canvas, materials

5
An open-back display window integrates the dynamics of interior activity and the merchandise array to attract shoppers. For this Banana Republic store in an enclosed shopping mall, wood provides a full-width outline of the store's front, peaking above the hanging fixture and wood-frame doors.

Design: Charles E. Broudy & Associates

6
The Milan unit of the Beltrami shoe store chain has crisp white retractable white fabric awnings. The left segment carries the distinctive "B" logo; on the right is the store name, repeated on the store window in a related type style and size.

44

7 & 8

Awnings can be made in a variety of materials, sizes, and shapes

such as glass, wood, metal, and plastic can be fabricated into bubble or arch shapes, as well as the standard 45-degree angle extension from the exterior wall.

In some urban areas, canopies extend to the curb line from the entry doorway to convey elegance as well as to provide overhead protection. At the Pavilions Shopping Center, Sacramento, fixed overhead canopies are part of the walkway system that connects clusters of stores.

Awnings can lend a unifying effect to rehabbed stores. In an existing streetfront setting, a merchant may take over an existing store or stores for expansion. If the the retailer does not wish to incur the expense of installing an entire new storefront, awnings can provide visual unity at far less cost.

Maintenance is vital; a shabby awning or canopy becomes a visual slur.

Canvas awnings and canopies have been approved for interior use in many enclosed malls because shopping center owners do not consider the material a permanent material. Check the tenant's criteria for stipulations if you are considering this type of storefront element. Requirements for retractable hardware as part of the design should be included in the budget.

Doorways and Entry Portals

Doorways make a very personal statement to the shopper. Doorways welcome people inside. They can also keep them out. They can make either a strong or subtle design statement. And they are a

7

cause for security concern.

Theoretically, doors are not needed for stores in enclosed malls during shopping hours. Some merchants opt for doors if they want more of a streetscape look. Doors can deter entry by potential nuisance makers such as youngsters with drippy ice cream cones. Often, retailers who prefer typical side-hinged swinging doors will keep them open during business hours. Furriers and jewelers who want to maintain an exclusive aura may prefer the closed door option.

Doors for retail stores

Swinging: Side-hinged glass doors can be framed with many different materials. Clear tempered glass with no frame is a popular style.

8

Glass awnings on a white metal frame provide protection to shoppers, and continue the same materials palette used for Gap store fronts at Post and Kearny Streets in San Francisco.

Design: Charles E. Broudy & Associates

4 Exterior Store Design

9, 10, 11, 12
The world of doorway design: historic, contemporary, or fanciful

Side and overhead: Often framed in aluminum or other metal, they are pushed open and stacked in side or overhead pockets. Open metal mesh is a popular material for doors which can be pulled from above as well as from the side. Tambour sliding doors, which have clear or opaque inserts adhered to a flexible backing, offer increased security over the open mesh variety. Automatic or manual operation can be specified from most manufacturers of side and overhead doors.

Accordian fold: An adaptation of the side sliding door, accordian fold doors can be fabricated of open mesh, or of solid panels which give the impression of a wooden or metal door.

Revolving doors: While they have excellent air-lock properties to control air and dust, revolving doors are not considered fire exits. A manually-operated door beside the revolving door is usually required for egress for emergencies and use by the handicapped.

Custom doors: Ornate wood and metal doors, gates, and antique doors can be converted to commercial use by replacing glass and other elements by careful repair work. Hardware should be reinforced to meet current security and fire code standards. Custom doors are an impressive technique to communicate style and quality.

Heated entrances: Some stores have experimented with open entries defined only by heat registers at top and bottom. They have proven to be energy inefficient and many have been replaced with solid partitions.

Automatic openers: Foot-activated treadles and sensors are frequently installed at supermarket and drug store entrances and exits.

Security at doorways is a major design consideration (see Chapter 9, "Systems"). Most stores with multiple entrances now have guards or electronic suveillance units to monitor traffic. A single entrance is recommended for small- and medium-size stores. Side and back doors that lead to a receiving dock, or installed to meet fire exit requirements, should be fitted with an alarm system.

Vestibules

Vestibules are windproof, weatherproof, coldproof enclosures that save energy. Vestibule flooring should collect shoe-borne grime before it is tracked inside.

There are a range of natural

9 Comme des Garçons/Shirt, New York City

10 Art gallery, Paris

46

11 Vidi Vici, New York City

12
Women's aparel store, Melbourne, Australia

and synthetic products that provide a nonslip surface undamageable by water, grit, or sand: natural flagstone; slate; nonslip aggregate; terrazzo; tile; rubber flooring and mats; and carpeting. A bi-level product provides slotted metal with carpet slat inserts that scrape foot bottoms. Grit and moisture are deposited underneath on a removable tray.

For mall stores, where vestibules are not needed, the recess between the mall walkway and the inside of the store should be of the same material. Mall maintenance crews use mechanical scrubbers and buffers to clean floor surfaces, and if the store's entry material is not compatible, it can be ruined by the powerful equipment.

Heat is sometimes introduced in store vestibules when the weather turns chilly. For a small store, a 3'6" space will probably get enough spillover heat from the store itself to keep it comfortable. For larger stores with deep enclosed recesses, separate provisions should be made for air handling in the vestibules.

The problem of how to relate the interior floor height to a lower sidewalk level is common in hilly cities like San Francisco and Seattle, or older cities where rehab is occuring. Many existing buildings that were once residential townhouses have steps within the vestibule. If the client wants to eliminate steps by installing a ramp, allow one inch for every foot of ramp length (a 6-foot-long ramp will eliminate a 6-inch-high step). When steps exist, the owner should check the store's insurance liabilitiy coverage and install a heavy-duty flooring product.

Lighting the Store Exterior

Exterior lighting is critical to a comprehensive, esthetically-pleasing master plan. A successful exterior lighting plan for a retail establishment will satisfy six important criteria:

▶ Safety

▶ Security

▶ Visual attraction

▶ Identification

▶ Landscape enhancement

▶ Design unity

(See also Chapter 6, "Lighting.")

Hemisphere

The Elements of a Store Exterior

1 Interior wood platform permits flexibility for display

2 Entrance pavers are compatible with mall flooring

3 Round wood column with contemporary trim defines doorway

4 Wood mullions and muntins become a visual bridge from the hard-surface verticality of the glass window to the warmly-lit friendliness of the interior

5 Halo-illuminated sign

6 Tempered glass doors extend the see-through quality of the store's facade

7 Curved glass display window with see-through back permits the ambience and activity inside to become a part of the store's overall exterior design

8 Recessed overhead lighting

9 Spotlighting for mannequins and displays

*Design:
Charles E. Broudy
& Associates*

Communicate the
merchandising
message.

49

| 4 | Exterior Store Design | 13 *The sign integrates the storefront design* |

Signs

Sign design is another area where the designer can do just about anything that is in good taste and legal. (See Chapter 7, "Signs and Graphics.") Successful signs are an intrinsic element in the overall exterior design theme, and harmonize with exterior materials, windows, and lighting.

Approvals needed for the exterior design may come from the zoning board, art commission, historical commission, residents' groups, and shopping center management. Before specifying a sign, the designer should have information on:

- Size: not-to-exceed maximum

- Suspension and mounting: rules and regulations governing hanging methods

- Illumination: internal or external lighting

Illuminated signs are important for suburban and highway stores. For downtown stores, street lighting often provides sufficient light for passers-by to read store signs.

Merchants who operate stores fronting on a highway may request a freestanding pylon-mounted sign to attract potential customers traveling in automobiles at 55 miles an hour. The design challenge here is to create a piece of "sales sculpture," a noticeable sign that communicates the store's image and at the same time is environmentally sensitive. Garish examples abound of what not to do.

13 So long as they are in good taste and legal, the designer has wide latitude in creating signs that can be proposed for the client's approval. This back-lit sign for the Ann Taylor unit in Beverly Center, Los Angeles, is set into a wood frame mounted on a glass-enclosed free-standing entry display.

Design: Charles E. Broudy & Associates.

Colors, Materials & Finishes

5

Just about anything goes for the store's colors, materials, and finishes plan that will not inhibit selling. Pulling together shapes, colors, patterns, and textures that will blend together successfully takes both flair and a keen sense of the combined effect of the final scheme on the shopper.

La Parfumerie at Bloomingdale's, New York is unabashedly dramatic. Inspiration for the cabinetry design came from a scene in the 1929 Greta Garbo classic, The Kiss.

Design: Fitzpatrick Design Group Inc., New York; Jay Fitzpatrick, principal in charge.

51

5 Colors, Materials & Finishes

1 *A skillful interplay of materials*

When it comes to selecting colors, materials, and finishes for a store interior, just about anything goes that will not inhibit selling. All combinations are fair game as long as they work together in the final scheme.

Here is where the designer's sense of flair and style can make an identifying statement. Sources of inspiration are virtually limitless. Exposure to art, music, travels, philosophy, food, psychology, and of course, people-watching, contribute to the molding of a personal pattern of spatial interpretation.

The making of a designer usually includes instruction on creating form. "Form" for interiors relates to the shape, color, pattern, texture and all aspects of the final product that the user's senses will be aware of. Intelligent form-giving and good design are never the result of a series of unrelated decisions based on arbitrary manipulations of form or scale or texture. All these facets are strongly interrelated.

Owners' Preferences

How do your clients *really* want to express their own sense of style and esthetic point-of-view? The designer may have to do a fair amount of probing to discover key preferences to augment the basic program requirements.

Query your clients about their esthetic likes and dislikes, their perceptions of their competition's store design. Have them

1 This elegant boutique area on the apparel floor of the new Nan Duskin store in Philadelphia combines marble, carpeting, wood, stainless steel, painted dry wall, exterior glass windows, and white lacquer pylons.

Design: Charles E. Broudy & Associates

verbalize what they believe is trendy, what is classic, what is contemporary, and give examples if they can. What do they mean by eclectic? Timeless? High tech? Contemporary?

Retail merchants are often quite visually literate. Indeed, color, line, and design are part of what they deal with in some manner every day. Their travels for buying trips and trade shows take them to the major cities of the world, and they make it a point to check out the latest crop of new and remodeled stores. They bring back ideas and photos for their own store's designer to review and possibly refine for their company's use.

You can even create an illustrated questionnaire to stimulate the communications process.

Charles E. Broudy & Associates used a mini-comic book format questionnaire as part of the information gathering process for the design of a chain of men's apparel stores. Interviews that had been conducted with management produced many ideas and concepts, but no clear direction emerged. They developed a 12-page comic-book that was a form of organized visual brainstorming. The executives completed the questionnaire by listing their responses to multiple-choice free-form association sketches. After the results were tabulated, the designers were able to establish a basic consensus on which they based their preliminary sketches.

Development of the Color, Materials, and Finishes Plan

▶ **Determine how much of the surface area will be covered by merchandise.**

Will the materials on walls and partitions be covered by shelving, cabinets, or hanging garments? Wall-mounted hang rods can cover two-thirds of a wall's surface.

Put your budget where it will have the most impact. Expensive materials that are hidden behind the merchandise is an example of wastefully poor planning.

▶ **Establish how much flexibility is needed to support the store's merchandising projections.**

Will space allocated for an aisle during the summer be turned into selling space for the holiday season? Changes in materials should be planned with clear foresight into departmental movements.

▶ **Calculate first costs versus life cycle costing.**

Can the budget handle higher first costs for floor coverings, wall covering, trims, and hardware in exchange for longer use? If it cannot, the designer and the store owner should establish wear priorities on which to base specifications.

Most merchants will not balk at replacing carpeting that wears down from high traffic; carpeting that looks shabby soon after installation because the designer did not present clear options for selection is another story. The client should be presented with the pertinent facts and the designer's knowledgeable recommendations, based on a realistic budget and solid data supplied by reliable vendors.

▶ **Materials as part of the security system.**

Angled mirrors and wall-mounted mirrors contribute to the visual control of the store by allowing visual monitoring by employees of areas that would otherwise be blind spots.

When an electronic surveillance device is placed near an entrance, designers should investigate whether certain materials under consideration, such as metals, will interfere with its operation.

▶ **Safety concerns**

Steps and floors at entryways should be covered with a slip-retardant material. Suppliers now offer attractive textured products fabricated of cocoa mat, ceramic tile, sheet vinyl, vinyl tiles, and rubber for use in these areas.

Local building codes and statutes concerning flame-spread and smoke generation should govern materials that will qualify for a store's interior.

5 Colors, Materials & Finishes

Ceramic tile or marble used with wood

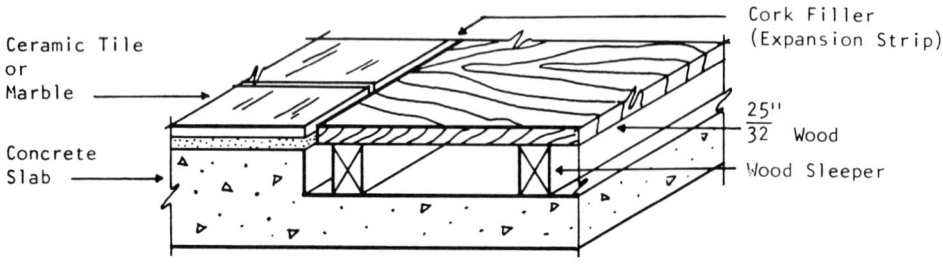

- Ceramic Tile or Marble
- Concrete Slab
- Cork Filler (Expansion Strip)
- $\frac{25}{32}$" Wood
- Wood Sleeper

Examples of dissimilar floors in retail environments. Store designers often utilize different flooring materials to indicate pathways or for visual interest. Careful detailing is important because of expansion and contraction qualities of materials, tripping dangers, worn edges, and cleaning and maintenance.

Carpet and resilient flooring

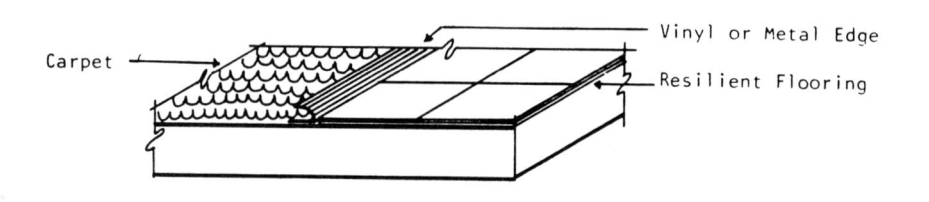

- Carpet
- Vinyl or Metal Edge
- Resilient Flooring

Carpet and wood

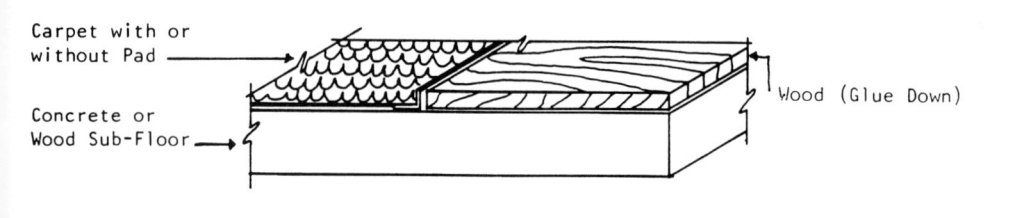

- Carpet with or without Pad
- Concrete or Wood Sub-Floor
- Wood (Glue Down)

Wood and existing flooring

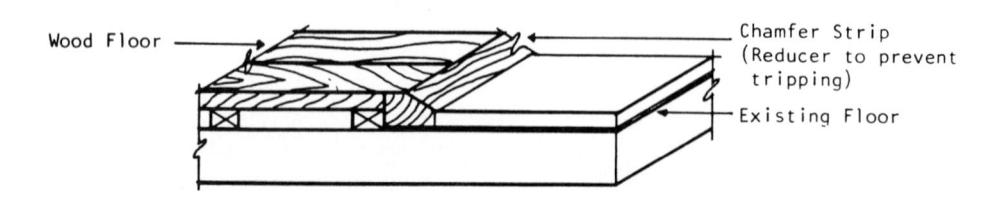

- Wood Floor
- Chamfer Strip (Reducer to prevent tripping)
- Existing Floor

Ceiling Types

Tin
Embossed metal ceilings have been revived for both soft and hard goods stores.

Metal
Available in brass, stainless, or enamel finish, a metal ceiling add a bright, clean overhead surface. They are popular in Europe.

Acoustic Tile
Many varieties of this material are available. Designers should keep the amount of framing to a minimum.

Wood
A wood ceiling can be hung on T-bars with wood tile inserts, or by panels and battens.

Drywall Cove
Drywall can be configured into a wide range of shapes and design themes. It can also be made to appear as a plaster moulding.

Glass or Plastic
By etching or frosting the surface, a skylight effect can be created.

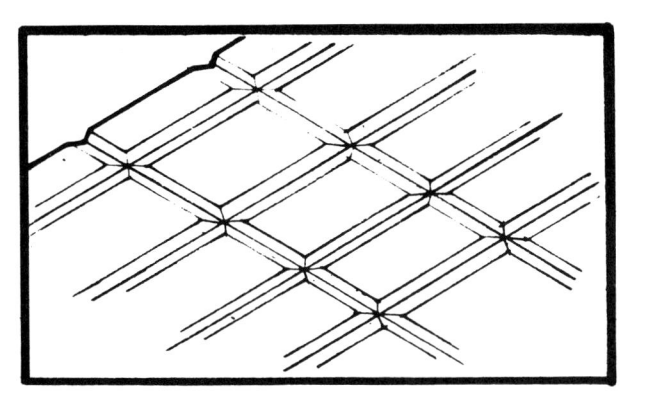

TIN

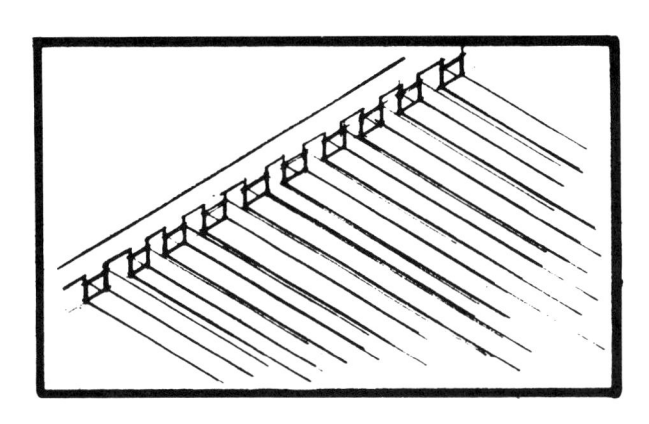

METAL

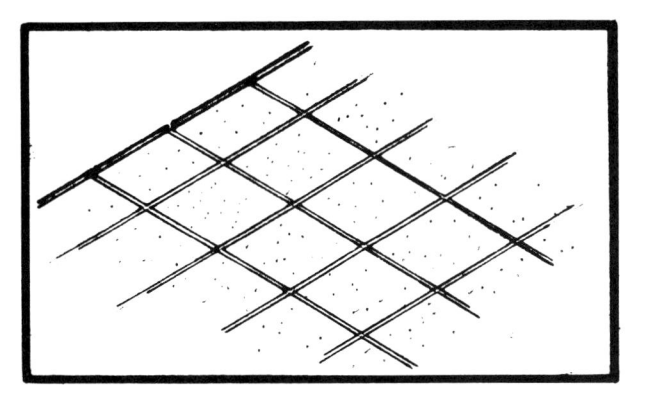

ACOUSTIC TILE

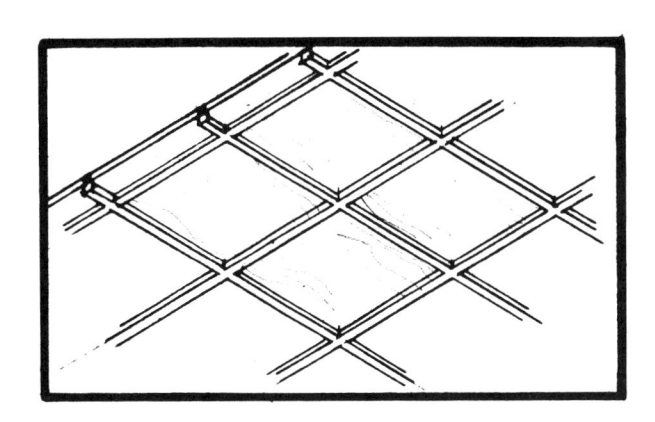

WOOD

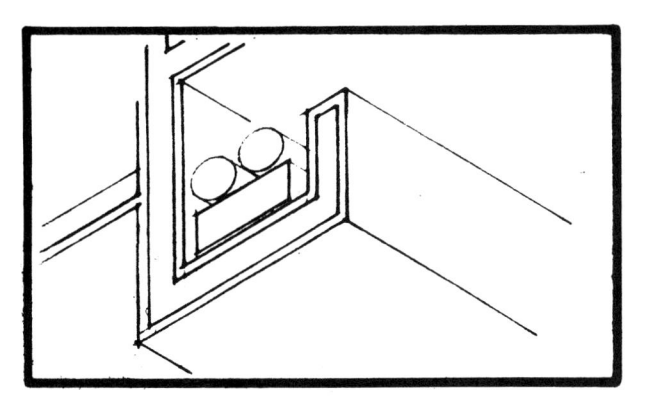

DRYWALL COVE

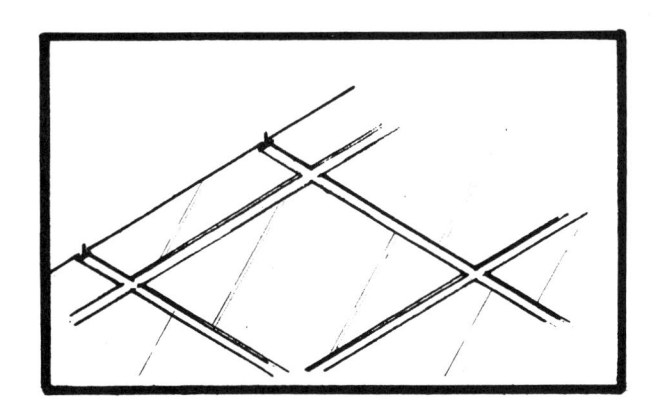

GLASS OR PLASTIC

5 **Colors, Materials & Finishes**

2
A long-wearing spray-on wallcovering

▶ **Early consideration of maintenance.**

"Why didn't you tell me that the brass has to be polished every other day?"

No, the designer does not want to face an unhappy client who has to deal with a maintenance factor that should have been discussed early in the materials selection process. Avoid this situation by submitting a maintenance schedule of first-choice items while the materials and finishes plan is still in its formative stage.

Take into consideration, for example, that painted walls in high traffic locations can quickly become scuff-marked. Merchants often opt for wall coverings with higher first costs and lower maintenance, such as fabric or paper. Wood, plastic laminate, or vinyl covering materials are suitable for dressing room walls not covered by mirrors.

▶ **Making substitutions**

Keep an open mind regarding product availability, particularly when you are in the midst of a fast-track job. Scurrying around to locate an acceptable substitute for original selections that have been discontinued, are out of stock, or have incurred a significant price increase is high on the designer's least-favorite-task list.

The designer must juggle both the project's integrity and delivery time constraints when deciding on substitute materials.

2

Zolatone is a synthetic resin sprayed on walls that is a long-wearing alternative to paint or vinyl. Up to five colors can be blended, and each will be distinguishable when applied. It was used here for the ninth floor at Saks Fifth Avenue, New York.

*Design:
Rubano • Mirviss • Associates, New York;
Lois M. Mirviss, principal in charge.*

56

Color Psychology For Store Design

Shape without form,
shade without color,
Paralyzed force, gesture
without motion.
  T. S. Eliot

Color and lighting are two of the most influential environmental factors in creating a distinctive store interior that adds to the salability of the merchandise. Color can soothe, excite, define space, provide visual cues to direct traffic, flatter the complexion, and give dimension to the products on display.

In a store composed of several departments or selling areas, color transitions should be smooth and subtle rather than abrupt. Customers should not be conscious that background colors are changing from one area to the next. Colors should nudge, rather than push the shopper from one part of the store to another. (Remember the "pin-ball effect.")

Table 5-1 contains additional ideas on the impact of environmental color on sales.

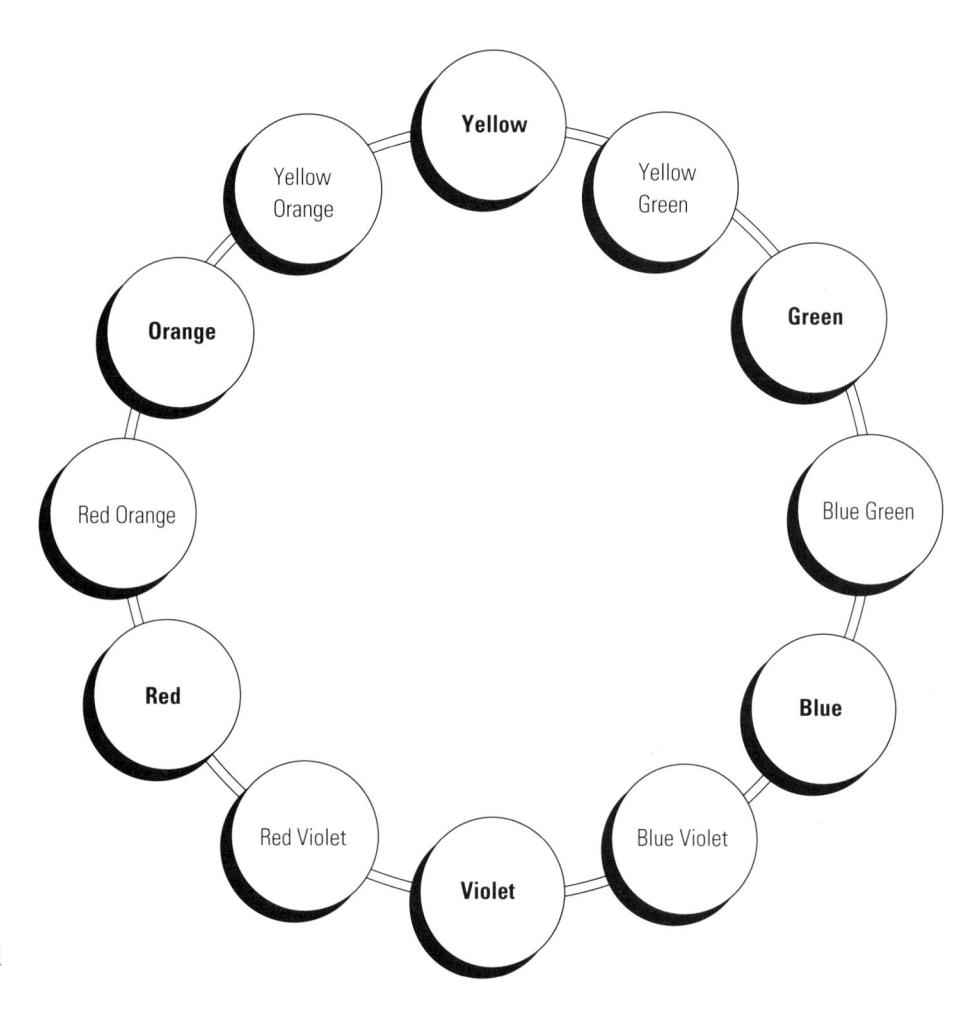

Color palettes

Color Terminology

The color wheel is a circular arrangement of 12 colors.

Analogous: Two or more colors that are next to each other on the color wheel.

Complementary: Colors that are directly opposite on the color wheel. Example: yellow/purple.

Double complementary: Two colors and their complements. Example: yellow/purple/green/red.

Intensity: A color's brightness or dullness.

Monochromatic: One color in different intensities. Example: pastel blue/medium blue/bright blue.

Primary colors: Red, blue, and yellow. (Mixtures of these are the origins of all other colors.)

Secondary colors: Orange (red and yellow); green (yellow and blue); purple (a blue and red).

Shade: The degree of darkness of a color.

Tint: A delicate color or hue.

Tone: A color's degree of modification.

Triadic: Three colors that are equidistant on the color wheel. Example: yellow/red/blue.

Value: A color's darkness or lightness.

5 Colors, Materials & Finishes

Table 5-1 Using Color as a Selling Aid

Type of Merchandise	Colors or Color Themes	Considerations
Men's apparel	Generally warm, Can borrow from gray flannel, blue pinstripe, herringbone, and tweed. Traditional colors such as brown, billiard green, wood tones. High-fashion colors.	Comfortable classic tones are cyclical and regularly return to favor. Brighter colors appeal to the youth market.
Women's apparel	Neutrals.	Women's fashions are bright and varied. Background should not conflict with merchandise and displays which should be made to stand out.
	Warm colors, including peach.	Flattering to skin and hair, particularly when seen in a mirror.
Children's apparel	Bright, primary colors.	Create a lively ambience.
Toys	Bright.	"Festive competition" works here. Bright and lively colored toys are enhanced by similar color scheme for fun atmosphere.
Jewelry	Cool or warm.	Create sparkle and clarity. For costly jewelry, give feeling of luxury. Enhance the product.
Books	Any color the designer wishes.	Keep the color plan simple so it will not compete with the jumble of book covers. Separate departments with contrasting color or colors.
Gifts	Neutral.	For varied merchandise.
	Punchier colors; complementary colors.	For merchandise with slower turnover and fashion cycle.
Shoes	Light colors for floors and walls.	Better for displays and for trying on merchandise in selling area. Dark or leather colors blend with many shoes and offer no contrast.
Fabrics	Neutral.	Colors should not clash or compete with colors and patterns of the fabrics themselves.
Electronics	Warm colors.	Contrast to hard-edge look or industrial look.
	Bright, bold colors.	Can be used because most of these products are small-scale.
Department store merchandise	Overall uniform scheme.	Gives feeling of unity, sophistication.
Discount store merchandise	"Jumpy" colors and textures; primary tones.	Convey a trendy, upbeat mood.

3
Continuing the wood theme

Ash was used for the exterior of the Pfaltzgraff store in the Oak Court Mall, Memphis. The interior design of the store, which sells tableware and gifts, also makes liberal use of wood.

Design: Charles E. Broudy & Associates

▶ **Timeless colors**
  Neutrals: beige, cream, off white, gray, greige, tan
Do not compete with merchandise.
Tasteful.
Can last many years.

▶ **Accent and jewel colors**
  Ruby, burgundy, emerald hunter green, navy, turquoise, teal
Use sparingly. Owners and customers can tire of large expanses of these colors.

▶ **Cool colors**
  Gray, blue blue-green, gray-green, blue-violet.
Conservative and adaptable.
Soothing and relaxing.
Good for home furnishings, men's wear.

▶ **Warm colors**
  Red, orange, yellow
Friendly and cheerful.
Add excitement to an area.
Appropriate for children's wear, active sportswear, housewares.

▶ **Pastels**
  Peach, mauve, lavender.
Flattering to complexions.
Good for lingerie, jewelry.

Materials and Finishes

Table 5-2 lists materials and finishes suitable for retail stores by "Characteristics and Considerations" and "Recommendations."

Space is limited in this volume for lengthy discussions of technical details and specifications for the many different types of materials, both natural and synthetic, that can be used to express the designer's concept for an attention-grabbing sales environment. Trade associations support the efforts of individual vendors to educate design practitioners in the latest methods and techniques utilized in the manufacture and fabrication of products for store interiors.

The type of information available from three trade groups is included here. Names of additional trade organizations are listed for the reader's reference.

Floor Covering Weekly's Specifier's Guide to Contract Floor Covering
Hearst Business Communications, Inc., FCW Division, 919 Third Avenue, New York, NY 10022 (212/759-8050); 80 pages; $15 single copy.

Lists producers of cushions; resilient flooring; ceramic tile; hardwood; and carpets and rugs. Carpets and rugs are further described by solid, multicolor, and patterned for loop pile and cut pile constructions; and solid and multicolor for cut and loop constructions.

Architectural Woodwork Institute
2310 South Walter Reed Drive
Arlington, VA 22206
(703/671-9100)

AWI has over a dozen publications for designers and specifiers in addition to the annual *Sources of Supply* that gives detailed information about services of AWI members nationwide. Listed here are two of the most requested AWI publications.

Architectural Woodwork Quality Standards, Guide Specifications & Quality Certification Program. Defines the three grades of architectural woodwork. Offers a system of reference specifications that enables architects and designers to specify all elements of architectural woodwork; 130 pages; $35.

3

Table 5-2		Materials and Finishes for Retail Stores	
Material		**Characteristics and Considerations**	**Recommendations**
Floors			
Wood	Parquet	Often set in mastic; checkerboard, herringbone patterns.	Can be a first-use, economical way to achieve the wood look. Can be glued down.
	Straight boards	Hardwood.	Will give an antique or "old floor" look. Effective in an accent area to set off an all-carpet floor.
	Acrylic-impregnated wood flooring	Glue-down parquet-like treated wood; very low maintenance.	Good for large shops or shopping centers. Can withstand moisture.
	Edge grain softwood	Very durable.	Expensive. Produces a deep, unique flooring look.
Marble		High gloss wears off quickly. Can be obtained 1/4-in. thick.	Rich-looking if maintained properly.
Terrazzo		Marble chips mixed with cement.	Expensive but long-lasting. Gives quality appearance. Good for aisles.
Granite		Available in 3/8-in. thickness; can be quick-set on subfloor.	Quality appearance combined with low maintenance. Appropriate for traditional and contemporary use. Good for heavy-traffic areas.
Flagstone		Can be used in grid or free-form design, single or multi colors.	Expensive. Gives a natural look. Effective even when used sparingly.
Ceramic tile	Quarry tile	Natural nonslip quality.	Good for aisles and corridors, and wet areas such as food preparation spaces.
	Glazed tile	Wear patterns can appear in heavy-traffic areas. Comes in a variety of colors.	Provides bright accent areas. Can be effectively used as a theme material to give a "continental" look. Walls and countertops are additional uses.
	Integral	Good wearing quality.	Use for aisles, floors, and traffic areas.
Carpet*	Wool and nylon blend	Durable.	Best used for quality shops and salons.
	Acrylic	Sturdy; less costly than wool and nylon blend.	Long-wearing, colorfast.
	Nylon	Carpet glued directly to subflooring.	Long-wearing. Colors have improved in new generations. Avoid shiny pile.
	Polypropylene	Moisture-resistant. Resists fading.	Not used as often as three types listed above.
	Padding	Rubber and jute.	Used extensively for large areas. gives softer, plusher underfoot feel. (Both forms of padding extend carpet life.)
Special-purpose	Area rugs	Antique or new orientals; patterned contemporary or solid movable rugs.	Effective over wood floors or neutral background carpeting. Creates quality atmosphere.
	Entryway flooring: Cocoa mat	Scrapes dirt off shoes.	Good appearance when new; replace when appears matted.
	Slats	Permit dirt to fall through to trap below.	Necessity for stores in frost belt. Good investment for all other climates, especially for entryways that lead to other flooring materials.

*Some synthetic carpeting needs stretching soon after laying.

Table 5-2 Materials and Finishes for Retail Stores (Continued)

Material		Characteristics and Considerations	Recommendations
Floors			
Carpet tiles		Easily replaced; owner should have reserve inventory of replacement tiles.	Good for heavy-traffic areas. Easier and less conspicuous to replace than patching broadloom
Resilient	Solid vinyl	Wide variety of colors and textures available. Glue-down installation. Minimum maintenance required.	Well suited for heavy-use areas such as aisles, corridors. Versatile style palette, from high-tech to elegant.
	Vinyl composition tile	Good selection of patterns and colors. Low maintenance.	Less expensive than solid vinyl. Long-wearing but lacks richness. Suitable for hard-use areas—discount stores, back-of-the-house spaces.
	Asphalt	Low cost	Less frequently specified as price spread between asphalt and other types of resilient flooring has narrowed in recent years.

Exterior Walls

Even though freestanding stores are the most challenging to the store architect, commissions to design them are rather infrequent. The designer has to communicate the store's personality to prospective customers primarily through the storefront. By using traditional or contemporary materials with flair and efficiency, the store's front can become the merchant's single most dramatic and effective "silent salesperson." The materials listed below can be used for both freestanding and shopping center stores.

Material	Characteristics and Considerations	Recommendations
Masonry	Limestone panels. Brick.	Has solid, quality appearance. Economical; available in many shapes and colors. Costly to ship long distances.
	Fieldstone, ledgestone.	For accent walls. Use regional materials.
Marble	Thin veneers will not give long use in harsh weather climates.	A rich, quality product that requires careful specification. Interesting and varied color selection.
Granite	Costly but durable. Veneers are becoming thinner. Low maintenance.	Limited colors but effective for traditional, classic stores.
Precast concrete insulated sandwich panels with exposed aggregate	Moderately costly, but reduce construction time.	Efficient material for large wall surfaces. Because material is manufactured, not natural, it works best with contemporary designs.
Anodized aluminum	Available with preinstalled windows and insulation.	Available in several price ranges and color ranges.
Stainless steel	Same as above.	Long-lasting and virtually maintenance free, material has austere, hard-edge look.
Porcelain enamel	On aluminum or steel base; prefabricated for window walls; or made in large panels with sealant joints.	Suitable to cover large expanses. Many colors to select from.
Cement plaster	Produced with insulation, gypsum wallboard, and metal studs. Cost efficient.	Scoring and jointing can easily create interesting slopes and shapes. Material is popular for covering large building expanses.
Glass reflective surfaces	A moderate-to-expensive prefabricated material. Colors are limited.	Most successful when used on a contemporary structure, as a visual integrator to reflect natural or artificial surroundings.

(Continued)

Table 5-2	Materials and Finishes for Retail Stores (Continued)	
Material	**Characteristics and Considerations**	**Recommendations**

Interior Walls and Partitions

For dividing and defining interior spaces, the retail store designer is involved with:

1. Permanent walls—load-bearing or structural walls

2. Floor-to-ceiling partitions—divide one selling or nonselling area from another when merchandise or service is dissimilar or intimacy or privacy is desired.

3. Freestanding partitions—dividers that separate spaces without blocking the view; should be easily relocatable and adaptable.

To cover wall and partition surfaces, there is a plethora of choices, with more entering the marketplace every year. From smooth and glossy marble to textured brick and from glittery mirrors to velveteen, the store designer can match atmosphere, mood, and budget to available products. Investigate wall systems that permit metal store fixture standards on the wall with panels of mirror, fabric, plastic laminate, or wall covering between the standards.

Material	Characteristics and Considerations	Recommendations
Permanent walls and floor-to-ceiling partitions		
Brick	Expensive.	Can be used in natural color or painted. Extends exterior experience indoors. Provides distinctive depth and texture.
Exposed concrete block	Inexpensive.	Split-face varieties and color can dress up this material.
Marble and granite veneer	Reinforcing produces larger blocks. Specify honed or polished finish.	Has distinctive richness. Popular for jewelry and other big-ticket item stores. Use to attain a varied wall texture.
Ceramic tile	Many sizes, textures, colors, and shapes for permanent installations.	Effective as overall background for housewares department or accents in other sales areas. Hand-painted scenic tiles can be focal points.
Plaster and stucco	Classic stucco, stipple, sand textures, and other imprints possible.	Carries out a warm climate theme. Deep texture can cover layers of previous finishes.
Sheetrock	Inexpensive basic interior material.	Joints need taping and proper spackling or they will show under glossy paint. Easily covered with paper or fabric.
Paint	Low cost and flexibility make paint the most used of all interior materials. Easily scuffed.	Merchandise and painted color background should not compete. Glossy and flat finishes create different backdrop effects. Painted treatments include supergraphics, stripes, stencils, contrasting panels.
Wood paneling	Modest to very expensive. Produced in boards or veneer.	Made in range or natural finishes or in lacquer colors. Can be natural barn look or elegant matched panels.
Plastic laminate	Colorful; easy to construct and maintain. corners are vulnerable to chipping.	Good for dressing rooms, as a long-term substitute for paint, and in hard-use areas.
Wall fabric, wallpaper, and wall vinyl	Price ranges from low to high but maintenance is often very low. Proper background preparation needed on substrate for thin or expensive materials.	Enormous variety, but designer should consider budget and product availability before making final selection.
Mirror	Can be used clear, gray or bronze colored, or smoked.	Visually enlarges a space or "stretches" a wall. Important to visual security program. Sparkle and luster of clear or tinted mirror can enliven a drab space.
Stained and leaded glass	Great variety of colors. Custom or stock designs.	For dividers, accent areas in hard or soft goods stores. Lighting from behind adds to visual punch.

Table 5-2 Materials and Finishes for Retail Stores (Continued)

Material		Characteristics and Considerations	Recommendations
Interior Walls and Partitions			
Etched glass		Can carry signage or decorative ornamentation.	Opaque or clear versions available. Most effective for "period" design themes.
Slotwall		Slotted wood panel with metal or plastic devices to support shelves or hangers.	For self-serve display of apparel, shoes, books, gifts, tobacco products, etc.
Free-standing Partitions	Grilles	Allow see-through effects.	Applicable to dividers of departments, and in some cases permit display and graphics to separate departments.
	Compressed spring systems	Can support hangrods or shelving.	Good for housewares; permit a see-through wall housing shoes, apparel, and home furnishings, etc.
	Homasote with wall Covering	Flexible display divider; easy to pin merchandise directly to surface.	For paper products, apparel, and light-weight accessory and houseware items.
	Wall cubes	Hollow glass or plastic cubes.	Shoes, hardware, small appliances, etc. placed in cubes make a combination merchandise exhibit and space divider.
	Stained, leaded, and etched glass	See listings under "Interior Walls and Partitions," above.	Panels
	Plastics	Clear or opaque color.	Can be suspended on wires from the ceiling or organized within frames. Used to break up space in large selling areas such as furniture showrooms or department stores.

Ceilings

Retail stores ceilings offer another design dimension. In offices, banks, schools, and hospitals, ceilings are a surface against which to bounce light or control sound. These aspects are certainly true in stores, but in addition, the designer can utilize materials, textures, and different height levels for stunning effects, or to restate a pattern used on floors or walls.

Acoustical tile	Exposed T-bar	Mineral or fiberglass panels, exposed metal track—2 by 4 ft or 2 by 2 ft.	Economical but "busy" ceiling.
	Concealed spline	Textured mineral tiles in concealed spline, usually 12-in square.	Even, unbroken ceiling appearance. Use for more sophisticated applications.
	Textured or scored	Scored panels in 2 by 4 ft, or 2 by 2 ft. Present linear and various geometric forms on surface.	Linear and grid-like in appearance. Use where ceiling interest is needed.
Luminous ceiling	Plastic	Plexiglass or acrylic in a variety of finishes and looks.	Can cause glare or shadowing from dust or dirt.
	Tiffany type	Plastic, colorful, decorative; costly.	Strong, powerful appearance.
	Egg crate	Metal or plastic; square or hexagon shapes.	Light can appear diffused.
	Low brightness	Parahex or square-shape grids. Colors: silver, bronze, gold.	Good way to reduce glare of fluorescent lighting.
	High-cell parabolic	Plastic or metal.	Creates a low glare, with various grid width openings.
Baffle ceilings	Insulated fabric	Foam board covered with fabric.	Helps conceal exposed lighting; has sound absorbent value.
	Wood baffles	Wood-veneer plywood or solid wood. Color or natural. Gridlike patterns.	Good for remodeling; creates either natural or contemporary feeling.

5 Colors, Materials & Finishes

4
Patterned floor of marble and terrazzo

Fire Code Summary. All-in-one source for fire code requirements and the use of architectural woodwork products; 36 pages, $12.

Italian Marble Center
The Italian Trade Center
499 Park Avenue
New York, NY 10022
(212/980-1500)

Sourcebook: Marble From Italy–United States Supplier of Italian Stone Products. Information provided by stock size; business type; stone types (alabaster, slate, onyx, and agglomerates); and marble, granite, and travertine by product (blocks, slabs, tiles, and finished pieces); 40 pages.

Full color posters: *Marble From Italy–The Natural Choice,* and *Marble From Italy–The World Source Of Natural Stone And Technology.*

Other sources of information:

National Association of Display Industries
470 Park Avenue South
New York, NY 10016
(212/213-2662)

National Association of Store Fixture Manufacturers
5875 West Sunrise blvd.
Sunrise, FL 33313
(305/587-9190)

Shop & Display Equipment Association
24 Croydon Road
Caterham, Surrey CR3 6YR
England
011-44-1-0883-48911

4 **For the regional shopping center that is part of the mixed-use New Orleans Centre at the Dome, the richly-configured marble and terrazzo floor on both levels evokes the mood of a continental arcade. The 100-foot-high skylit atrium has exposed steel space frames.**

Design: Hellmuth, Obata & Kassabaum, P.C., New York; Till Wendel, AIA, principal in charge for the shopping center.

64

Lighting

6

The illumination of a merchandising area is an integral part of the design. When the space begins to take form in the designer's imagination, it should be "seen" with the merchandise in place and the lights on.

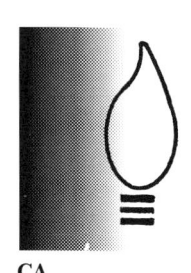

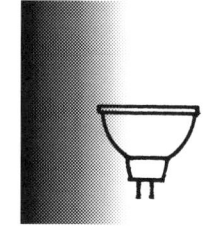

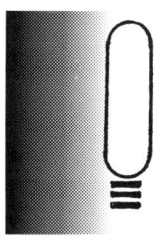

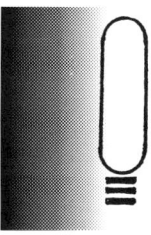

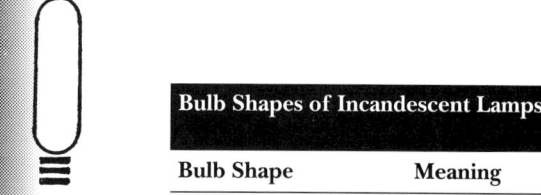

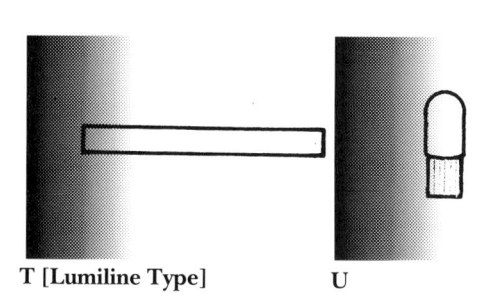

A CA F

G GT MR P PAR PS

R S T

T [Lumiline Type] U

Bulb Shapes of Incandescent Lamps	
Bulb Shape	**Meaning**
A	Standard
CA	Candle
F	Flame
G	Globe
GT	Globe tubular
MR	Multireflector
P	Pear
PAR	Parabolic reflector
PS	Pear straight neck
R	Reflector
S	Straight side
T	Tubular
U	Mini low voltage

6 Lighting

1
Lighting helps to create an energized upscale image

One of the most imporant questions that retail store designers should ask themselves as soon as the store's form begins to evolve is:

▶ **How do we light it?**

Architectural programs for other types of building programs place lighting further down on the design decision-making list. But a retail space virtually lives and breathes by the success of its lighting plan. It is a prime factor from the inception of the design process.

"Lighting is the most important decorative item in the store," said the former CEO of a New York women's specialty store. "The quality of lighting can make or break merchandise. If the lighting is great, it does not make any difference if the merchandise is on mannequins, pinned up on a display, or presented as a still life."

Effective store lighting creatively accomplishes these objectives:

▶ attracts shoppers

▶ moves merchandise

▶ dramatizes ceilings, floors, walls

▶ flatters merchandise and customers

▶ minimizes eye strain

▶ is energy-efficient

1

Topaz is a junior and contemporary apparel, shoes and accessories chain targeted to the 18-35 age group. The 2,500-sq. ft. unit in the Willowbrook Mall, Wayne, N.J., is 18 feet wide. High ceilings and indirect uplight from a continuous light cove give an impression of spaciousness. To conserve energy, 90 watt capsylite bulbs that are the equivalent of 150 watt bulbs were used.

Design: Dorf Associates, New York; Martin E. Dorf, principal in charge.

Attracts Shoppers

Light attracts. It is the quickest and most direct form of nonverbal communication.

The quantity, quality, and effect of the exterior and interior lighting will be evaluated in an instant by shoppers. If they are intrigued, they will let the light help guide them into and through the store, and into the next level of merchandise evaluation and selection. Light can be subtle or overt. It can divert and influence, whether the shopping trip is made because of today's great sale prices, or if the shopper is casually browsing for a wedding gift.

There are very few "standard" retail lighting solutions because nearly every store (other than "formula" chains) is unique: merchandise mix, trading area, customer profile, and image combine to give it the personality that the design, including the lighting, must communicate. *Just about the only constant is that initial impact is critical.*

The human eye adjusts to the light level even before it begins

2
Layers and curves at Lerner New York

to transmit to the brain information about the the merchandise. Consider the impression of a store with bright (100 footcandles or more) ambient light created by unbaffled fluorescent lamps, versus a store where ambient lighting is discreet, accent light complements the merchandise, and architectural details are enhanced by lighting elements. Both stores are sending out clear messages that shoppers quickly perceive.

Moves Merchandise
Retail store lighting is not a space lighting problem; it is a merchandise lighting problem and should be conceived with a solid sales orientation.

Lighting and merchandise presentation work in tandem to differentiate products to the customer.
- Items are complemented by their physical environment while at the same time standing out from the background.
- Merchandise on display is determined by a hierarchy; focal objects are enhanced by compelling displays and lighting techniques.
- Integrated store design and merchandise presentation add value to products on display.

The techniques by which the designer can add sales appeal to the merchandise by lighting effects, while still staying within the constraints of the project's budget and applicable energy codes, can provide the client with a noticeable competitive edge. In the retail store design field, many designers have built their reputations as

2 **The Limited, Inc. introduced Lerner New York to appeal to an upscale shopper. At The Gardens, W. Palm Beach, Fla. store, layered and curved ceiling drops with concealed illumination define perimeter merchandising areas. Mannequins are strategically placed along main traffic aisles and in windows.** *Design: The Limited, Inc., in association with Jon Greenberg & Associates, Berkley, Mich.; Ken Nisch, principal in charge.*

67

6 Lighting

3 & 4
Sparkle plenty

Effective retail store lighting complements merchandise presentation at Addis and Dey's in the Great Northern Mall, Clay, N.Y., near Syracuse. In the Glassware Dept. (rt.), downspots add brilliance to fine crystal. On the main floor (below), natural illumination from the skylight combines with overhead and showcase lighting to produce extra overall depth.

Design: Pfeiffer & Miro Associates, New York; Ken Pfeiffer and Fidel Miro, principals in charge.

3

4

much on their ability to deliver a volume-building store on the basis of their lighting design talents as on their more traditional architectural and planning skills. They view the project from the outset *with the lights on, the merchandise in place, and customers in motion.*

Dramatizes Ceilings, Floors, Walls
Lighting is an extremely malleable as well as precise design tool. A store planner can highlight, sculpt, signal, wash walls, or subdue–all within the frame of an overall plan.

Excellent retail architectural lighting plans will echo the floor plan, create a visually-dynamic ceiling (overhead zone), and define wall surfaces (perimeter zone). Here are some techniques:

▶ Cove lighting

▶ Dropped ceiling outlined with lighting

▶ Neon accents

▶ Showcase lighting

▶ Lighting at mirrors

▶ Spot lighting above displays

▶ Wall washing

▶ Lighting under shelves

68

5
Use a palette of lighting techniques to differentiate merchandise, and guide the customer.

Elements of a Lighting Plan

5

Former Alcott & Andrews store, New York City

Design:
Charles E. Broudy & Associates

1	Two-level fluorescent cove lighting	**6**	Pale-color wood adds light reflectance to main aisle, helping to draw the customer to the back of the store
2	Texture of tin ceiling is accentuated by cove lighting		
3	Angled cove visually directs traffic flow to rear of store	**7**	Dark carpet, a design contrast feature to balance lighter tones of adjacent materials, maximizes reflectance on merchandise
4	Incandescent downlighting illuminates merchandise	**8**	Lighting above center pediment is both architectural and directional, to lead customers to merchandise area beyond lattice divider
5	Concealed fluorescent perimeter lighting draws customers to hanging merchandise displays	**9**	Track-type accent spotlighting gives drama and dimension to mannequins

A & S

Landmark Lighting

Location:
New York City

Size:
**A & S Plaza:
1 million sq. ft.;
A & S department store:
300,000 sq. ft.**

6

7

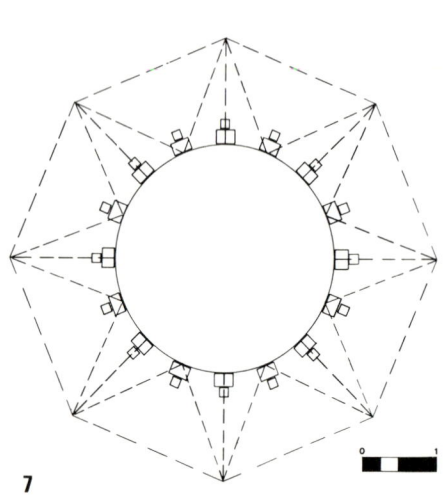

The exterior design for A&S Plaza makes it a major retail landmark. On the facade near Herald Square, 40-foot high neon marquee signs provide glitter and dimension, establishing a high level of customer excitement for the shopping experience inside.

Design Architect: RTKL, Baltimore, Md.; Leonard Kagan, AIA, principal in charge; HVAC/electrical engineers: Syska & Hennessy, New York.

6
Neon pizzazz on Herald Square

7
Plan view of column capitals

8
Crowning glory

Located on the site of the former Gimbel Bros. store, a block from R. H. Macy & Co., this Abraham & Straus unit is the first department store on the New York scene in two decades. The original structure was designed by Daniel Burnham in 1909. The current rehab sheaths the facade facing the Avenue of the Americas with 100-foot-high glass windows that bring the movement and activity of the new 11-level A&S Plaza to one of the country's busiest intersections.

In addition to the A&S unit, which is eight levels, the building houses four levels of office and showroom space, and a 1,000-seat food court. Developers were Melvin Simon & Associates, Inc., Silverstein Properties, Inc., and the Zeckendorf Companies.

The massive project was fast-tracked to open in time for the 1989 holiday selling season. For the A & S design team, this meant a telescoped timetable requiring the production of design development drawings and construction documents at the same time.

Some lighting goals
- Help organize the spaces by defining the perimeter and giving customers direction through the spaces.
- Energy-efficient and easy to maintain.
- A 40-50 average maintained footcandle level on the merchandise. Accent lights provide higher levels on specific displays.

8

Constraints
- Wattage limitations: 3.0 for the lighting, and .5 for power and signal.
- Other than the first floor, the average ceiling height was 9'-10'.
- Irregular column spacing dictated the lighting patterns.

Solutions
- Delux tri-phosphor fluorescent lamps with a high color rendering index.
- Electronic ballasts. Capsylite energy efficient lamps. A 90 watt lamp is roughly equivalent to a standard 150 watt PAR lamp.

The 15-foot-high first floor ceiling of the A & S store is dramatized with glowing column capitals. Lightweight acrylic plastic was tinted to resemble glass; inside are long-life PL lamps. The sponged ceiling is outlined with a cove fluorescent. A grid of downlights and accent lights is focused on the merchandise.

Design:
Norwood Oliver Design Associates, Inc., New York.

Lighting consultants:
Cline Bettridge Bernstein Lighting Design Inc., New York.

71

6 Lighting

Flatters Merchandise and Customers

Light and color are interdependent. The visible spectrum of energy consists of varying wavelengths of color (red, orange, yellow, green, blue, violet). When a source contains energy throughout the visible spectrum, it is seen as "white" light.

Objects have no color in themselves. Their color can be seen only by means of the source illuminating them. The source must emit those wavelengths of light corresponding to the object color. A red object under a "white" light will appear red because it reflects only those wavelengths of light corresponding to its own particular color. The same red object under a green light source will appear black because the green wavelengths are absorbed and there is no red energy in the source to be reflected.

The choice of a light source will control the color appearance of objects and people. Since most stores use a variety of light sources, the designer's lighting plan should assure a balanced color rendition to flatter merchandise and customers. See Table 6-1, "Color Rendition Comparison," below.

Minimizes Eye Strain

Brightness is the sensation produced either by light from a light

Table 6-1	Currently Recommended Illuminances for Lighting Design in Merchandising and Associated Areas—Target Maintained Levels		
Areas or Tasks	**Description**	**Type of Activity Area**	**Footcandles**
Circulation	Area not used for display or examination of merchandise	High activity Medium activity Low activity	30 20 10
Merchandise (including showcases and wall displays)	The plane area, horizontal to vertical, where merchandise is displayed and readily accessible for customer examination	High activity Medium activity Low activity	100 75 30
Feature displays	Single item or items requiring special highlighting to visually attract and set apart from surroundings	High activity Medium activity Low activity	500 300 150
Show windows	Daytime lighting	General Feature	200 1000
	Nighttime lighting Main business districts	General Feature	200 1000
	Secondary business districts or small towns	General Feature	100 500
Support spaces	Alteration room		100-200
	Fitting room	Dressing areas Fitting areas	20-50 100-200
	Locker rooms		10-20
	Stock rooms, wrapping and packaging		20-50

Source: *Recommended Practice for Lighting Merchandising Areas*, Illuminating Engineering Society of North America, New York, 1986, pp. 17 and 18.

source, or by light reflected from a surface. When quantitatively measured, it is called "luminance." A balanced luminance ratio between the merchandise and the environment will make it easy for customers to see quickly in the selling area, including examining product details.

Glare is a distraction to shoppers and fatigue-producing to employees. It is caused by either overly-bright light sources or reflected surfaces that are within the visual field. Glare can be avoided by adjusting the luminance of lighting equipment; changing the angle between the source and the line of sight; or increasing the general brightness of the space. Table 6-2 on page 74, "Currently Recommended Illuminances for Lighting Design in Merchandising and Associated Areas," provides practical guidelines.

Energy Efficiency
Merchants consider costs associated with illumination as a selling tool as well as an expense. They see it as an expenditure on which they will receive a return on their capital outlay.

Massachusetts, California, and New York have stringent laws governing illumination levels (lumens/square foot) in retail stores. Local codes relating to overall energy management and retail store lighting may also apply.

Guidelines for lighting energy conservation in the design and operation of merchandising facilities are described in the *Lighting Energy Management Series*, published by the Illuminating Engineering Society of North America (345 East 47th Street, New York, NY 10017 (212) 705-7926).

"Conserving Energy Through Lighting" appears on page 80.

Developing the Lighting Plan
The lighting plan can be developed after these factors have been determined:

▸ Type of merchandise to be carried in each section

▸ Size and shape of departments

▸ Ceiling height

▸ Colors and materials for walls, ceilings, floors, and fixtures

▸ Type of display windows (closed back or open back)

A well-planned and well-executed lighting plan will meet these objectives:

Motivate the customer to purchase.
An effective lighting plan heightens the sense of excitement and discovery that adds to the shopping experience. It is one of the most powerful design tools available, and can influence customers' behavior and decisions. Lighting works in unison with the floor plan and background materials to create a sales-stimulating merchandising environment.

Light the merchandise.
Visualize the lighting plan with the product displays in place, and then specify the lamps and fixtures where they will carry out their intended purpose: to effectively light the merchandise. Do not give the same intensity to expanses of the walls or floors. If customers cannot easily examine the merchandise and read product information, chances are they will not buy it.

Divide up the merchandise area.
Pendant lights and other types of hanging fixtures can visually delineate a space. This is one way that the designer can sculpt space with light. Other techniques at the designer's disposal include cove lighting using wood or drywall enclosures, and integrating lighting with crown molding.

Direct the shopper to the merchandise.
Lighting can influence traffic flow to specific displays or to sections of the store, particularly to the back and perimeter walls. High intensity lighting can be utilized to highlight a specific area, as a focal point, or to emphasize a feature wall. Merchants favor focal point and display lighting to draw the shopper to the newest and the best merchandise and coordinated displays.

(continued on page 76)

6 Lighting

Table 6-2 Color Rendition Comparison

Light Source/Lamp Type	General Rendition and Effect	Design Considerations	Colors Emphasized*	Colors Grayed*
Natural light	Adds spatial interest. Customers like to view merchandise in natural light. Skylight can introduce light to store's center.	Fading from ultraviolet rays. Windows reduce interior hanging and shelf space. Heating/cooling load has to be balanced.	All	
Incandescent	Very good rendition (warm) Flexible. Most easily controlled.	Higher energy consumption. Shorter life means increased maintenance.	Red; orange; yellow	Blue
Fluorescent				
CW–Cool White	Good rendition (cool). Economical.	Cold and unflattering. Not recommended except when color rendition does not add to product's salability.	Orange; yellow; blue	Red
WW–Warm White	Fair rendition (warm). Suitable for some selling areas, and non-selling depts. such as offices.	Effect on products to be illuminated should be tested so color rendition is accurate.	Orange; yellow	Red; green; blue
CWX–Cool White Deluxe	Very good rendition (cool). Simulates north light.	Good for fabrics, natural materials.	All	None
WWX–Warm White Deluxe	Good rendition (warm). Blends well with incandescent.	Flatters complexion.	Red; orange; yellow	Blue; green
Ultralume 3000	Approximates standard incandescent lamp.	Higher first cost.		
Multireflector (MR)	Can sometimes be used in place of incandescent. Good for spotlighting, track, and recessed applications.	Cost-efficient. Low voltage reduces energy use. Higher first cost. Requires special housing with transformer.		
Color Improved Mercury	Fair rendition (cool).		Red; yellow; blue	Green
Metal Halide	Good rendition (fairly cool). Specify color-corrected lamps.	Energy-efficient. Powerful. Good for high-ceiling spaces.	Yellow; green; blue	None
Sodium Vapor	Fair rendition (yellowish).		Orange; green; yellow	Red; blue
Halogen	Very good color rendition (white light).	Good for apparel and brightly colored merchandise.	All	

Sources: *Recommended Practice for Lighting Merchandising Areas*, Illuminating Engineering Society of North America, New York, 1986, p. 47; all other information, Charles E. Broudy & Associates.

Ann Taylor

Lighting Solves a Space Problem

Location:
Philadelphia

Size:
3,500 square feet

Designer:
Charles E. Broudy & Associates

A two-level Ann Taylor unit in downtown Philadelphia now occupies a space that originally was deep, narrow, and high: 20 feet wide by 125 feet long with a 20-foot-high ceiling. To make the space work for a women's apparel store selling quality, fashion merchandise, the design program solved these problems:

▶   Create additional selling space by constructing a mezzanine connected to the main floor.

▶   Attract customers to the mezzanine. Make the staircase a design element by curving it at the bottom.

▶   Make the store appear wider than it actually is. Light oak and off-white colors provide good reflectance values and create an open feeling.

▶   Draw traffic to the rear of the store.

▶   Make the mezzanine seem higher from floor to ceiling.

9   **A palette of lighting techniques made this deep and narrow bi-level space work.**

Here's how lighting was integrated into the design plan to achieve each objective:

1   Recessed fluorescent lamps in a dropped trough define mezzanine selling area.

2   Adjustable pulldown incandescent spotlights focus on the merchandise and also provide ambient lighting for the mezzanine. Placement of overhead fixtures makes mezzanine seem higher and wider.

3   Lighted sign helps to identify store name behind cashwrap.

4   Skylight well surrounded by downspots leads customers to rear of store.

5   Perimeter lighting illuminates merchandise and adds visual width to the space.

6   Recessed lighting in beam provides ambient first level illumination, emphasizes a dominant architectural element, and pulls the customer's eyes upward to the mezzanine.

6 Lighting

10
Track-mounted pendants at Crabtree & Evelyn

Minimize structural deficiences.
Lighting can help designers solve tricky space problems. Examples are given in the following section, "Refining the Lighting Plan."

Provide accurate color rendition to merchandise and flatter customers.
Tungsten-halogen is the newest lamp technology in retail use. Halogen, which is a type of incandescent lamp, does not muddy or cast grey overtones on colors; apparel store owners like the way halogen makes clothing colors look more vibrant and realistic. Fluorescent lamps introduced in recent years such as SP30, SP35, SPX30, and SPX35.

Make shoppers and employees feel comfortable.
Low wattage and low voltage lighting reduces the amount of heat transferred to the store environment, and cuts down on the cooling load handled by the mechanical system. For example, some 90 watt tungsten-halogen lamps are equal to a standard 150 watt incandescent lamp. To reduce glare, aim the luminaires so that they are not in the direct line of vision of either employees or customers, or provide shields or deflectors.

Avoid boredom.
An unrelieved expanse of a selling floor illuminated only by fluorescent lamps will give a flat look to the space and the merchandise. Diffuse light from wide distribution downlights or large area light sources, such as fluroescent luminaires or indirect lighting systems, tends to reduce the variations that relate to form and texture. Three-dimensional merchandise benefits from directional lighting, so provide for enough diffusion to counteract harshness.

Refining the Lighting Plan

▶ **Enhance the merchandise**
Use the following as a checklist to fine tune the lighting plan with the client.

Have you identified all the feature areas?
• Along the main and secondary aisles? On the perimeter zones?

Is the footcandle level at the back of the store high enough to draw customers without appearing garish?

Movable fixtures suspended on long cords are placed at eye level above merchandise at the Crabtree & Evelyn store in Toronto's The Promenade.
Design: The International Design Group Inc., Toronto; Nella Fiorino & R. MacLachlan, principals in charge.

Has the color rendition quality been checked for the range of products that will be carried in the department? Food? Clothing? Furniture? Flowers? Accessories?
• Basic stock
• Seasonal merchandise
• Holiday items

Does the stock have a typical color quality?
• Men's business clothing is usually dark.
• Children's clothing, toys, and major appliances are usually bright, pastel, or white.

76

Lamps of learning

11
Lighting for Olssen's Books and Records, Washington, D.C., encourages brousing.
Design: RTKL, Baltimore; Laurent Myers, AIA, principal in charge.

Does merchandise salability depend on glitter?
- Jewelry?
- Crystal?

Emphasize the dazzle! MR lamps beaming from above, or in-the-case illumination are two basic and effective solutions. Other options the designer can consider include fluorescent, MR's, and special incandescent strips with lamps.

Have you allowed for flexibility in the lighting plan to accommodate movable display items?
- Gondolas?
- Racks?
- Tables?
- Will pre-packaged merchandise be stacked on the selling floor?
- Will shadows created by the packages affect readability of product information?

Solve unusual space problems

▶ **Expand or retract space.**
Some stores should be made to appear larger; others should seem less cavernous. The designer can create these optical illusions through the use of colors and materials, by the lighting plan, or by combining colors, materials, and lighting.

To make a small space seem bigger, use bright, light colors. At the same time, emphasize the height of the ceiling with uplighting.
- Floor-mounted fixtures will direct bright light toward the ceiling without interfering with a person's line of vision.
- Ceiling-mounted fluorescent tubes contained in a cove project light upward, and often make a distinctive architectural statement.

Lighting projected on wall areas will add to the expansive feeling of the space.
- Wallwashers can be recessed into the ceiling, or surface mounted
- Cove lights around the perimeter will conceal the source of the light while casting illumination on the wall surface.

To visually reduce the space, specify a dark color for the ceiling and walls.
- Spotlight the merchandise, and reduce ambient and feature lighting.

▶ **Make low ceilings seem higher and high ceilings appear lower.**
To add height to a ceiling, use wall-washing up-lights on a light color surface.

- Pendant lights which project illumination downward will make a ceiling appear lower to the viewer. Spaces also seem to be more intimate when pendant lights are introduced.

▶ **Make a narrow store seem wider and a wide store look narrower.**
When the objective is to create the impression that there is more floor space between walls or partitions than actually exists:
- Specify a light color with a reflective surface.
- Wash the walls with light.
- Project light by specifying adjustable ceiling fixtures such as track lights.

▶ **Make a store seem less wide.**
- Use dark colors.
- Direct sources of light on merchandise with a narrow-beam pattern created by track and spotlighting.

6 Lighting

12
Track lighting for an open-back window

Window Lighting Techniques

Show windows send out multiple messages to the shopper. The arrangement and design of the show windows are a panorama of messages about the store's image, its point-of-view, and the merchandise being featured. Store windows can:

- impress
- influence
- inform
- amuse
- entertain

In some U.S. stores, show window design has reached the level of an art form (Tiffany's and Barneys New York are two examples). Merchandise displayed in the windows of promotional stores often indicate price; up-scale and fashion-oriented stores do not. In Europe, store windows of even the most fashionable shops are very straight forward and unadorned; they consist mainly of simple displays with the price of the merchandise typically shown.

Retail store display windows face out onto a street; a level of an enclosed or open shopping mall; walkway; parking area; or highway. There are two basic types of display windows: closed back and open back. Store designers should work closely with their client's visual merchandising director to provide sufficient outlets, power supply, and structural supports for them to have the flexibility to create shopper-stopping windows.

12

Simple, flexible illumination of the open-back The Elder Craftsmen shop in New York City was provided by overhead track lighting.

Design: Bennett-Wallace, New York; Anne E. Bennett, ASID, Gordon T.H. Wallace, partners.

▸ **Closed-back windows**
Behind the glazing, the display area is enclosed on three sides. Some merchants favor this approach, believing that the viewer's attention should focus on the staged scenario depicted in the window without any of the peripheral views presented by open back or partially open back windows.

▸ **Open-back windows**
Here, the store interior is visible behind the mannequins, props, or other display elements. Proponents of the open-back genre believe that the depth and selection of the merchandise within the store, and the movement, color, and illumination of the store's interior are attractions in themselves and augment the window display.

Window-lighting Techniques

▸ **Track lighting**
Tracks, which are the most popular form of window lighting, can be mounted horizontally or vertically. Most frequently specified lamps are 150-watt spotlight and low-voltage pin spots.

Overhead tracks can cause apparel to appear winkled. Footlights that shine upward can counterbalance down lighting. Tracks and individual floor-mounted lights that beam illumination upward to mannequins create a subtle elegance.

▸ **Stage lighting**
C-clamps, Kleigl lights, or barndoor louvers add drama to store windows. They are integrally theatrical, and help to rivet the viewer's attention on the setting.

▸ **Combination lighting**
Windows that contain displays of many small items, such as calculators, tape recorders, or cameras, are best lit with an even, high-footcandle level. Fluorescent and incandescent used in combination can measure from 100 to 300 footcandles.

▸ **Pin spots**
High-power, high-output pin spots can aim a circular beam measuring from 6 to 12 inches at specific items of merchandise. Products such as jewelry or small art objects benefit from judicious pin spot lighitng. Framing projectors create many shapes, including rectangles and squares.

13
Coordinated approach at Owings Mills (Md.) Town Center

Entry to the food service Conservatory is framed by pole-mounted lamps that define the walkway restate the theme of the Center.

Design: RTKL, Baltimore, Md.; Paul Jacob, AIA, principal in charge.

▶ **Filters and colored lamps**

Entire displays can take on a specific hue–warm or cool–by use of gel filters placed over incandescent bulbs, or by replacing white lamps with colored ones. This display technique successfully adapted from the theater by visual merchandisers adds allure to both the merchandise and the background setting.

Exterior Lighting

Check the local codes before you specify!!

Municipalities and other lawmaking bodies establish codes relating to exterior lighting, and they vary all over the country. In most cases, there is still enough latitude to be both functional and artistic.

For stores which face the street, are located in a strip center, or are freestanding, the designer's will best serve the client with a lighting plan that is in good taste and in sympathy with the environment. Check the minimum light levels for parking areas.

Developers of shopping centers and malls normally impose restrictions for storefront lighting. Here, it becomes mostly a matter of window and signage illumination.

13

▶ **Best frontage forward**

There is usually one side of the building housing a store in a strip center or facing a street which will benefit from traffic-attracting lighting. A free-standing store may have other facades which face the parking area or walkways.

▶ **A coordinated approach**

Lighting of the front facade should complement the sign or signs carrying the store's name. If the sign itself is not illuminated, the sign should be used as the focal point and lit with ground-mounted floods, or from lighting mounted above and/or below the sign.

A coordinated approach combining signs, windows, and facade will produce the most successful final product. To prevent possible annoyance to pedestrians or motor traffic, the lower portion of the building should have less illumination. Typical values for exposed concrete facades are between 5 and 10 footcandles.

▶ **Emphasize texture**

If the store exterior has an interesting texture, use lighting to emphasize it. The surface interest of wood, brick, stone, and stucco can be accented by HID (high-intensity discharge), waterproof high-output fluorescent lights, and spot lighting.

▶ **Emphasize architecture**

One method of emphasizing architectural details such as arches, awnings, or canopies is sparkle lights. These are small, usually white bulbs that have an appealing, festive quality when used with care and moderation.

▶ **Parking areas**

The lighting plan for parking areas serving free-standing stores or shopping centers is part of the design plan for the site. A lighting consultant can offer assistance in the selection of floodlighting, bollards, and lamppost illumination.

▶ **Nighttime lighting**

Create your own evening and nighttime images with color, either as an all-over wash or for accents. An investment in landscape lighting is particularly important in warm climates.

A retail structure with distinctive architectural elements –historical renovations with such details as columns, friezes, or sculptured forms–takes on a new life after dark with monumental lighting. The store becomes a landmark, and amplifies the merchant's public image.

6 Lighting

14
Sculpting with light

14 The monumental entry to Saks Fifth Avenue in Boca Raton, Florida is made more dramatic after dark with lighting mounted on the building and from fixtures at ground level. The store is a mall landmark.

Design: Bridges & Lavin Architects AIA, New York; Robert J. Bridges, AIA, partner in charge.

▶ **Sign lighting**
In municipalities where internally illuminated signs are banned, provide for illumination from an outside source, mounted either on the ground, wall, or on a pole.

▶ **Security lighting**
Protect: 1/ the customer; 2/ the building.
1. *Provide sufficient illumination* so that customers feel safe in parking areas, open and covered walkways, and on stairs. Major suppliers of lamps for such purposes, including General Electric, Sylvania, and Philips can provide assistance.

2. *Focus on entry points,* such as windows and doorways. For outdoor merchandising spaces, such as garden centers, lights can be mounted on poles or along an adjacent roofline.

Security lighting is often controlled by electric timers so that they shut down automatically during daylight hours when natural illumination is sufficient. Manually-set time clocks need seasonal adjustment. Systems triggered by electronic photo cells that "read" daylight levels self-adjust throughout the year.

Conserving Energy Through Lighting
Lighting consumes about five percent of the nation's energy. The discipline of lighting energy management has evolved, and it is concerned with, among other aspects of lighting, the quality and quantity of light required for productive performance, including retail uses.

The merchant and store planner can together plan and implement a long-term program to get the most out of the lighting plan, for as long, and as cost-effectively, as possible.

Recommended Practices To Cut Lighting Costs And Conserve Energy

1. Prepare a cost analysis. In one section, list original cost of material and labor, controls, and wiring. In another section, include operating cost of power consumption, air conditioning load, maintenance, relamping, etc.

2. Select luminaires based on proper lighting distribution for the application. The efficiency of a luminaire is one indication of the quality of its design.

3. Establish a lighting maintenance program that includes periodic cleaning and relamping.

4. Use energy-conserving fluorescent lamps where possible. Most save about 15 percent of the electrical energy used by standard lamps.

5. Fluorescent and HID ballasts made for the higher-voltage, 227-volt service are now in use in retail stores. Where codes permit and 277-volt is available, operational savings result from reduced wiring and distribution equipment costs.

6. Use a single larger incandescent lamp instead of two or more smaller lamps.

7. Use long-life-rated lamps.

8. Use higher-power factor ballasts.

9. Install diffusers which provide special light distribution coverage.

10. Install timers and photocells to turn off lighting when areas are not in use.

11. Provide selective switching and, where applicable, local control of lighting.

12. Apply light-reflective finishes for walksways and other surfaces.

13. Investigate auxiliary relays for lighting that interface with computerized energy management programs.

Signs and Graphics

7

Storefront and mallfront differentiation is a major identity strategy. Merchants and shopping center developers allocate more budget to sign programs and identity programs than ever before; they want their signs to stop shoppers in their tracks, and then keep reminding them why they stopped.

Retail signs and symbols have evolved into an important form of mobile communication, appearing on shopping bags, bus enclosures, mass transit advertising cards, packaging, and direct mail pieces.

Main project identification for Bayside Marketplace, Miami, is an illuminated roadside marquee with 12-foot-high dimensional letters in pastel colors. The logotype was translated into posters, mugs, caps, shirts, carriers, yo-yo's, and other promotional items. Bayside is a project of The Rouse Company.

Design: Communication Arts Incorporated, Boulder, Colorado.

7 Signs and Graphics

3 *Shopping center adaptation of a landmark storefront*

4 *Illuminated arch to Atrium Shops*

5 *Scribner's image goes with the customer*

Image continuity is a major theme when a retail project's sign program is formulated. Merchants and shopping center owners and developers want the public to be aware of their image at just about every turn.

In the past few years, the lines of distinction between signs as store identification and signs as advertising have overlapped. Store signs, never a timid specialty of the graphic design discipline, have assumed the additional task of selling the store outside of its physical boundaries.

Competition for the consumer's attention—and dollar—has never been more fierce. The merchandising graveyard is littered with once-famous names of department stores and chains that are now gone from the scene. Retail managers consider signs and graphics as a visual insurance policy to support their investment in inventory and the physical plant, and as an adjunct to their advertising and promotion efforts.

What Retail Signs Do

There are two basic types of retail store signs:

▶ exterior signs that identify the store and attract traffic

▶ interior signs that act as a "silent salesperson" and point-of-sale technique to directly influence customer buying

Sign programs created for institutional and other types of commercial structures are primarily concerned with space identification and user wayfinding. Unlike retail signs, their success does not

3
Storefront design for Scribner's Bookstore in The Fashion Centre, Pentagon City, Va., was influenced by the former Fifth Avenue Beaux-Arts flagship store in New York City. B. Dalton Bookseller Inc. operates Scribner's Bookstores.

Design: Hambrecht Terrell International, New York.

4
Thematic archway sign at St. Louis Union Station draws on traditional railway type styles, lights, and structural elements.

Design: Communication Arts Incorporated, Boulder, Colorado.

5
The identity program for the Scribner's Bookstore shopping center chain includes logotype, stationery, point-of-sale displays, and packaging materials.

82

6
Standing Motherhood on end

depend on boosting sales revenues. Because a store's sign and graphics program is so critical to the success of a retail operation, it offers more challenge to the designer, is more time-consuming, and needs early integration into the overall store design concept.

Point-of-sale signing should provide customers with answers to three basic queries:

▸ What is it?

▸ Why should I buy it?

▸ How much is it?

"The most successful signs are those that promote additional purchases," said Joseph Weishar, president of New Vision Studios, Inc., New York, a store planning and merchandise presentation consulting firm. "Signs are a vital part of the communication process. Whether mounted or freestanding, they are an integral part of the balance of the store's space, merchandising, and marketing strategy.

"Signing rationale must be based on consumer interpretation," he stressed. "The Limited is one retailer that uses signs effectively, in size, location, and color. It excels in its creative use of words, too," Mr. Weishar said.

Basics of Retail Sign Design

Signs created for retail use have to solve communication, circulation, and visual problems. Leslie Blum, a New York City architect and principal of Leslie Blum Design, Inc., wrote in a recent issue of *Identity* magazine, that the skills

An 18-foot, 2-story-high painted metal panel carries the store name, Motherhood, turned on its side in 8-foot-high white lettering. The store is located in Santa Monica Place, Santa Monica, Cal.

Design: Charles E. Broudy & Associates

6

required to design signs that are functional, understood, made correctly, and fit their environment require skills that cross the lines of all the design disciplines. For retail, this refers to:

▸ how to spec type

▸ how to create mechanical art

▸ knowledge of materials

▸ understanding of fabrication processes and methodologies

▸ how to analyze traffic patterns

▸ how to evaluate solutions from both the customer's and the merchant's perspectives.

"It also means that your work can be beautiful, brighten its surroundings, or it can be whimsical, if appropriate," said Ms. Blum.

Store planners and designers also have to be knowledgeable and sensitive to sales and buying psychology: how scale, proportion, color, illumination, placement, and materials are perceived and evaluated in the macro- and near-environment by shoppers. Customers' behavior in retail spaces is an area that both marketers and scientists are now studying and evaluating.

7 Signs and Graphics

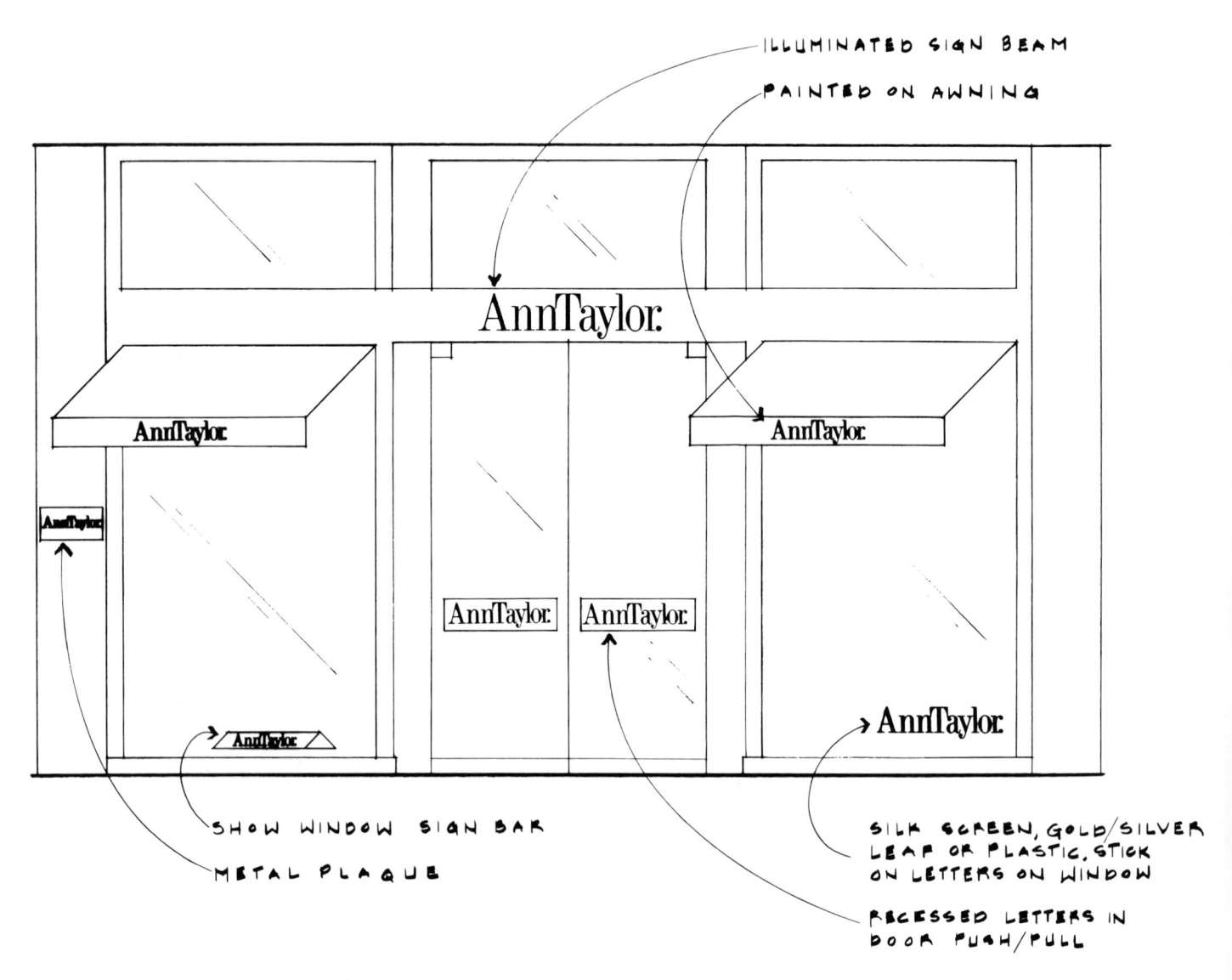

ILLUMINATED SIGN BEAM

PAINTED ON AWNING

SHOW WINDOW SIGN BAR

METAL PLAQUE

SILK SCREEN, GOLD/SILVER LEAF OR PLASTIC, STICK ON LETTERS ON WINDOW

RECESSED LETTERS IN DOOR PUSH/PULL

Alternative techniques to "sign" a storefront.
- show window sign bar
- metal plaque
- illuminated sign beam
- painted on awning
- silk screen, gold, or silver leaf, or plastic stick-on letters on window
- recessed letters in door push/pull

7
Signs as an organizing element

8
PRO + owner for outdoor sign

A store's sign program is an important extension of the overall store design theme to:

▶ attract

▶ stimulate

▶ dramatize

The interior sign program should include:

▶ hanging signs

▶ supported signs

▶ holders

▶ dividers

Until recently, data on customer behavior in retail settings was scarce. A competitive edge can be gained by practical application of the explicit and implicit forces at work that guide, direct, and motivate customers to enter a store, and influence their movements once inside.

Signs as Image Continuity
Merchants allocate considerable funds to promoting their logo: on the storefront; in media advertising; on direct mail pieces; on hangtags; and on shopping bags and totes. The graphics "package," in both two and three dimensions, static or kinetic, extends the reach of the store's advertising.

Now, retail sign programs are consciously integrated into an ongoing program. The Banana Republic carried this idea to its limits, with jungle themes, camouflage patterns, and flora and fauna suspended everywhere to link its visual identity to its casual and hunting clothes merchandise specialty. The concept was rolled out nationally with much skill and good humor.

The identity package can be expanded to include tee shirts, baseball hats, mugs, frisbees, yo-yos, posters, book protectors, umbrellas, and just about anything else that has a surface upon which the retail establishment's name and logo will adhere.

People appreciate visual order. They understand a logical and related progression of information linking the store and the merchandise. The relationship that extends outside the physical confines of the store–to visually supplement the store's message or the shopping center's market position with a consistent graphic approach–is a very solid way to maintain a competitive edge.

7

A new logotype and modular sign system were part of PRO Hardware's visual upgrading for 1,500 stores in the U.S. and Canada. Interior signs identify departments, aisles, and services.

Design:
Gerstman + Meyers Inc., New York;
Richard Gerstman, partner in charge.

8

7 **Signs and Graphics**

9 *High tech for Timex*

10 *Sports shop knows how to score*

The 400-square foot Timex store in the Trumbull (Conn.) Shopping Park carries over 300 styles. Signs and mannequins are part of the high tech look. Above the showcases are video monitors and the widely-promoted Timex logo highlighted by track feature lighting.

Design: Vinick Associates, Inc., Hartford, Conn.; Barbara Ebstein, FASID, principal in charge.

9

Retail Sign Trends

Electronic Signs and Displays
The latest news flashing across Times Square in New York City like an electronic ticker tape was once considered a deft engineering feat and a popular tourist attraction. Now, the local convenience store has LED signs; video screens meet customers at every turn in department stores and specialty stores; and computer programs control the timing of sales-stimulating messages.

Designers should consider electronic signs and displays as pieces of equipment that require appropriate wall space and power supply. Because of the technology and costs inolved, their budgets should be carefully assembled, with estimates gathered from reliable vendors and consultants.

Safety Zone, a chain of security system stores, uses LED signs bechind the cash wrap to communicate with customers while they are waiting to complete the sales transaction. The signs carry statistical information relating to thefts; news stories about the benefits of security systems; and case studies emphasizing security product performance.

Illuminated Awnings and Canopies
Backlit awnings are a cost-effective method of combining communication and illumination. They can be used outdoors or indoors, and fabricators are happy to relate success stories resulting from their installation.

10

Plan for a proposed spoerts shop has electronic scoreboard-type signs. Designers should consider electronic signs and displays as pieces of equipment that require sufficient wall space and power supply, and budget accordingly.

Design: Charles E. Broudy & Associates

86

11
Lucky's backlit awnings stimulate traffic

Table 7-1	Do's and Don't's of Retail Signage and Graphics
Do's	**Don't's**
In dark areas, provide for light on the sign or internal illumination.	Don't be too tricky with typeface or graphics that will prevent instant recognition. Keep it to the point, and make it simple to read.
When using removable letters, make sure the sign background is a hard surface, so the sign can be removed and a new one installed without a "ghost effect" remaining from the original sign.	Do not specify a highly reflective surface or background that will distort the sign or allow readability from one viewing location.
Do consider baked-enamel, porcelain enamel, or metal that is available in many colors, to introduce variety into the palette.	Do not use a grade of plastic for the face of a sign box that will wave or "oil can."
For stores in shopping centers and malls, maintain storefront criteria. Many developers provide manuals, explicit instructions, and information regarding signs and graphics on the exterior of the stores.	On exterior signs, do not specify threaded screw mountings that will rust.

Some basic properties are:

- translucent vinyl coated polyester fabrics offer translucency and strength

- surface treatment resists soiling, provides ease of cleaning, and enhances graphic applications

- wide variety of colors

- contain internal fluorescent tubes and transmit light efficiently

There is no single nationally-recognized fire code for awning fabric. The California State Fire Marshall's flammability test is the most broadly recognized code and the most stringent (Title 19, Subchapter 8, Article 4, Section 1237.1).

Backlit awnings are especially popular with food stores, hardgoods ratailers, and chain operators. Bill Hodges of Nashville Tent & Awning, a major fabricator, cites case studies where the installation of backlit awnings influenced a sales upturn: Lucky's Supermarket in the center of a

11

Lucky's Supermarkets in Alabama increased its visibility and sales following the installation of backlit awnings. The lightweight, flexible vinyl-coated polyester fabric efficiently transmits light. Used outdoors, backlit awnings are visible from a distance of a quarter-mile. With normal maintenance, awnings should provide 8-10 years of service.

Fabricator: Nashville Tent & Awning Co., Nashville, Tenn.

7 **Signs and Graphics**

12
Animated neon at a shopping center

northern Alabama shopping center stimulated more night traffic; Hunters Cee Bee, a small suburban Nashville independent grocer, increased nighttime shopping while reinforcing security; the backlit awning design for Super D, a Southeastern drug chain, accents window graphics to present a stronger visual statement.

Etched Glass
Logos or symbols are subtle and elegant when translated into the medium of etched glass. They are especially effective when the glass panel is set into a screen or divider. Glass-etched signs are most effective as a support-level sign system, reinforcing primary modes of identification.

Neon
Once shunned as tawdry by architects and designers, neon was rediscovered in the late 1970s as a classy and colorful retail sign medium. Neon now spans a wide spatial range to highlight architecture and merchandise. It has been used to outline glass entryways and atriums of shopping centers; for interior and exterior environmental signs; on store fronts; to dramatize displays; and as point-of-sale graphics.

Discovered in 1910 by the French inventor Georges Claude, neon signs literally stopped traffic when first introduced at a Los Angeles auto dealership in the 1920s. Its popularity as a sign medium dipped in postwar years and through the 1960s, and glitzy Las Vegas-like overuse caused designers to seek other mediums to

12 **An animated neon sign identifies the Campus Level at Bridgewater (N.J.) Commons, a project** **of The Hahn Company. Retail uses for neon include point-of-sale, directional, and architectural.** *Design: Communication Arts Incorporated, Boulder, Colorado.*

88

13
Incised neon and photomurals at a supermarket

Kroger Supermarkets, together with the Kraft Dairy Group, have tested in-store boutiques selling hand-dipped superpremium Frusen Glädjé ice cream. Sub-titled "Fantasy," the section is identified by three types of signs: mounted photomurals hung at a 90 degree angle; incised bright pink neon; and surface painted.

Design: Gerstman + Myers Inc., New York; Richard Gerstman, principal in charge.

13

interpret their sign ideas for retail clients.

The great neon revival was spurred by such factors as MTV, *Miami Vice,* and the interpretation of neon as an art form by such artists as Larry Rivers and Jasper Johns. In 1987, architect Helmut Jahn's dramatic United Airlines Terminal at Chicago's O'Hare Airport unequivocally established neon as a legitimate contemporary medium: Michael Hayden's 800-foot-long, million-dollar installation, "Sky's the Limit," was a breakthrough for neon.

▶ Miniturization of transformers has eliminated the bulk and buzz of neon signs.

▶ Over 150 colors are available.

▶ Neon is lively, eye-catching, and offers high contrast with surroundings.

▶ Neon tubes are fragile and emit heat when in use; they should be protected from customer contact by recessing the sign into a wall or other frame, or covered with glass or plastic.

Fabrication

There are approximately 30,000 commercial sign shops in the U.S. and Canada–woodcarvers, tube benders, gilders, pinstripers, etc. Another 4,000 companies are involved in producing and installing electrified signs, an industry generating estimated annual sales of over $2.5 billion.

Many sign fabricators will help designers to develop their sketches, and produce shop drawings for approval. Sign companies may also offer the services of an in-house designer who can give valuable advice on color, texture, and patterns, and in the use of such materials as steel, stainless steel, aluminum, a variety of plastics, woods, concrete, glass, gold leaf, paints, and more.

Electric sign companies can guide the designer in specifying appropriate fixtures and lamps: direct, indirect, and silhouette lighting modes; proper illumination from traditional fluorescent and incandescent lamps; the best electrified gas for luminous tubing signs (there are five, including neon); and practical application for laser and fiber optic technologies.

| Table 7-2 | Retail Store Signage and Graphics |

Type	Characteristics, Considerations & Recommendations

Exterior

Wall

Pinned off

Pin mount; individual letters. Sophisticated; for quality store.

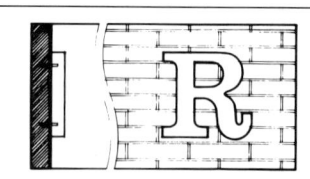

Direct mounted

Screw mount to wall. Easy installation.

Rear illuminated

Neon tube creates glow on wall; letters are in silhouette. Quality appearance; background wall material should be receptive to light halo.

Direct mounted plaque

Brass or stainless steel; non illuminated.

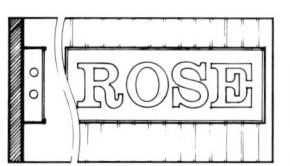

Box sign

Flourescent tubes behind plastic face in a metal box. Economical; easy to change sign face.

Canopy

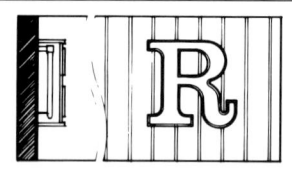

Illuminated letter

Individual letter mount; metal, plastic. Surface applied. Glowing letter is more elegant. Usually used on quality stores.

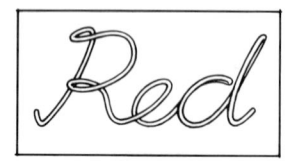

Neon

Neon or fluorescent; behind plastic face. Individual, distinctive. Not applicable on all types of stores.

Pylon or tower

Freestanding

Illuminated; heights vary. Flashing of blinking lights are usually not permitted.

Used for highway recognition, for shopping centers or larger stores. Sometimes lists tenants.

Hanging

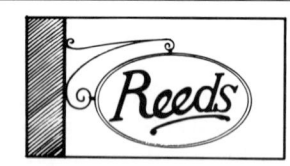

Wood

Carved wood often with gold leaf lettering. Used when a traditional, antique, or casual appearance is desired.

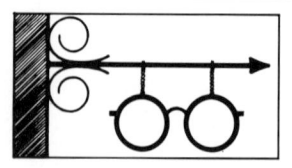

Metal

Wrought iron, often with scroll work. Identifies a craft shop or tradesperson.

Glass applied

Glue-on or rub-on letters for show windows; cutout letters of thin plastic or plaster.

Changeable signage for show windows.

90

| Table 7-2 | Retail Store Signage and Graphics (Continued) |

Type	Characteristics, Considerations & Recommendations	
Awning	 Canvas or metal; graphics can be painted.	A lightweight and semipermanent device to unite multifacade stores. Stripes, patterns or solids are appropriate.
Banners	 Fabric or canvas. May have plain or patterned background.	Can be temporary or long term. Can be changed seasonally.

Interior	Characteristics, Considerations & Recommendations	
Departmental and directional signs or graphics	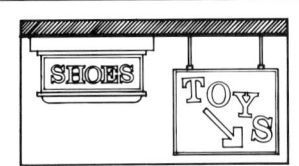 Can be suspended from ceiling or valance mounted. Illuminated or nonilluminated, depending on effect to be created. Directional arrows and signs should not confuse customers.	In department stores or large stores, identification signs should be properly located for easy reading. A variety of surface backgrounds and types of letters create and extend the mood of the environment.
Name brand or product category	 Can be placed above merchandise on a valance or suspended from above. Designer logos can be used.	Can be temporary or permanent, depending on the store's policies. Surface background is important if names will change. Letters can be cut out of any material that is appropriate for the solution.
Directories	 In large stores and department stores, directories are needed to help customers get to the proper merchandise or service area quickly and easily.	Directories can be wall- or floor-mounted, or suspended from ceilings. Maps may also be employed; most are rear-illuminated.
Photomurals	 Large photo enlargements (prints or transparencies) are used to encourage patrons to buy toiletries, lingerie, jewelry, etc.	These photos may be black and white or color, front-illuminated or rear-screen color transparencies.
Point of purchase	 Table-top graphics and displays play a large part in retailing. They range from TV monitors of fashion shows, to nameplates, to mirrors custom-frabricated with a trade name.	Cosmetics, jewelry, sporting goods, foods, children's apparel, shoes.

International Signs

United States
New York: Abraham & Straus (Design: RTKL, Baltimore); Banners in Soho; Robert Lee Morris Gallery; Honeybee (Design: Charles E. Broudy & Associates) *Philadelphia:* Bailey Banks & Biddle (Design: International Design Group, Toronto)

England
Maidstone, U.K.:
Royal Star Arcade
(Design: International
Design Group,
London)

Spain
Madrid:
Bucarian;
Antonio Parriego

7 Signs and Graphics

Signs provide visual unity at strip center

The renovation and expansion of Plainview Centre, Plainview, N.Y., a successful strip center, included a continuous horizontal signband, canvas canopies, and banners hung from ornamental lamp posts.

Design: Planned Expansion Group, White Plains, N.Y.; Kenneth D. Narva, partner in charge.

Consultants

Some store design architects and designers are also fine graphic designers; others are not.

If, in the original scope of work, it appears that the signing aspects of the project are greater than can be comfortably handled within the lead design firm, or if the firm does not have the expertise in-house, the fee for a graphics consultant should be built into the budget. Sign programs for major projects, such as large stores, chains, or shopping centers, are often designed by environmental graphics specialists.

For stores that will have built-in or freestanding video monitors or other types of electronic signs requiring dedicated lines or special power sources, the project's electrical engineer should be advised as early as possible. A well-conceived signing program can be negated by estimated cost add-ons to rewire the project because the budgetary information was delayed.

Sign Ordinances and Codes

Design proposals for signs which face a street or other public thoroughfare can be subject to review by a community's zoning commission, planning board, historic district overseers, and various organizations concerned with esthetics. The Philadelphia Art Commission, for example, must approve the size, style, color, and illumination technique before a major sign can be installed in certain of the city's districts.

The designer may have to prepare for nearly as many hearings for sign approval as for the original zoning permit. Presentations to groups can involve samples, photos with the new sign superimposed over the existing structure in the case of a remodeled store, and elevations and detail drawings. If the reviews take an inordinate amount of time, the designer should be compensated for the time spent beyond the typical contract agreement.

Signing restrictions for stores located in shopping centers and malls are detailed within Tenants Criteria guidelines and handbooks.

Displaying Merchandise

8

What it means:
dis-play (verb)
to put or spread before the view

display (noun)
an eye-catching arrrangement by which something is exhibited

What the designer does:
Integrates merchandise into a shopping environment that is organized, exciting, and enjoyable for the customer.

The result:
Makes merchandise sell by itself.

1 *Revlon's 80 square feet of floor space in department and specialty stores is an example of retail-oriented industrial design. Beauty products are treated as small jewels; display elements are engineered to highlight the appeal of the sophisticated packaging and customer accessiblilty to the merchandise.* *Design: Revlon Creative and Communications Group.*

95

Typical Merchandise Display Analysis

	POSTCARDS	STATIONERY	TOYS/GAMES	GLASSWARE	JEWELRY	OBJECTS	TOTAL
SALES AREA (SQUARE FEET)							
Service							
Self Serve							
Plan of Space							
Siting Consideration							
MERCHANDISING							
Number of Items							
Seasonal Increase							
Item Pricing							
Sign Consideration							
MERCHANDISING SPECIFICS							
Wall Display-Accessible							
Wall Display-Above 80"							
Island Display-Accessible							
Secure Display, Under Glass							
Manufacturers' Displays							
STOCK							
Concealed in Floor Display							
Drawers/Doors behind Sales							
Stockroom/Backup Areas							

GIFT SHOP (EXAMPLE)

	POSTCARDS	STATIONERY	TOYS/GAMES	GLASSWARE	JEWELRY	OBJECTS	TOTAL
SALES AREA (SQUARE FEET)	10%	15%	20%	15%	18%	22%	100%
Service	—	—	10%	20%	60%	25%	
Self Serve	100%	100%	90%	80%	40%	75%	
Plan of Space	LINEAR	OPEN	U-SHAPE	LINEAR	ENCLOSED	RANDOM	
Siting Consideration	NEAR CASHIER	REAR	MID-SHOP	PERIMETER	EASY VIEWING	NEAR FRONT	
MERCHANDISING							
Number of Items	200	420	500	175	300	100	1695
Seasonal Increase	HOLIDAYS	600	XMAS	200	350	130	
Item Pricing	●	ON PRODUCT	ON PRODUCT	PARTIAL/SALE	●	●	
Sign Consideration	●	●	●	BRAND NAMES	—	—	
MERCHANDISING SPECIFICS							
Wall Display-Accessible	●	●	●	●		●	
Wall Display-Above 80"	—	●	LARGER ITEM	●	—	●	
Island Display-Accessible	●	●	●	●	—	●	
Secure Display, Under Glass	—	—	EXPENSIVE FRAGILE	EXPENSIVE		●	
Manufacturers' Displays	50%/50%	—	AUTO MODELS	—	EARRINGS	—	
STOCK							
Concealed in Floor Display	●	●	●	●	●	●	
Drawers/Doors behind Sales	—	●	●	●	100%	●	
Stockroom/Backup Areas	BOX STOR.	●	●	●	—	●	

Source: Charles E. Broudy & Associates

2
Dimensional display for Accessory Place

2

The targeted customer for the Accessory Place chain operated by Plymouth Lamston Stores is the fashion-conscious woman in metropolitan markets. White elements form a unified backdrop for the varied types, sizes, colors, and shapes of the merchandise displayed: white slatwall around the perimeter; white perforated metal shelving and bins; white wire grid display baskets; white laminate feature fixtures; and white-speckled granite floor tile.

The tubular fixtures which support circular rotating displays and shelving bins also direct the traffic flow through the center of the store.

Design: Jon Greenberg & Associates, Inc., Berkley, Mich.; Kenneth Nisch, principal in charge.

Modular Multiplication

Create the casework or fixtures that will fit the dimensions of the goods to be sold. In apparel stores, 85 percent of the total space on the selling floor is devoted to housing the merchandise in racks, shelves, bins, or freestanding units.

To obtain efficient housing, designers must physically measure the products to be displayed on the sales floor and stocked either on the selling floor or in back-up areas. *This is an absolute requirement,* whether the items are postcards, books, blouses, shoes, men's shirts, overcoats, glassware, or furniture. The designer converts these measurements into housing and display units that provide the most arresting setting for the merchandise.

8 Displaying Merchandise

3
Dole Kids Shop

Project the Merchandise "Appeals"
Analyze the merchandise to determine its "appeals," the characteristics that will determine how it will be received by the buying public. How should the display theme make the products stand out from their surroundings?

Catch the mood of the merchandise and project it! Identify its personality and create an enhancing envrironment. What message do you want the displays to communicate?

▶ Timeless

▶ Conservative

▶ Trendy

▶ Kicky

▶ Classic

▶ Au courant

▶ Charming

▶ Restful

▶ Lively

▶ Elegant

▶ Cute

▶ Bizarre

3 The second floor Village Shops at Honolulu's Dole Cannery Square is part of an adaptive reuse project which turned 35,000 square feet of former warehouse space into retail stores. The main display in the Kids Shop is an orange and yellow train running on tracks inscribed in the vinyl flooring tile.

*Design:
AM Partners Inc.
Brian T. Takahashi, AIA, project manager.*

98

4
Marshall Field's Luggage Dept. recreates O'Hare Airport

Coordinate the Environment
A display does its job when it draws customers to the merchandise and then invites product investigation. The arrangement created for the merchandise should make it easy for shoppers to locate, examine, and evaluate the products.

Background colors, materials, lighting, and display fixtures all must present a unified, cohesive visual impression.

The store designer should create settings to enhance the merchandise. They should be appealing visual compositions, in which the merchandise appears to be framed. Front-facing apparel has more sales appeal than garments shown shoulder-out. Handbags on pedestals and platforms draw more customer response than bunches of hook-hung bags.

Provide an area where samples can be isolated for customer examination.

Develop Distinctive Display Approaches
A dramatic display can give additional dimension to the merchandise.

▶ Add panels made with an interesting fabric, mirror, wood, or metallic material.

▶ Play matte and reflective surfaces against each other.

▶ Build in lighting to create special effects.

4 The Luggage Department in Marshall Field's downtown Chicago flagship store was inspired by the gleaming high-tech environment of the United Airlines Terminal at O'Hare International Airport. The circular merchandise display here is enlivend by a space-suited mannequin. A reflective ceiling adds to the impact of the setting with its undulating back-lit walls and overhead neon sculpture.

Design: Hambrecht Terrell International, Inc., New York; Marian D'Oria, project manager.

99

⑧ Displaying Merchandise

5 *An atrium for Gap Kids*

6 *Geometry for floor fixture*

5

Change of Levels
Change of levels of the major horizontal planes. Create forms with beams, recesses, and dropped ceiling areas. Add geometric shapes with solid materials and pools of light to focus the shopper's eyes on the groupings of merchandise displays around the sales floor.

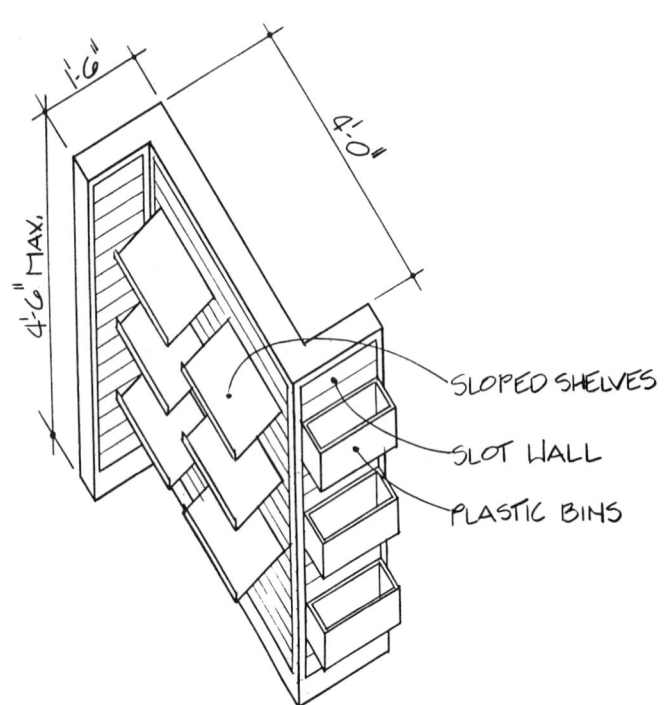

The vaulted atrium of this San Francisco Gap Kids store creates an architecural link between the two levels.

Shoppers on the stairway get a variety of perspectives of the multi-color merchandise and movable fixtures.

Design: Charles E. Broudy & Associates

Display Merchandise Sculpturally
Triangles, rectangles, circles, arches, squares, rhomboids–all can be translated into two- and three-dimensional effects for display units, walls, and floor and ceiling surfaces. Create levels with ziggurats, dropped ceiling panels, and wall treatments.
    Enclose or frame the merchandise with lighting, pedestals, platforms, screens, or contrasting materials or colors. Take advantage of solid/void and negative/positive opportunities to focus attention on the merchandise.

6
Z-shaped floor fixture with slotwall plastic holders and shelves.

Design: Charles E. Broudy & Associates.

100

7
Samuel Pepys

Add Value to the Merchandise
Create a setting that will increase the shopper's perception of the value of the products on display, and the implied benefits gained by ownership. Investigate stock items that can be customized, or design a system that will show the merchandise to its best advantage.

7 **The Biedermeier style favored in the era of the seventeenth century diarist Samuel Pepys was translated into elegant wood fixturing displaying writing materials, cards, address and appointment books, and related items in this 250-square-foot Toronto shop. Inlaid burl and cherry veneer accented by black lacquer columns and fittings form the display and storage units.** *Design: The International Design Group Toronto; Nella Fiorino, project director.*

101

8 Displaying Merchandise

D. F. Sanders

Specify Flexible Display Systems

Build flexibility into the display system, using the basic project program as the foundation to support the merchandising plan. Specify adjustable shelving and racks that can be rearranged by employees rather than a master carpenter.

Retailers have a predeliction for stacking merchandise on tables, display islands, and movable horizontal surfaces in the highest traffic locations. Store aisles that are six to eight feet wide can accommodate customer traffic and a merchandise display. The rule is: Do not put anything in the way of the customer unless it is an appealing display!

The Boston store of D. F. Sanders, an upscale housewares and home products retailer, fitted baker's racks with glass shelves to hold floor stock. Units in the foreground are on wheels. Industrial carpeting covers the floor. Frosted glass wall panel is illuminated from behind to silhouette the merchandise displays.

Architectural Design: Craig Jackson and Charles E. Broudy & Associates

9
The cashwrap station

The cashwrap station (cash desk) can combine function with impulse merchandising opportunities. The station's design allows for sophisticated electronic registers, credit card machines, writing surfaces, and spaces for wrapping materials. At Lerner Woman, Miami, a circular display case is integrated into the cash desk unit.

*Design:
Jon Greenberg & Associates, Inc.,
Berkley, Mich.*

Working with Visual Merchandisers

Esthetic structure and control

Joseph Weishar, President, New Vision Studios, Inc., New York City

The most productive selling floors result from successful team collaborations between the store planning and visual merchandising consultant, the merchant, and the in-house visual merchandiser. The store planner should establish the structure; the VM maintains the attractive shopping atmosphere. Both should base their programs on data provided by the merchant:
1. sales history of the department
2. inventory value/sq. ft.
3. market-niche projection
4. width and depth of inventory to carry the line for a minimum of two weeks
5. proportion of basic merchandise to total selling space

The visual merchandiser has the long-term esthetic control of the store and makes day-to-day decisions on the optimum use of space. For example, within the fixturing system, the VM can display more stock without making the sales floor look like a warehouse. In addition, the VM:

▸ glamorizes the basics

▸ dramatizes the presentation of promotional goods

▸ maintains an ambience that accommodates the customer.

The VM should understand the dynamics of customer traffic and circulation patterns, and their impact on sales volume.

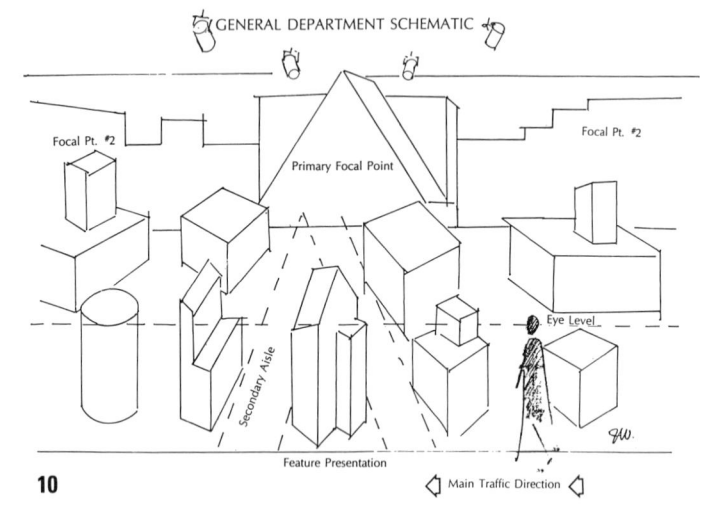

10 Lead customers to the merchandise. Presentation of stock is sculpted around a central point to create a merchandise signature for the department. That point on the main aisle is the "feature presentation." It should:
- be simple and make one major statement
- be lit from the front and if possible, the back
- be higher than other presentations
- be visually arresting, combining stock with mannequins, photos, signs, and/or props

11 Antique display fixtures lend warmth and grace to career wear at Ed Mitchell's 600-sq. ft. store in the Merritt 7 office complex, Norwalk, Conn. Armoires are lit internally and from ceiling-mounted track fixtures. Walls are painted a classic forest green which complements both the merchandise and the display elements.

10 *Create a feature presentation*

11 *Antique armoires become display fixtures*

12 *Neon drama at a 4-aisle intersection*

Point-of-sale's full potential

Norwood Oliver, President, Norwood Oliver Design Associates Inc., New York City

At Hess's in the Greenbrier Mall, Chesapeake, Va., an 8-foot-high, neon-outlined "Discus Thrower" marks the intersection of four aisles and separates Young Men's from Juniors. The predominantly white center field creates a stage-like effect; the 12-foot-high dark grey ceiling and black marble aisles heighten the contrast. Stripes of white neon over the display follow the aisle pathways.

12

Visual merchandising is an indispensable, required tool in many segments of the retail market. Every business day, visual merchandising displays communicate non-verbally with customers, like silent salespeople; mold store point-of-view; and offer important product information.

The visual merchandiser plays a vital role in creating effective point-of-sale dynamics. The relationship between the in-house VM and the store planning consultant should be a close partnership, not a creative competition. We have worked with many VMs who are talented, dedicated display specialists, eager to contribute; they have a special insight into what is right for their store, and can provide valuable assistance in shaping the store's overall display plan. Their active support smooths the transition from the conceptual phase to a fully-stocked in-store position.

A store that is over-designed and inflexible inhibits effective merchandising. Avoid by specifying design elements that are flexible, which means that they can be adapted with equal effectiveness throughout the year's seasonal promotions.

The planning consultant and the VM together can implement point-of-sale displays that achieve their full potential as powerful sales stimulators–displays that will reinforce and enhance the store interior design. Manageable components, impressive visual aids, and ease of maintenance are the program's foundations.

13
Power of suggestion

This entrance to the Menswear Department at Joslin's Colorado Springs branch store is a visual magnet into the area. Staggered windows at the entrance opening and a strong mannequin staging in the center of the aisle presentation draw customers deeper into the department.

Design: Jon Greenberg & Associates, Inc., Berkley, Mich.; Michael Crosson, principal in charge.

Moving merchandise

● *Ron D. Gosses, Director of Visual Merchandising, Joslin's, Denver, Colorado, a division of Mercantile Stores.*

Visual specialists today have to be more involved with the total presentation of goods. Display is more than just making something look nice. The objective is to move merchandise.

Placing the merchandise next to the display has an extremely positive effect on the self-sell process. We place the displayed merchandise next to a mannequin on the sales floor so that the customer can easily find the items. If we do a form, or have a display on the back wall, the merchandise must be right next to it.

We work very closely in the planning stage with our design consultants. Anything that is used to hold merchandise–mannequins, forms, abstracts–should relate to the design of the department. We try to give separate identities to each area. The designer department will look different–more austere, more elegant–than the junior section.

Classification and colorization

13

are two of the most imortant elements we employ to create a visually stimulating presentation on the selling floor. We group a classification of goods in one area. For example, some vendors have a very strong name which is a classification in itself, such as Liz Claiborne. Once we have a classification, then we colorize within the department.

Each individual fixture or rack is colorized light to dark, left to right. We also colorize vertically, never horizontally. When customers stand in front of shelving or cubing, they can look up and down for colors, rather than have to walk back and forth.

Systems

9

HVAC
Support Areas
Security

10 Most Important Retail Store Maintenance & Operations Procedures

1. Lower thermostat during heating season; raise thermostat during cooling season.
2. Install and use programmed digital heating and cooling thermostats.
3. Check temperature control system for proper calibration.
4. Keep condenser coils, evaporator coils, and filters clean.
5. Inspect fans annually and clean if necessary.
6. Use self-contained units only when needed.
7. Inspect tension and alignment of all belts and adjust as necessary.
8. Where applicable, lubricate motor bearings and all moving parts as manufacturer recommends.
9. For central heating and/or cooling plants, operate only the mininum number of machines (boilers, pumps, and chillers) necessary to satisfy the load requirements.
10. For central heating and/or cooling plants, maintain the heat transfer medium (air or water) at a minimum temperature that will still maintain comfort conditions.

9 Systems

HVAC Systems and Their Applications

This section was written by Ken Meline, PE, of DFW Consulting Group, Inc., Irving, Texas.

A retail store's heating, ventilating, and air conditioning system (HVAC) is designed by the consulting mechanical engineer to meet these criteria:

▶ the architectural designer's concepts

▶ the type of merchandise to be sold

▶ number and type of employees

▶ hours of operation

▶ project lease terms

▶ projected energy budget figure based on gross sales

▶ plans for operating and maintaining the system's equipment

From this information, the mechanical designer determines the system's degree of sophistication and the quality of the equipment that will comprise the system. For example, a merchant with knowledgeable maintenance personnel and a long-term lease can consider a more sophisticated system that offers more energy options, will require fewer replacement parts, and will be more cost-effective over the life of the lease.

The architectural designer sets the plan, specifies the materials, and advises the engineers on 1) space available for HVAC prime mover equipment, and 2) space available for energy distribution equipment and the preferred terminal equipment.

Major tenants occupying spaces over 100,000 square feet in shopping centers may have the option to design their own energy plant, complete with boilers, pumps, and chillers. Most large national retailers have standard design parameters for HVAC. Stand-alone buildings also allow the mechanical designer to compare the full range of options and recommend those which best fit the structure and the type of retail business.

Checklist for Determining a Retail Store's HVAC Requirements

▶ What type of merchandise does the store carry?

▶ What is the total size of the store, and what are its physical limitations?

▶ If the store is located within an existing shopping center, what are the landlord's design criteria?

▶ What services will the landlord furnish?

▶ If the shopping center or building does not furnish primary and secondary energy utilities, what fuel source is available?

▶ Where is it available?

▶ How can it be used in the design?

▶ If the store is not in an enclosed shopping mall, what are the anticipated seasonal conditions?

▶ Will the merchant control the store's environment after closing hours?

▶ Is documentation available if the proposed space is located in an independent building with an existing HVAC system that served the previous occupant?

▶ Is chilled and hot water piping provided?

▶ Is the engineer restricted to a system which can employ these services?

Small Tenants (0 - 5,000 sq. ft.)

Small tenants normally use the type of HVAC system existing in the mall. A few of the systems and their characteristics are listed below.

Rooftop Packaged Unit

This system is a direct expansion, self-contained unit located on the roof (it may also be located adjacent to the space). The heating source may be either gas or electric. Supply and return air must be ducted to the unit on the roof. Characteristics:
- common
- may be used in almost any climate
- low first cost for the landlord
- high maintenance cost
- short life expectancy
- not energy efficient unless the heat pump version and/or economizer version is used

DX Split System

This is a direct expansion system that normally will have a condensing unit located outdoors and a fan-coil unit located indoors, either above a ceiling or in a mechanical room. The heating source may be either gas or electric. Refrigerant lines must be routed from the condensing unit to the fan-coil unit. Supply and return air must be ducted to the fan-coil unit.
Characteristics:
- common
- may be used in almost any climate
- low first cost for the landlord
- high maintenance cost
- short life expectancy
- not energy efficient unless the heat pump version is used

Water Source Heat Pump

The landlord-provided condenser water loop is the basis for this system. Heat may be rejected to the loop or heat may be extracted from the loop to give heat to the retail store space. The water source heat pump must be connected to the condenser water supply and return mains normally located above the ceiling.
Characteristics:
- somewhat common
- may be used in almost any climate
- moderate first cost for the landlord
- low maintenance cost
- long life expectancy
- energy efficient

VAV Cooling Only

This system relies on the landlord-provided central air distribution system. The VAV valve will be connected to the landlord's ductwork system and the tenant usually provides the ductwork and diffusers downstream of the VAV valve.
Characteristics:
- common
- may be used only when there are no exterior walls, roofs, or windows
- low first cost for the store operator
- low maintenance cost
- long life expectancy
- requires no energy consumption on the part of the tenant

VAV Reheat

As with the VAV cooling only system, this system relies on the landlord-provided central air distribution system. The tenant provides the ductwork, diffusers, and reheat coil downstream of the VAV valve.
Characteristics:
- somewhat common
- may be used when there are exterior walls, roofs or windows
- low first cost for the tenant
- low maintenance cost
- long life expectancy and
- an energy inefficient system

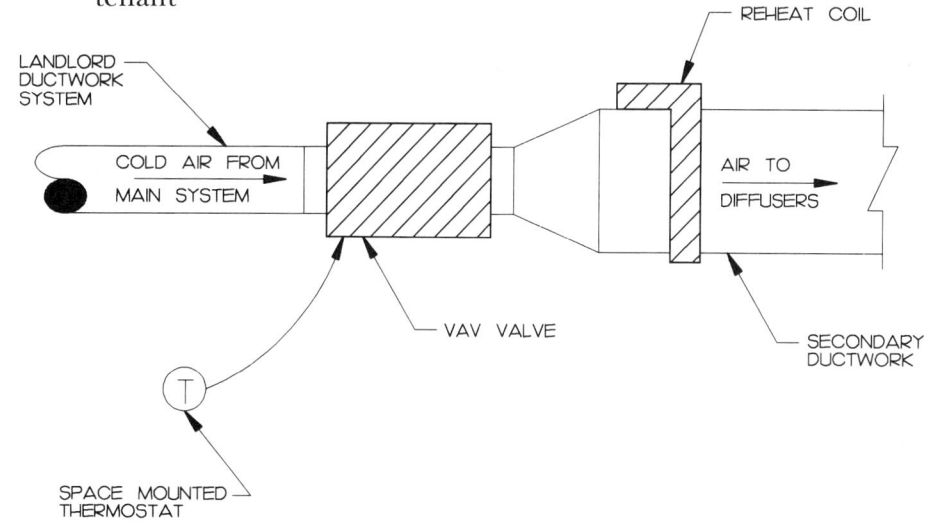

**Figure 9-1
VAV Reheat System**

The central air distribution system provided by the landlord is the basis for VAV reheat. Ductwork, diffusers, and reheat coil are supplied by the store owner.

Source: DFW Consulting Group, Inc.

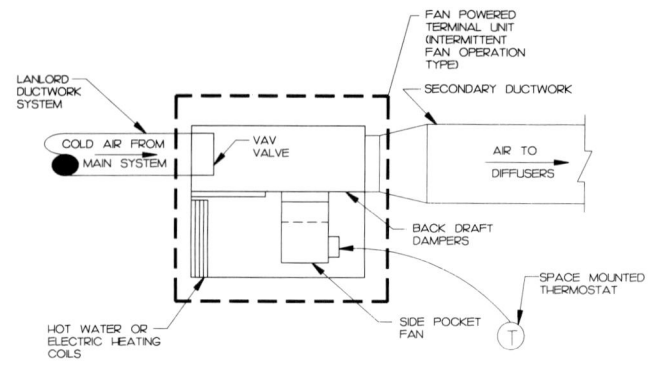

**Figure 9-2
VAV Fan-Powered
Box System**

This system relies on the central air distribution system provided by the landlord. The store owner provides ductwork and diffusers.

Source: DFW Consulting Group, Inc.

VAV Fan-Powered Boxes

This system also relies on the landlord-provided central air distribution system. The tenant provides the ductwork and diffusers downstream of the Fan-Powered Box.
Characterisitcs:
- common
- may be used when there are exterior walls, roofs or windows
- low cost for the tenant
- low maintenance cost
- long life expectancy
- energy efficient

Chilled Water Fan Coils

A landlord-provided chilled water loop is used here. Heat is rejected to the chilled water loop. The chilled water fan coil must be connected to the chilled water supply and return mains normally located above the ceiling. Heating is accomplished with electric heaters in the ductwork or with hot water coils if the landlord provides a hot water system.
Characteristics:
- common
- may be used in almost any climate
- high first cost for the landlord
- low maintenance cost
- long life expectancy
- energy efficient

Medium-Size Tenants (5,000 - 50,000 sq. ft.)

Medium-size tenants may use several of the systems listed above for small tenants. Depending upon various other requirements, some of the central systems may be used. For example, if the tenant desired a VAV system, a large rooftop VAV unit may be used to serve any of the VAV systems described in this chapter. A 50,000-square-foot tenant may, however, be too small to consider a central utility plant with boilers and chillers. Economic factors in making this decision equipment costs and space vs. operational costs.

Large Tenants (Over 50,000 sq. ft.)

Large tenants may use several of the systems listed for the small tenants; in addition, some central systems may be considered .

Air Distribution Schemes

VAV: This scheme uses a VAV valve to vary the airflow to the occupied space to maintain comfort conditions. Usually the supply air is maintained at a constant temperature of approximately 55 degrees F. As the space heat gains rise (lights come on, more people are present, or sunlight raises the interior temperature), the thermostat will sense a rise in temperature and cause the VAV valve to open and therefore provide additional cooling capacity. When the space heat gains lower , the thermostat will sense a reduction in temperature and cause the VAV valve to close.
Since this scheme does not provide a source for heat, the applications for the system are limited to those spaces that do not have exterior exposures, with no walls, roofs, or windows to the outside.

VAV With Reheat: This scheme uses a VAV valve to vary the airflow to the occupied space to maintain comfort conditions. Usually the supply air is maintained at a constant temperature of approximately 55 degrees F. As the space heat gains rise, the thermostat will sense a rise in temperature and cause the VAV valve to open and therefore provide additional cooling capacity. When the space heat gains reduce to a level where heat may be required, the thermostat will sense a reduction in temperature and: 1) cause the VAV valve to open to a preset position and; 2) cause the reheat coil to come on therefore providing heat to the space.
The reheat option is very energy inefficient and should be used only where the frequency of heating is minimal.

VAV With Side Pocket Fan: Common references to this system are: VAV with powered induction boxes, VAV with fan-powered terminal units, or VAV with fan-powered boxes. The fan-powered boxes come in two different configurations; the "Constant Operation Fan" type and the "Intermittent Operation Fan" type. Both types, however, do not use the 55 degree cooling air for heating purposes. The fan draws air from the return air cavity above the ceiling for the heating air.
Since the fan-powered boxes do not reheat the cooling air, this system may be used in almost any climate with excellent energy efficiency.

VAV With Independent Heat Source: There are several systems that fall within this classification. Basically, these systems are similar to the VAV system with side pocket fan, but have a wide range of options available for heat sources. Some of these sources are: baseboard heaters, ceiling radiant heaters, and unit heaters.

Constant Volume: Constant volume systems differ from VAV systems in one major way: The VAV system utilizes a constant supply air temperature (about 55 degrees F) and varies the supply air quantity, whereas the constant volume system utilizes a constant supply air quantity and varies the supply air temperature. The typical constant volume system will have the heat source located at the air conditioning unit as opposed to the VAV systems which have the heat sources located in the VAV valves or in the ductwork.

An example of a constant volume system is the rooftop-packaged air conditioning unit which supplies both heating and cooling from one packaged unit on the roof of a structure. The heating can be either gas-fired or electric.

Heat Rejection Methods

Refrigerant: The use of refrigerants as the heat transfer medium is the most basic of all methods and is used in each of the following heat transfer methods. Heat is transferred from the indoors to the outdoors through a series of phase changes, expansions, and compressions of the refrigerant. Examples of systems using only refrigerant as the heat transfer medium are: window units, rooftop packaged units, and split systems.

Chilled Water: A chilled water system uses water (between 42 and 48 degrees F.) as the heat transfer medium. A remotely-located water chiller supplies chilled water to chilled water coils that may be located in small "fan-coil units" suitable for small (0 - 4,000 sq. ft.) retail stores or in large "central station air handlers" that are normally part of the shell building HVAC system. Larger retail stores may also use multiple fan-coil units.

Both the fan-coil system and the central station system may be combined with any of the above air distribution systems to form a complete HVAC system.

Condenser Water: A condenser water system also uses water as the heat transfer medium. The major difference between a condenser water system and a chilled water system lies in the refrigeration system. As stated above, the chilled water system uses a remote chiller to chill the water to approximately 42-48 degrees F. The condenser water system circulates water in the 80-95 degree F range. The higher water temperature in the condenser water system necessitates the use of compressorized units (Water Source Heat Pumps) for air conditioning.

As with the chilled water system, the condenser water system may be combined with any of the above air distribution systems to form a complete HVAC system.

Definitions

Air-To-Air Heat Pump
A system that produces both heating and cooling with refrigerant heat exchanges. The heat from the space is rejected directly to the outside. This type of system typically offers a reasonable energy efficiency and requires supplemental emergency heat in cold climates.

ASHRAE
American Society of Heating, Refrigeration, and Air Conditioning Engineers.

DX
Direct Expansion or Direct Exchange
The method of heat transfer in the HVAC system. In a DX system, the refrigerant (Freon) exchanges heat directly with the air through a DX cooling coil. There is no intermediate heat exchange as in chilled water systems.

Economizer Cycle
An air conditioning cycle normally occuring on packaged units that use cold outdoor air for air conditioning purposes. This cycle is required on certain units in California.

Fan-Powered Terminal Unit
A type of VAV valve that utilizes a side pocket fan and heating strips or coils for heating.

HVAC System
Heating, ventilating, and air conditioning system

Packaged Unit
An air conditioning system that contains both the condensing and cooling sections in one unit. The units may be located on the roof or on grade adjacent to the building.

Reheat
A heating system that heats the cooling air for heating purposes.

Split System
A direct expansion air conditioning system that utilizes a condensing unit located outdoors and a fan-coil unit located indoors. The two units are linked by a set of refrigerant lines.

VAV: Variable air volume
An air distribution system that varies the volume of air delivered to the space to maintain comfort conditions.

VAV Valve
Device used to vary the air flow to the space.

Water Source Heat Pump
This system, which produces both heating and cooling with refrigerant heat exchanges, offers a high energy efficiency. The heat from the space is rejected directly to a condenser water loop.

9 Systems

The Four Basic Retail Store Support Functions

- **Merchandise movement**
- **Customer services**
- **Staff functions**
- **Operations and building functions**

The cashwrap station

- TRANSACTION FORM DIVIDERS
- CASH REGISTER WELL
- RECEIPT DRAWER WITH LOCKS
- ADJUSTABLE SHELVES

These are often referred to as "back-of-the-house" activities because most are out of customers' sight. A major exception is the cashwrap station, or cash desk. This is usually the end of the customer's shopping excursion, where cash, check, or credit cards are exchanged for goods, receipts prepared, credit checked, and purchases packed for the trip home.

Space designated as off-the-floor storage has been steadily shrinking. Merchants have recycled areas that previously housed back-up stockrooms into sales areas because of:

1. High cost of inventory. Because debt servicing on unsold goods bites deeply into merchants' profit margins, they prefer to place reorders on fast-moving items rather than gamble on heavy back-up inventory.

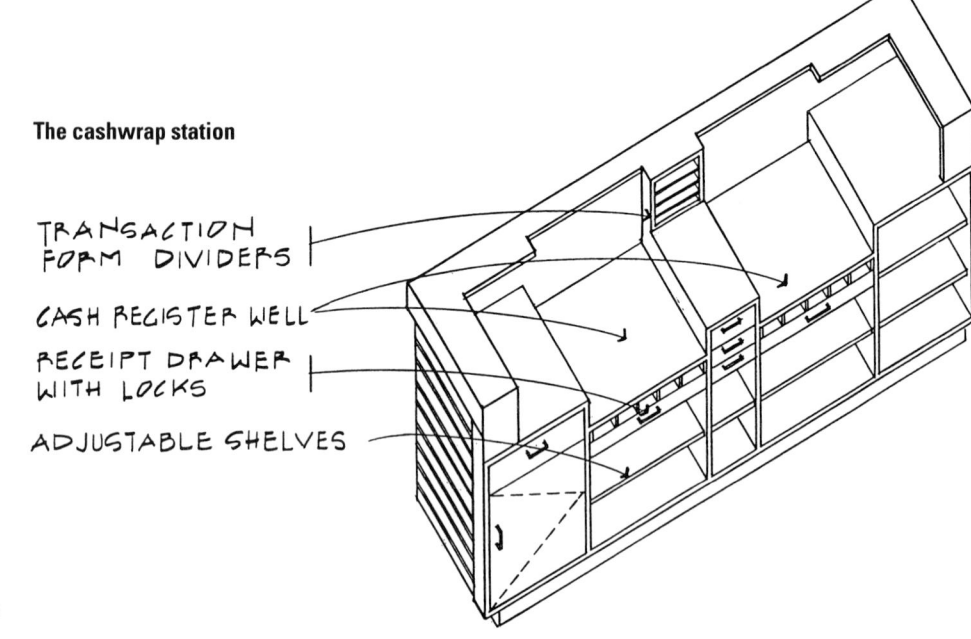

2. Lack of trained help. If the goods are not on the sales floor, clerks today are often reluctant to check a back stockroom or holding area to locate an item for a customer.

3. Impact of merchandise density. Stacked "boxed" goods, such as housewares, small appliances, make their own effective displays, and show customers depth of selection and immediate availability.

Planning Support Areas

The store designer should identify the required support spaces *before* the sales space is allocated. This part of the overall planning process may take just 5-10 percent of the total time, but a major omission or miscaulaltion can cause hours of redrafting.

- For a small soft goods store, 15 percent of total gross floor area will handle most support functions: receiving and shipping; stock; toilet area; general storage; office; and lockers.

- Stores that carry a wide range of products, such as hardware, require a large stockroom.
- Stockrooms for shoe stores can occupy 50 to 70 percent of total leased space, because shoe profits are generated by the amount of stock on hand, rather than the number of seats on the sales floor.

Solving storage problems can challenge the designer's creativity. Space-saving devices, bins, shelving units, and rack systems can be customized to handle specialized storage needs.

Receiving

Based on their past experience, most operators of medium and large stores will tell the planner the type of equipment preferred for initial merchandise handling.

1 & 2
Vertical customer transportation systems

Escalators, elevators, and stairways are major investments in funds and space for multilevel stores.

Or, if the designer is asked to research new vendors and systems, manufacturers can offer assistance with layout and basic flow patterns. Some will create a layout at no cost; others will charge a fee for these services.

Merchandise Transfers

Sturdy equipment is a prerequisite for moving goods between levels of a store or between units in a chain.

Within a multilevel store, merchandise can be moved vertically either by a freight elevator or, in small shops or boutiques, by a manual or electriaally-powered dumbwaiter.

For one chain's intrastore shipments, the planner devised a system that included a vestibule where the containers holding the items to be moved at the end of the business day are picked up by the trucker. At the destination store, the storage vestibule is unlocked from the outside, the goods unloaded, and the vestibule made secure overnight. In the morning, employees unlock the vestibule from the inside and wheel the containers into the store.

Marking and Pricing

Factory or warehouse supply houses offer a large selection of metal equipment suitable for retail marking and pricing. Basic components include tables with drawer options, and storage shelves with files or door units.

For odd-shaped spaces, get competitive bids from millwork shops or carpenters to determine the most cost-efficient method for procuring the equipment.

1

Stock

Merchants today are operating on close demand-and-supply cycles, not unlike the "just-in-time" industrial manufacturing process. Apparel retailers hold merchandise in areas close to the selling floor for short periods, and then move it directly onto the sales area in racks and carts.

For goods creased from shipping and handling, a preparation area for steam irons, pressing machines, or dry cleaning equipment may be required.

In gift shops, a work space to clean glassware or other items is often provided. Shoes stores need an area for stretching, touch up, inserting pads, etc.

Storage for back-up of boxed goods can be housed on movable shelving units that ride on tracks or trolleys, similar to those used for office file storage. They can be operated either manually or electrically. Shoe stockrooms also adapt well to this system.

2

Curved escalator at Nordstrom, San Francisco Centre.

Design: Whisler-Patri, San Francisco.

Curved staircase at Episode, San Francisco.

Design: Charles E. Broudy & Associates.

Table 9-1	Support Spaces in Retail Stores: For Customers, Staff, Operations, and Building Functions	
Area	Considerations	Functional and Design Requirements
Customer Services		
Cashwrap desk	Often in customers' view; multipurpose; for writing, cash handling, packing merchandise.	Outlets and wire management for cash register, phone, credit check-charge input; storage for sales books, bags, and boxes, etc.
Wrapping station	May be seasonal or permanent.	Storage bins for boxes, bags, wrapping material; holding area for sends; phone outlet.
Return desk	May be seasonal or permanent.	Holding area for returned items on shelves, bins, or movable carriers (may need to be secured); storage area for credit books and other supplies.
Fitting rooms	Trend to smaller, tighter spaces; average range; 12 to 18 sq. ft.	Lighting flattering to skin tones; materials and finishes that are simple, attractive, durable; may need security control-locks on doors of dressing rooms to prevent entrance by other than legitimate customers and staff; control desk at entrance to group of fitting rooms.
Credit offices	Privacy to make applicants feel comfortable.	Basic office environment for lighting, desks, chairs, counters, files; outlets for phones, computer terminals; employee storage of coats and valuables; cash handling and security for customers who pay bills by cash or check in this area.
Layaway and alteration pick-up	Medium to large stores need separate spaces; smaller stores can set aside part of a stockroom.	Storage for hanging and boxed goods; may need security for merchandise, cash handling; surface for writing and wrapping merchandise; phone outlet.
Repair service	Same as above.	Same requirements as layaway-alterations, plus work station if repair of jewelry, china, watches, etc. is carried out on premises.
Community rooms	For larger stores, shopping centers, and malls.	Appropriate acoustics, lighting, seating, based on owner's intended uses. May include serving kitchen.
Parcel checking	For security or as service to customers carrying briefcases, luggage, parcels.	Storage bins or spaces; counter with storage for tags, receipts, phone outlet.
Toilet rooms	Check local codes for size, separate male and female, separate personnel and employee, special food store codes.	Locate near plumbing; check codes for venting and air handling, handicapped requirements.
Staff Functions		
Toilet rooms	Same as above.	Same as above.
Lockers and checking areas	For security and employee convenience.	Storage bins and spaces; attendant desk; storage for tags and receipts; athletic-style lockers for coats and personal items; seating for changing of shoes.
Office	For merchandising staff, for accounting staff.	For departmentalized stores, buyer's office usually in or near department; can be 6 by 6 foot cubicle with desk, chair, file; accounting can be near credit office; outlets and wire management for phones, office machines, computer terminals; safe; cash drawers.
Lunchroom	Recommended for stores in areas where restaurants are remote.	Tables and chairs; vending machines are optional. Large stores may run their own employee cafeteria.
Lounge	Employee rest area; can also be used for informal meetings.	Chairs, tables; cot or equivalent (health code).
Training rooms	For medium and large stores.	Tables, chairs; instructional aids; cash register; storage space for sales books and other supplies; phone outlet.

Table 9-1 — Support Spaces in Retail Stores: For Customers, Staff, Operations, and Building Functions (Cont.)

Area	Considerations	Functional and Design Requirements
Operations and Building Functions		
Elevator	Self-service. Departments and corresponding floors should be listed above door opening.	Cab interior can be fitted with display system for ads, posters, even television.
Escalator	Requires valuable sales floor space but is a very efficient people mover. Customers are visually exposed to merchandise and displays as they ride.	Owner must evaluate budget versus benefits to determine the absolute need for this conveyance.
Dumbwaiter	An efficient and low-cost material mover. Size of objects to be transported is important factor.	Takes up relatively small amount of space. Can be manually or electrically operated.
Heating and cooling	See pages 108 to 111.	
Telephone service	From a wall-mounted panel board to separate room.	Contact phone company as early as possible in the planning stage.
Trash and garbage	Type of refuse: clean-paper goods and boxes; hazardous - glass, plastic, spray cans.	Trash-garbage room near exit; trash compactor, bailer; dumpster is outside, sometimes screened with optional roof covering.
Janitor's closet	Medium and large stores.	"Slop sink" with plumbing connection; storage for mops, buckets, cleaning preparations, polishes, and cloths.
Supply room	Separate or space in general "back room."	Storage for extra lamps, bulbs, air-conditioning filters. Merchandise-related supplies, such as sales books, tickets, bags, boxes, wrapping paper, etc. Small stores may keep seasonal displays and signs here.
Display/carpentry/sign making	Medium and large stores.	Storage and equipment for building of window and sales floor displays; spray painting; fabrication of backdrops and platforms; outlets and ventilation for fabricating equipment.

9 Systems

The Basic Objectives of a Retail Store Protection Plan

▶ Control store entrances

▶ Know where the patrons are

▶ Protect the merchandise from theft

Inventory shrinkage in the U.S. is currently running at $27-billion-a year clip, equal to 2 percent of total sales. Stores of all sizes fall prey to shoplifters and burglars. Marshall Fields' vice president for loss prevention Lewis C. Shealy told *The New York Times* that "every tenth of a percent saved is worth $1 million toward profit." The Knogo Corp., makers of electronic article surveillance equipment, reports that for every $10 lost to a shoplifter, the retailer has to increase sales by $500 just to break even.

Faced with such sobering statistics, store designers should make provisions for merchandise protection early in the planning process. There are five major aspects for store security:

1. **Merchandise protection on the sales floor**
   - Visual surveillance by sales personnel
   - Physical hindrances
   - Mechanical protection equipment
   - Electronic protection equipment

2. **Back-of-the-house merchandise protection**

3. **Currency protection**

4. **Building protection**

5. **Night and after-hours lighting**

Merchandise Protection on the Sales Floor

▶ **Visual surveillance by sales personnel**

More self-service stores and fewer salespeople on the selling floor have contributed to the increase in losses from shoplifting. Medium and large stores may station uniformed security personnel at entrances, escalators, and along heavy-traffic aisles.

▶ **Physical hindrances**

- Control the width of open front stores in shopping centers with merchandise displays, plants, or free-standing signs.

- In apparel stores, a check station that is monitored by an employee tracks the number of garments customers take to fitting rooms, using a numbered voucher or other numerical system.

- Fitting rooms that are locked when not in use prevent shoplifters from hiding merchandise in bags or on their person. Salespeople open the doors for legitimate customers.

- Design fitting rooms with floor-to-ceiling partitions between rooms to prevent shoplifters who work in teams from passing garments from

Table 9-2 Do's and Don't's of Visual Surveillance

Do	Don't
In small stores and large store departments, place the cashwrap where fitting rooms and entrances can be seen.	Do not put a display fixture higher than 4'6"–a short person's sight line– in the middle of the floor.
Create openings in partitions.	Avoid spaces that force a difficult floor plan, such as a Z plan, dog leg, or broken-back plan.
Place convex mirrors for visibility in hard-to-view places, like corners or down hallways. On the sales floor, specify full-size mirrors that can be angled.	Do not add a second entrance from a parking lot or the street unless mechanical or electronic devices are installed, or a guard is positioned.

one fitting room to another. Advise the mechanical engineer to allow for an extra load on the HVAC system.

- Resourceful shoplifters can hide electronic article surveillance tags or strips behind mounted mirrors. Keep surfaces smooth, or seal off dead spaces with mastic.

- To prevent "grab-and-run" thieves, specify locks for display cases containing such items as jewelry, small electronic items, or expensive handbags.

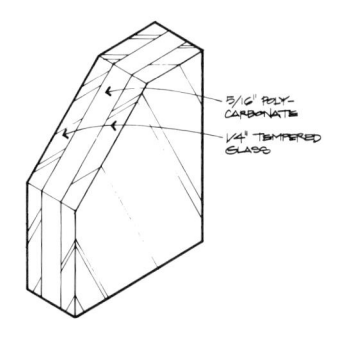

Security glass

For glass showcases, and for glazing exposed to the exterior as windows or doors, laminated glass combines the durability of glass with the strength of plastic. Manufacturers have single-ply	compositions as will as multi-plys that consist of polycarbonate plastic and glass layers. Some brands carry time ratings based on forcible entry and bullet-proof resistance.

- "Smash-and-grab" attacks on glass showcases are curbed by using impact-resistant glazing, which is made by sandwiching a layer of polycarbonate plastic between two outer layers of regular glass.

- "Hit-and-run" thefts have been controlled with cable lock systems for hanging garments, lock-equipped T-stands, and hidden switchpins for countertop items.

- Pilfering of accessories from mannequins has resulted in some retailers enclosing the displays within glass cases.

- Safes and vaults, up to room-size, protect furs, jewels, artworks, and other big-ticket items.

▶ **Mechanical protection equipment**

Rolling and side-folding grilles are used extensively in enclosed shopping malls as security gates in place of doors. The openings between links is sometimes enclosed with snap-in, high-strength plastic panels.

For stores with street frontage, rolling grilles are frequently installed to protect show windows and door openings. They can be installed either on the outside of the building or on the inside, behind the windows or doors. Both manual and electrically-operated versions are available.

▶ **Electronic protection equipment**

Retailers are investing in electronic devices that can scan, buzz, talk, chime, and record customer's movements as part of their long-running battle to cut losses from theft.

- Closed circuit television can be as basic as one camera focused on the checkout counter, or as complex as multiple cameras feeding data to a central monitoring station.

    As a visual deterrent to would-be shoplifters, the retailer can install ersatz TV cameras which have a blinking red light and move as if scanning the area, but have no recording mechanism.

- Cash registers can be equipped with a button that activates a signal to summon security officers when the clerk suspects a shoplifting incident.

- Hidden cameras and recording devices have been implanted in mannequins, one model of which is marketed under the name "Anne Droid."

- In the late 1960s, systems were introduced Electronic article surveillance (EAS) into stores and have proven to be an effective investment in the retailer's arsenal of theft-deterring efforts. Knogo Corporation advertises that a business can get a 100-150 percent return on their investment within the first year.

9 Systems

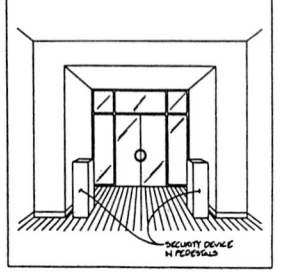

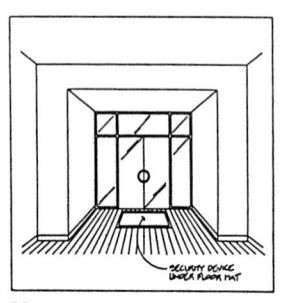

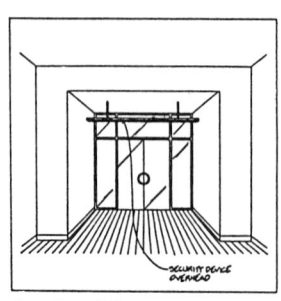

Pedestal **Mat** **Overhead Scanners**

EAS Detectors

Electronic article surveillance (EAS) utilizes low-level radio or microwave signals to detect wafers or tags on merchandise that have not been removed or deactivated before the shopper reaches a store entrance. Mechanisms that translate the signals into alarms are contained within pedestals, mats, or overhead scanners.

The original EAS used low-level radio frequency technololgy. A plastic tag is fastened to apparel and other soft goods with a wafer locking mechanism. Clerks use a decoupler at the checkout or cashwrap to remove the tag; tags not removed are detected by equipment in pedestals, underfoot, or overhead, and set off an alarm.

A radio frequency circuit can now be laminated to a piece of paper that resembles a label or price tag, and can be deactivated by the clerk. If not, the tell-tale tag activates an alarm system.

Back-of-the-house Merchandise Protection
Merchandise that disappears before it reaches the sales can be an "inside job" planned and carried out by dishonest employees, or a heist by outside thieves who track merchandise and employee movements and then illegally remove the goods. Tight inventory control and surveillance starting with the arrival of the merchandise at the store is as important as sales floor theft-deterring procedures.

▶ **Secured delivery areas**
Merchandise unloaded after store hours from trucks into a delivery vestibule that is secured by locked doors which can be opened from the store side only. Stores often provide truckers with toilet rooms and drinking fountains in the vestibule space.

▶ **Locked stockroom cages**
High-risk merchandise is separated from other goods and stored behind locked floor-to-ceiling mesh cages.

▶ **Electronic surveillance**
Monitored closed circuit TV provides visual control. An additional feature is combining life safety indicators and HVAC controls with an alert signal activated by an illegally-opened door.

▶ **Insurance-approved construction**
Input during the programming phase from an insurance expert can favorably influence insurance premium rates. Payback for following insurance-approved constrction guidelines is estimated at five years.

Construction

10

Five-point checklist for retail construction:

1. **The schedule**
   Tight, but realistic

2. **Contracts**
   All agreements in place

3. **Environmental studies**
   No surprises from "hidden" hazards, underground or within the existing structure

4. **Project documentation**
   A system in place for memos, confirmations, and other correspondence

5. **Quality control**
   Site visits, site meetings, review of shop drawings, final punchlist

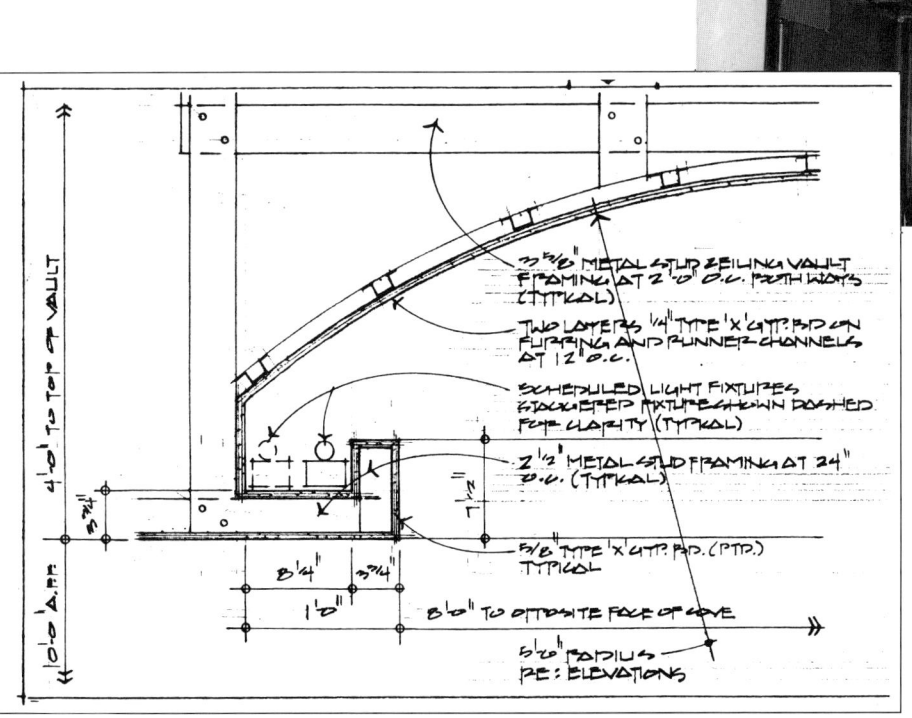

Installation of steel framing studs to support vaulted ceiling, cove, dry wall, and walls at 2,500-sq.-ft. Pasadena, Cal. unit of Pea in the Pod, a 25-store maternity wear chain.

Design: Charles E. Broudy & Associates, Dallas, Texas; Michael Malone, AIA, project designer.

10 Construction

Retailers are prodigious builders and rebuilders. According to the F. W. Dodge Division of McGraw-Hill, the the value of new retail space rose from 1987 to 1989, while the total amount of new retail construction peaked in 1987.

Stores are becoming more expensive to build, according to *Chain Store Age Executive's* Physical Supports Census for 1989. For new construction, compared to 1988:

- apparel specialty stores jumped 20 percent, from an average of $26.50 per square foot to $31.90

- discount stores rose 12 percent, from $25.60 per square foot to $31.90

- drug stores now cost $30.80 per square foot, compared to $29, a 6 percent increase

- supermarkets cost $38.14 per square foot, compared to $31, a 23 percent gain

- department stores now cost $44.60 per square foot, versus $38.20, a 17 percent hike

The "Right" to Retail Profit

Not long ago, successful merchandising relied on having the right store in the right place with the right goods. Today, merchants are redefining the components of "the right store" to include "the right environment" to support the salability of the merchandise.

Table 10-1	Store Construction Activity 1987-1989		
	1987	1988	1989
Stores: Area (millions of square feet)	250.0	238.2	244.9
Stores: Value (millions of dollars)	13.301	13.404	13.967

Source: *F. W. Dodge Division, McGraw-Hill, Inc.*

Store design and redesign have become prime differentiation tools that are part of the arsenal of consumer appeal techniques employed by retailers to attract and hold targeted segments of the marketplace. Retail giant K mart Corp. announced early in 1990 that it was accelerating its $2.3 billion program to modernize all of its 2,300 stores, compressing it from five years to three.

Industry leader Sears, Roebuck & Company has invested in Sears Ltd. stores, specialty units with brand name merchandise. Slicker and contemporary, they represent Sears' strategy to tailor the units to individual communities, establishing a strong presence in new or underperforming areas.

Pre-Construction Concerns

Three basic retail store construction categories:

- new
- renovation and rehab.
- alterations and additions

for:

- retail stores in malls and shopping centers
- stores in typical downtown retail shopping districts

Since the publication of the First Edition of this book in 1985, environmental considerations have added a whole new layer of pre-construction planning for both new and existing retail facilites. Expenditures to correct environment-related situations is one of the causes for the escalation in store construction costs.

Environmental engineers and specialists have joined the cadre of consultants needed to contribute to a retail building project. Buyer, seller, landlord, tenant–all should proceed with utmost care when evaluating a parcel of land or the renovation of an existing structure.

Toxic waste, asbestos, radon, fire ratings of materials, and fire protection requirements should be investigated by experts before the bid package is assembled. They will provide the owner with a report explaining the severity of any problems encountered, and a cost estimate to correct them.

Toxic waste materials: From buried gas or chemical tanks; PCB's; lead paint
Asbestos: Asbestos floor tile, or insulation for ducts and pipes
Radon: Trapped underground gas seeping into structures

Fire resistance and retardancy: Structural materials and materials used in interiors. *Smoke and fire spread ratings of finished materials.* The presence of vinyl materials–PCB's, paints, and coatings–should be pointed out.
Fire protection and sprinkler systems: Conform to local codes; mandated by insurance industry.
"Sick" buildings: Some buildings with non-operable windows retain substances that can be health hazards; HVAC system overhaul may be required.
Drainage: Government bureaus like the Environmental Protection Agency are concerned with long-term effects of air and water quality; run-off from parking lots and internal roadways is an example.

The Retail Construction Package
This package includes:

1. Basic building, including HVAC, electrical, plumbing, sprinkler, and elevators
2. Perimeter, partitions, drywall, wings, soffits, bulkheads, and valances
3. Fixtures that fit into the walls, and floor fixtures that are removable and portable: racks, tables, gondolas, display stands
4. Carpet and wall coverings (optional)

For a large store or a complex of stores, outline drawings are prepared showing the basic building shell, partitions, stairways, elevators, and drywall.

Prepare an illustrated fixture "bible" showing all the store fixtures for the particular job: shelves, bins, racks, rods, movable floor cases, and all other freestianding floor fixtures. The "bible" can be bound in a standard ring binder, or in large drawings.

Large retail operations have staff specialists who are assigned as liaisons for the construction phase. They often have their own systems of specifying and bidding, and can act as a construction manager. If this is the case, they will divide the four basic construction packages to suit their own procedures. Sometimes signs and furniture are let as separate contracts.

For small jobs, it is not unusual to put all four packages together and give it to the general contractor to bid and implement. Many GCs who do retail work have their own custom woodworking, metal, and glass fabricating operations. Or, they can choose to subcontract them.

Schedules and Time Constraints
Construction deadlines for retail stores are closely linked to seasonal events: year-end, spring, and back-to-school are examples. Since stores can account for up to 40 percent of their annual gross sales in the five weeks before Christmas, they will push the design team hard to meet deadlines for new construction or renovation before the holiday selling season sets in.

It is more the rule rather than the exception for small- and medium-size jobs to have very little lead time. Designers should not waste time anguishing over the fact that the owner should have retained them two months ago. A small store can be designed in three weeks, and built in six weeks. So start compressing the time schedule, charge up the creative motors, and convince your vendors and the contractor to cooperate.

For larger stores of 100,000 square feet and over, a six-month construction timetable is not impossible, but it is very tight. Considering the amount of interior work involved, plus any customization, completion could be more like 8-12 months.

Fast-tracking
A successful fast-tracking of the design and construction phases takes skill and determination, but can mean the difference between meeting and missing an opening deadline.

To tighten the timetable,

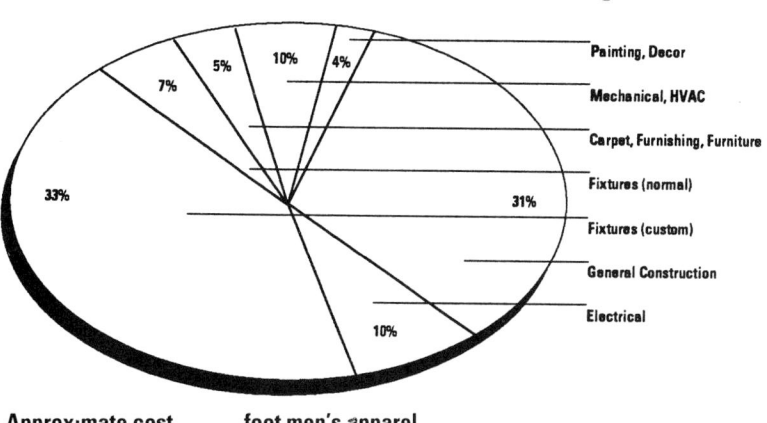

Approximate cost breakdown for a 10,000-20,000-square-foot men's apparel store.

Painting, Decor — 4%
Mechanical, HVAC — 10%
Carpet, Furnishing, Furniture — 5%
Fixtures (normal) — 7%
Fixtures (custom) — 33%
General Construction — 31%
Electrical — 10%

Job Schedule

Job #:
Name of Job:
Address:
Date:

Project Architect:
Contractor:
Start Date:
Completion:

Trade	Sub-Contractor													

Figure 10-1
A sample job schedule for a 3-month construction project, prepared by the store designer. Scheduling by week for the subcontractors' activities is indicated by the shaded areas.

Job Schedule

Job #: 123
Name of Job: XYZ STORE
Address: 1001 G. ST. N.Y.C.
Date: 12.2.88

Project Architect: CHARLES BROUDY & ASSOC. P.C.
Contractor: JONES CO.
Start Date: 12.5.88
Completion: 3.2.88

Trade	Sub-Contractor	12.5	12.12	12.19	12.26	1.2	1.9	1.16	1.23	1.30	2.6	2.13	2.20	2.27
CONCRETE FLOOR	J. WILLIAMS	▨												
DRYWALL	D. BROWN			▨	▨									
CARPENTRY	JONES CO.		▨	▨	▨							▨		
CEILING	ABC CO.						▨	▨						
GLASS & STOREFRONT	ADAM INC.							▨	▨					
CABINET & FIXTURES	FRANK CO.										▨	▨	▨	
HARDWARE	SMITH LTD.									▨	▨			
PAINTING/WALLCOVG	HIGH & DRY											▨	▨	
CARPET/FLOORING	JANSEN & BROS.											▨	▨	
HVAC	H. HALL & SONS		▨	▨	▨						▨	▨		
PLUMBING	SMITH BROS.			▨	▨	▨						▨	▨	
ELECTRIC	CENTRAL ELEC.				▨	▨					▨		▨	
SPRINKLER	AAA SPRINKLER				▨	▨								▨
LOOSE STORE FIXTURES	FRANK CO.											▨	▨	

122

develop the fixture design and perimeter design while the shell is under construction. Fixtures have long lead times for design, fabrication, and installation. Elevators, escalators, special hardware, special lighting, and roof skylights are other items that should be specified as early in the project as possible.

To prevent time-consuming misunderstandings between the GC and the outside fixture sub, set up a communications system so that they are working on parallel, rather than divergent, tracks.

Scheduling

With all good intentions, plan a realistic schedule, but be equally realistic that it will probably be revised. There are myriad reasons: a strike at the carpet mill; the sign maker's delivery truck was hijacked; fabric for the banquettes is tied up in customs; the fixture shop overestimated it production capabilities. Or somebody didn't pay the electrical sub on time and he won't finish the wiring.

Don't panic!! Remember, the contractor's value to a client is his expediting capability, to keep the job running, sometimes, it may

Table 10-2 Typical Store Design and Construction Activity Times

Size (sq. ft.)	Design Time (from signing of design contract to start of construction)	Construction Time (from start of construction to store opening)
2,000	6 weeks	6-9 weeks
20,000	3 months	4 months
50,000	6 1/2 months	4-5 months
100,000	7 1/2 months	6-13 months

Figure 10-2
Layout diagram of phased construction for a 10,000-20,000 square foot apparel store

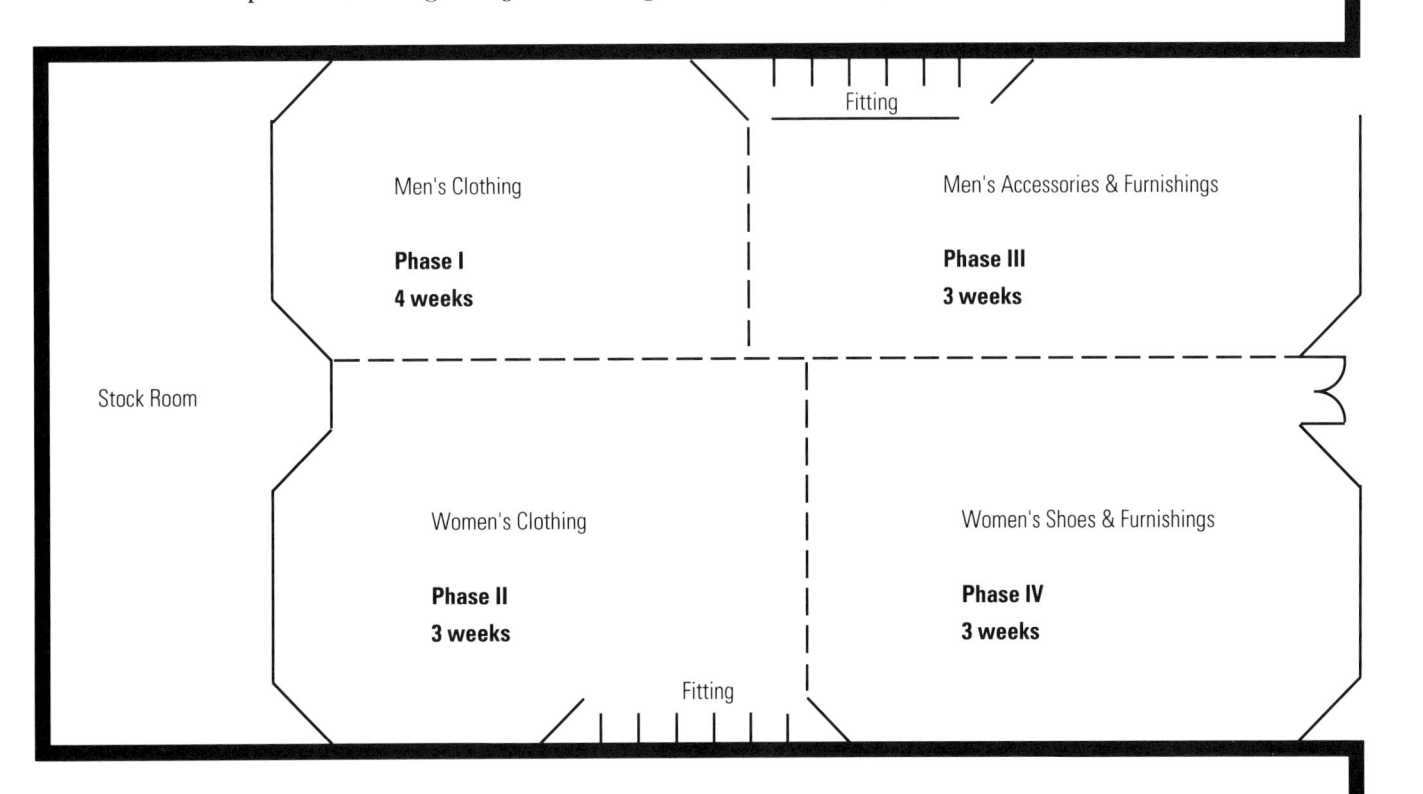

Men's Clothing
Phase I
4 weeks

Men's Accessories & Furnishings
Phase III
3 weeks

Stock Room

Women's Clothing
Phase II
3 weeks

Women's Shoes & Furnishings
Phase IV
3 weeks

Fitting

10 Construction

seem, in spite of itself.

Establish a construction schedule for a remodeling or renovation job that allows the merchant to remain open for business. Few retailers want to lose even one day's proceeds. Plan a phased construction timetable with the contractor so that parts of the store are in operation while he works in one area.

Dividing a sales floor into quadrants for phased contruction has proven to be an effective plan. Another method is to split the store down the middle. If the trades have to be brought in two, three, or four times, be sure that the contractor figures this expense into the price, and confirms it in the bid.

Protective measures

Agree with the contractor on procedures for dust protection at the site, and frequent removal of dust and trash. Include in the budget an allowance for an enclosure to contain the construction activity and reduce the noise and general disruption levels.

It is wise to take progress shots of the job before, during, and after construction. The photographs should be taken from the same vantage points and dated. Black and white film is satisfactory. Use film with an ASA rating of at least 400; available lighting may be scant.

Substitutions

Substitutions during construction are the bane of a designer's existence. Whatever the cause for a substitute product, it must perform and look like the product proposed originally, or the design firm will have an unhappy client or owner's representative on its hands.

The most serious types of substitutions involve building products like the facing or roofing materials. If the product to be respecified is covered or behind the walls, the situation may be quickly resolved. Searching for an new upholstery fabric or wood veneer that everyone is happy with and that can be obtained on short notice combines luck, perseverence, and a sense of humor.

Keep the owner advised of the situation, and have the client or owner's representative help you with the final approval. The designer should make recommendations and then back them up with data.

Fixtures: New and Renovated

There are two major considerations:

▸ **Is the cost to renovate considerably less than buying new? Accurate estimates should be obtained from several contractors.**

▸ **Will a renovated fixture be as esthetically desirable as a new fixture? If it does not augment the philosphy of the new store design, it is no bargain.**

If existing showcases qualify for physical upgrading, these techniques will prove effective:

▸ Change the color by spray painting the entire unit, or by covering with new wood or metal laminate.

▸ Change the ends of the unit by applying mirrors, wood, or plastic laminate.

▸ Install new lighting.

▸ Refit the interior of the unit with a new material.

Unless the fixture is critically fitted into a wall, the fabricator will take it out to work on in the shop. Bid each item or group before awarding the contract.

New fixtures or display pieces can be stock, modified stock, or custom. If the design firm is creating custom fixtures for the project, an orderly record of the receipt, processing, and disposition of shop drawings and samples is recommended. The American Institute of Architects publishes Document G712, "Shop Drawing and Sample Record," for this purpose.

In addition, the Office for Professional Liability Research of Victor O. Schinnerer & Co. recommends the following to avoid professional liability losses relating to shop drawings:

▸ Be certain that the contractor and sub-contractors fully understand the agreed on procedure for handling shop drawings.

▸ Do not approve shop drawings in a manner that indicates approval for other than conformance with the specifications and drawings prepared by the designer.

Neiman-Marcus Lenox Mall, Atlanta

Custom Platform

Design:
Rubano•Mirviss• Assoc., NYC;
Lois M. Mirviss, principal in charge;
Earl E. Carpenter, project coordinator.

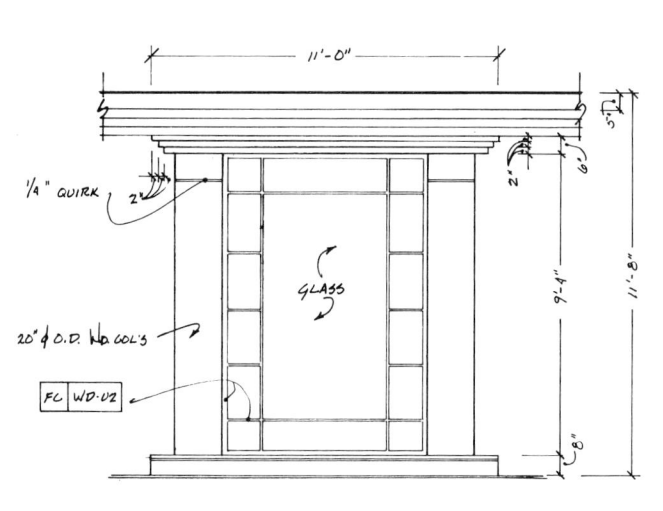

The overall design themes for the remodeling of the 154,000-square-foot branch focused on: updated traditional elegance; innovative use of forms and materials; improved departmental flow; and reconfiguration of the main and upper floors while adding a third selling floor on the lower level.

For the upper level fashion apparel floor, mahogany unifies the floor visually and provides the primary architectural element. The major custom displays are framed in mahogany with columns on each side; free-standing double mahogany columns mark each corner of the court; and the displays along the central court's sides are framed with mahogany end panels and base. The displays which feature mannequins have glass backs defined with mullions, and built-in overhead illumination.

125

10 Construction

3
St. Louis Union Station now a mixed-use facility

Adaptive Reuse
Viable older buildings and complexes have been reclaimed and literally given new leases on life by creative developers and designers. There are some rather spectacular examples of retail complexes rising from the skeltons of underutilized railway stations in St. Louis and Washington, D.C., outmoded food distribution centers in Boston and New York, an empty Federal Government building in Washington, an abandoned chocolate factory and a cannery in San Francisco, and a former hotel in Philadelphia.

Warehouses, with their high ceilings and long spans, are favorite targets for successful retail makeovers. Other smaller adaptive reuse projects demonstrate ingenious solutions to difficult existing conditions.

Many structural and architectural features of older properties can make unique design statements in the new retail environment.

Walls
Exposed stone: Cleaning and repointing enhance appearance.
Exposed brick: Cleaning by sand blasting or power wash, or by chemical restoration reveals hue and texture.
Existing arches and bearing walls: Make for interesting space dividers and display walls.
Wood: Paneling, wainscots, and moldings can be stripped to base material.

Ceilings
Beams: Rough-hewn, old wood beams can be restained, sanded, or sand-blasted.

3

Pressed tin: Original pressed tin ceilings can be integrated into both formal and casual design themes.
Brick or concrete: Arched brick or exposed concrete ceilings give a feeling of height and are enhanced by innovative lighting.
Moldings: Exposed wood or plaster moldings often reveal decorative details.

Floors
Wood: Sanding and staining can bring wood floors back to life.
Tiles: Restored ceramic and marble tiles can make a dramatic overall surface, or contrast to carpeted areas.

Other features
Lighting fixtures, bars, and back bars
Old signs
Stained glass windows

The conversion of the historic St. Louis Union Station created a mixed-use development from the c. 1894 structure that was once the largest single level passenger train terminal in the world. Restoration of the 822,000 square-foot-structure included the Bedford limestone headhouse exterior, red tiled roof, and barrel-vaulted grand hall. Shops and restaurants occupy 275,000 square feet; Hyatt Regency operates a 550-room luxury hotel. Developer of the project, which was completed in 1985, is The Rouse Company.

*Design:
Hellmuth, Obata & Kassabaum, St. Louis; Gyo Obata, FAIA, partner in charge.*

4
A new higher ceiling at Nan Duskin, Baltimore

4

Alterations & Additions

Raising of the orginal ceiling from the standard 9 feet to 17 feet gives exciting visual character to this upscale women's apparel store. Located in Cross Keys Village Shopping Center, six small service shops formerly occupied a 7,500-square-foot space. Construction took four and one-half months.

- The original flat ceiling was demolished. The new sloping ceiling follows the roof line.
- Air conditioning ducts and wiring for lighting were relocated.
- Skylight with perimeter lighting was installed.
- Walls originally separating the six former shops were removed.
- Flooring of service-grade vinyl and carpet was removed. Highly-polished Andes granite, wood, and quality carpeting were installed.

Design: Charles E. Broudy & Associates

127

10 Construction

5, 6 & 7
Eddie Bauer
Southcenter Mall
Seattle

5

6

7

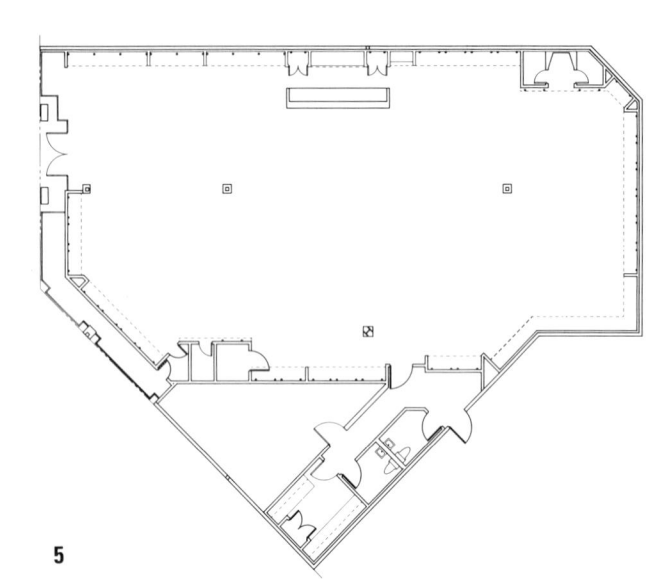

Multiple Stores

Eddie Bauer plans an aggressive rollout of stores in the 6,000-square-feet category, for a total of 250 rollouts by 1993. The prototype design has many typical standards for store layout, fixture arrangement, retail/stock square footage proportion, etc.

Computer applications have made the task of adapting the prototype to each location more time- and cost-efficient. According to Paul Humes of NBBJ/Retail Concepts, the approved preliminary plan is transferred to the computer. It serves as the basic floor plan for the demolition plan, main floor plan, fixture plan, and mechanical/electrical plans, and has application to the reflected ceiling plan.

Mr. Humes said that the computer-generated plans improve quality control as design and drawing quality are consistent. "We can also isolate portions or entire plans to print out at larger or smaller scale for various uses on construction documents or for client communication. We are expanding the computer's use for area take-offs for construction materials and store layout analysis," he added.

Design: NBBJ/Retail Concepts, Seattle; James Adams, design director; Craig Hardman, project director.

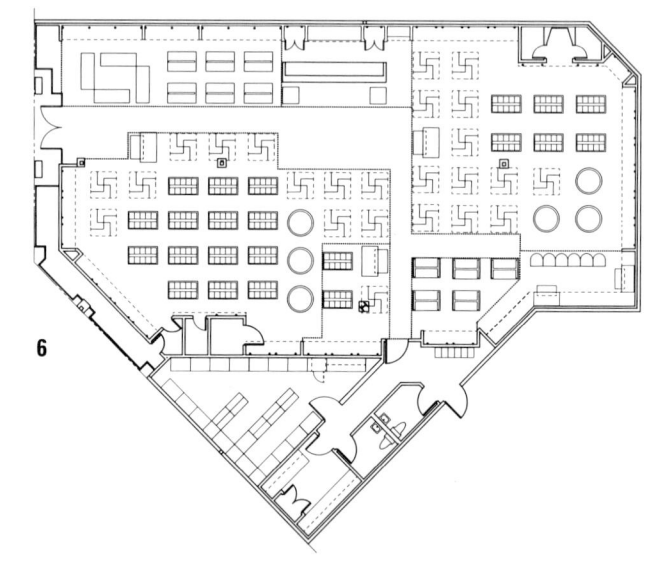

128

Table 10-3 — Do's and Don't's of Construction Communication

Do's	Don't's
Memoranda of informal conferences and telephone conversations	Avoid all references to personalities. Do not use statements which will debase another person.
Documentation of the owner's authorization to enter into the contract with the design professional	Do not record opinions or conclusions as to the cause of the incident or how it could have been avoided.
Copies of owner-furnished data	Do not volunteer or perform gratuitous services. Communications with third parties (i.e., parties other than the client) should be limited to and in accordance with the requirements of the professional service contract with the client.
Documentation of key design decisions, and the owner's response	
Documentation of the owner's written approval to proceed from one phase of professional service to the next.	Don't be vague when stating which party is responsible for activities noted in minutes of construction site meetings.
Copies of all contracts entered into by the design professional and the client, whether the client is the owner or another design professional.	

Source: *Guidelines for Improving Practice*, Vol. VI, No. 8, published by Victor O. Schinnerer & Company, Inc., Chevy Chase, Maryland.

Legal Considerations for Retail Store Design: Roles, Responsibilities, and Procedures

This section was written by Charles R. Heuer, Esq., AIA, The Heuer Law Group, Somerville, Mass., a practice concentrating in design and construction law. Mr. Heuer is the author of *Means Legal Reference For Design & Construction* (R. S. Means Co., Inc., Kingston, Mass., 1989).

Project Participants

The major participants involved in retail store construction projects follow the traditional role identification that characterizes most building jobs: the owner; design professional(s), general contractor and/or construction manager, subcontractors, manufacturers, and suppliers. They are the individuals and entities who work together to design and then construct, renovate, or otherwise improve real property, here for retail distribution activities.

Their relationships, including the way that responsibilities are allocated between them by operation of law and by their own contracts, contribute to the successful conclusion of their mutual endeavors.

▶ **Owner**

The term "owner" refers to the individual or business entity who commissions the design and construction of the project. The owner may be a partnership, corporation, joint venture, trustee of a trust, governmental entity, or individual. The owner may own the real estate on which the project is to be constructed and will often own the actual construction itself.

Sometimes, however, the owner is not the legal owner of the construction and property, but instead assumes the role of project initiator. For example, a developer who does not own the real estate on which the shopping center will be built is nevertheless referred to as the owner because he creates the project and assembles the financial resources to build it.

Similarly, a retail tenant does not own the shopping mall into which its store will go. Yet, with respect to the designer and contractor hired, it is the owner.

With minor project variations, these are the typical owner's duties:

- obtain access to the project site or premises
- secure financing
- develop information on project needs, goals, and objectives
- select and hire a design professional and other consultants

129

10 Construction

- procure soil tests and geotechnical engineering services, if necessary
- hire a construction manager and/or construction contractor
- obtain required approvals
- provide necessary insurance
- pay the design professional(s), the construction manager, (if any), and the contractor(s)

▶ **Design Professionals**

A commonly used definition of a "design professional" is an individual licensed in at least one state to perform design services. Design professionals, therefore, include architects, engineers, landscape architects, and land surveyors, and in some states, interior designers. The laws that apply to them are generally the same, even though their services, training, and experience differ to some degree.

It is also common for many unlicensed designers to refer to themselves as "design professionals." Subject to the specific provisions of state licensing laws, that is fine since they make extremely important contributions to the total design process.

For retail construction jobs of any significant size, the architect is often the prime design professional who contracts with the owner to provide all of the professional services for the project. As the prime design professional, the architect is responsible for all of the design decisions for the architect's firm, as well as for those made by other design professionals engaged as consultants. For example, an architect may hire engineers to design the structural, plumbing, electrical, and the heating, ventilating, and air conditioning (HVAC) systems.

An architect doing retail work may need to hire additional design consultants, such as store planners, interior designers, visual display specialists, and graphic designers. The services provided by consultants should be coordinated with the services provided for in the architect's contract. Ideally, the consultants should be hired with the understanding that they owe the same responsibilities to the architect or other prime design professional as the architect owes to the owner, within each particular discipline.

The architect is usually responsible for producing the documentation which describes the design. Such documentation includes drawings, specifications, schedules, and other contract documents. Among other tasks during the construction phase, the architect generally:

- interprets the contract documents
- observes the progress of the work
- reviews and comments on shop drawings and other submittals
- prepares change orders
- inspects the construction work at substantial and final completion

▶ **Prime (General) Contractor**

A prime contractor has a contract directly with the owner. Often, there is a general contractor under contract with the owner to provide all of the construction services for the project, and remains responsible to the owner for all construction under that contract.

The general contractor normally subcontracts part of the construction work to other contractors (referred to as "subcontractors"). In the traditional relationship the general contractor does *not* have a contractual relationship with the architect. The general contractor is normally responsible for:

- construction means, methods, techniques, sequences, and procedures
- site safety programs and precautions
- scheduling and coordinating the work of all subcontractors

▶ **Construction Manager**

Some owners prefer to use a construction manager rather than a general contractor. The construction manager may provide to the owner (during pre-construction activities) professional advice on construction issues, e.g., availability of materials, cost of construction, and constructability of design details. During the construction phase, the construction manager may maintain the professional role by managing multiple prime contractors (the trades) who are all under contract directly with the owner.

Alternately, the construction manager may actually hold the trade contracts itself. If so, the construction manager operates essentially like a general contractor.

8
Arched entrance for Macy's branch

8   At the R. H. Macy & Co. branch in the River Chase Galleria, Birmingham, Ala., the tone-on-tone, **massive arch entrance combines rough aggregate** block and terra cotta tiles.

Design: GSGSB, New York; Michael G. Bobick, AIA, project architect; Paul Rudolph, consulting architect.

10 Construction

▶ Subcontractors

Subcontractors contract with the general contractor (or, perhaps, the construction manager) to provide labor and materials for construction of the project. They are often trade contractors who do specific work such as masonry or plumbing. Subcontractors do *not* have a contractual relationship with the owner or architect.

The usual terms of the contract with the general contractor require the subcontractor to assume toward the general contractor all of the duties that the general contractor assumes towards the owner via the prime contract. This tends to aid in administration of the construction contract for all involved.

▶ Manufacturers and Suppliers

Manufacturers and suppliers actually provide the products and materials installed on the project. Many of the legal principles to which they are subject are codified in the individual states' (except Louisiana) versions of the Uniform Commercial Code (UCC). In particular, the UCC affects warranties, with which designers should be familiar, especially for major installations.

Agreements

Two major types of agreements are applicable to the design and construction process:

- ▶ professional services agreements
- ▶ construction agreements

Although, generally neither of them must be in writing to be enforceable, it is in the parties best interests to make written agreements. Otherwise, it is very difficult to prove the terms of the understanding reached by the parties. Agreements may take several forms.

1. *Letter agreements* are often favored for small and/or simple projects because they are non-threatening and usually easy to understand.

2. *Standard form agreements* are produced and distributed by the various professional societies and trade organizations, such as the American Institute of Architects (AIA), the Engineers Joint Contract Documents Committee (EJCDC), the American Society of Interior Designers (ASID), and the Associated General Contractors of America (AGC).

Standard form agreements usually try to strike a balance between the parties' interests while reflecting current practices and procedures in the industry.

3. *Custom agreements* are made by the parties to suit their individual circumstances, and have the advantage of being highly focused and specific. They also require considerable effort by the parties.

▶ Professional Services Agreements

The construction process usually begins with the owner's selection of a design professional to plan and design the project, and with whom a contractual relationship is formed. While the contents of the owner's agreement with the design professional vary depending on the project, the following topics or issues should be addressed.

- design professional's scope of services and other responsibilities
- owner's responsibilities
- scheduling of services
- methods of compensation
- payment schedules
- ownership and use of documents created by the design professional
- provisions for termination of the agreement
- dispute resolution procedures (e.g., arbitration)

Commonly used forms of agreement include:

AIA Document B141:
Owner–Architect Agreement
AIA Document B151: Abbreviated Form of Owner–Architect Agreement
AIA Document B171: Interior Design Agreement
AIA Document B177: Abbreviated Form of Interior Design Agreement

Users should verify that they have the most up-to-date edition in every case.

▶ **Construction Contracts**
A number of different methods may be used to contract for construction services.

Traditional
The owner contracts with a *single prime* contractor who takes responsibility for all construction on the project. The prime contractor then contracts with trade contractors who perform part of the actual construction work.

Multiple prime contractor
The owner directly hires a number of trade contractors to perform the required construction work. The owner may be capable of managing those contractors with its own staff or may require the assistance of a construction manager.

Design/build
One individual or entity is responsible for *both* the design and construction services for the project. Design/build contracts have some of the attributes of both professional services agreements and construction contracts.

The specific terms of construction contracts vary depending on the project and the construction method, but should generally address the following topics or issues:
- contractor's responsibilities
- owner's responsibilities
- methods of compensation
- owner's and design professional's procedures for administering the construction phase of the work
- procedures for handling changes in the work
- a schedule for the work
- procedures for handling delays in the work
- requirements for insurance and bonding
- procedures in the event of breach of contract and other defaults

The forms of agreement listed here are the most commonly used in the industry.

AIA Document A101:
Owner–Contractor Agreement (Stipulated Sum) or
AIA Document A111:
Owner–Contractor Agreement (Cost of the Work Plus a Fee)
To be used in conjunction with:
AIA Document A201: General Conditions of the Contract for Construction
AIA Document A107: Abbreviated Form of Owner-Contractor Agreement (including General Conditions) (Stipulated Sum) or
AIA Document 117: Abbreviated Form of Owner-Contractor Agreement (including General Conditions) (Cost of the Work Plus a Fee)

AIA Document A101/CM: Owner-Contractor Agreement (Stipulated Sum, Construction Management Edition
To be used in conjunction with:
AIA Document A201/CM: General Conditions of the Contract for Construction, Construction Management Edition

AIA Document A171: Owner-Interior Contractor Agreement (Stipulated Sum), Furniture, Furnishings and Equipment, or
AIA Document A177: Owner-Interior Contractor Agreement (Cost of the Work Plus A Fee), Furniture, Furnishings and Equipment
To be used in conjunction with:
AIA Document A271: General Conditions of the Contract for Furniture, Furnishings and Equipment
and
AIA Document A191: Owner-Design/Builder Agreement.

Here too, users should verify that they have the most up-to-date edition in every case.

10 Construction

Table 10-4   Design and Construction Checklist for New and Remodeled Stores

Area or Service		Considerations
Storefront		
Show windows	Platforms Backgrounds	Type and size. Fixed or portable. See-through or enclosed.
Bulkheads above storefront in interior malls		Drywall.
Vestibule	Type of HVAC Floor Walls	Size and location. Nonslip or removable grille. Glass or maintenance-free; see-through or solid.
Entrances	Entrances and doors	How many and where? Consult building code.
Awnings		Sun coverage or cosmetic.
Canopies		Metal or plastic; sun and customer protection.
Exterior lighting		Security and ornamental.
Demising strips for separation of stores		In strip centers or malls.
Signs		Location and type.
Interior		
Walls		Some are load-bearing in old buildings.
Partitions		Freestanding or permanent.
Blocking within partitions		For hangrail, shelves, etc.
Partition materials		Gypsum, or other.
Curtain walls		Suspended or projecting valances.
Doors, hardware		Location, type use, color.
Ceilings		Acoustical or smooth, painted or not.
Special ceiling detail		Drops, rises.
Floor finish		Material, thickness.
Depressions in floors		Change in materials.
Base	Cove Wood Carpet Marble or other natural stone	Vinyl. To match floors. With cap cove or straight. How fastened to wall.

Table 10-4 Design and Construction Checklist for New and Remodeled Stores (Continued)

Area or Service		Considerations
Stairs	Customer	Ease and comfort of movement from place to place.
	Service	Building code compliance; back-of-house uses.
Fixtures	Perimeter	Wall-type or departmental dividers.
	Freestanding	Loose, portable type.
	Specialty	Unusual display units.
Backroom storage	Furniture	Seating, tables.
	Shelving	Wallhung, individual, floor-mounted.
	Hanging	How supported.
	Equipment	Marking, tagging tables, repair bench.
Lunchroom	Employees' use	
Toilet rooms	Flooring and base	Type of material.
	Walls	Paint, wallcover, ceramic tile.
Toilet partitions	Fixtures	Metal or plastic laminate.
and baffles	Accessories	Toilet, lavatories, urinals.
	Drains	Towel, waste, soap dispensers.
		For overflows.

Painting and Decorating

Clearly define scope for walls, ceilings, curtain walls, fitting areas	Specify flat, semigloss, or gloss paint or wallcovering.
Preparation of surface	Spackling, sanding, sealing.
Display window interiors	Material selection.
Nonselling areas	Specify where required.
Toilet rooms	Type of finish.
Trim and doors, frames, exposed metal	Clearly specify for paint or wallcovering.

Receiving and Shipping

Loading platform	Doors, levelers.
Bumper	Truck bumpers.
Climate-control enclosure	HVAC retained at truck loading dock.
Mesh enclosure	For see-through storage.
Conveyors	Materials-handling equipment.
Forklifts	Provide for storage and maintenance space.
Slick rails	Pipe rail overhead to move hanging merchandise.
Overhead automatic carriers	Dry cleaning-style movers.

| Table 10-4 | Design and Construction Checklist for New and Remodeled Stores (Continued) |

Area or Service		Considerations
Vertical Conveyances		
Elevators	Structure	Structural design of openings and support.
	Hoistway	Masonry or gypsum walls.
	Mechanical room and equipment	Provide adequate space.
	Penthouse	Sometimes not required.
	Glass enclosure screen	For glass-enclosed cabs or freestanding elevators.
	Type	Hydraulic or electric.
	Cab design	Material finishes and ceiling.
	Doors and jambs	Painted or nonferrous metals, such as stainless steel.
	Controls and signals	Up and down; pushbutton.
	Escalators	Allocate proper space and size in preplanning.
	Dumbwaiters	Electric or manual.

Electrical System		
Service		Adequate incoming electric power.
Meters		In malls, landlord submeters the smaller stores.
Panel boards		Provide adequate space and location for proper function.
Transformers		In small malls, stores are sometimes required to have these.
Time clocks		Usually for HVAC system and sign and window light.
HVAC wiring		Power to supply equipment.
Outlets, receptacles	Location	Wall or floor.
	Type	Provide for task and portable types for future use.
	Equipment	Flush wall and floor use; underfloor conduit.
	Signage	Special-use motors and display equipment.
		Required for illuminated signs.
Cash registers		Proper wiring for complex registers.
Telephone		Panel board receptacle; check for other communication uses.
Intercom		Very important for large store.
Sound system		Includes piped-in music. Ceiling or wall speakers connected to microphone, radio, recording equipment.
Equipment requiring electricity		Provide spares in panel boards or future equipment conduit.
Contactors		Various types - one switch can turn off lighting or equipment.
Bells, chimes		Doorbells, annunciators, and call systems.
Lighting fixtures		All fixtures; general, ceiling spot, display type, etc.
Emergency lighting		Provide for illumination of exit pathways.
Fire alarm system		Detection of fire.
Smoke detection equipment		Can prevent loss of life by smoke.
Computers		Many are being used, from personal size on up.
Tailor shop		Sewing machines and pressers.
Energy-saving devices		Timer switches and body-actuated devices.

Table 10-4	Design and Construction Checklist for New and Remodeled Stores (Continued)

Area or Service	Considerations
Heating, Ventilating and Air-Conditioning	
Air-conditioning equipment and system	Type of air-cooled or water equipment and equipment locations.
Heating system	Heat from lights can be recovered and reused.
Ducts and insulation	Carefully specify size and location, especially vertical and horizontal runs.
Diffusers and grilles	Coordinate reflected ceiling plans.
Exhaust systems — Display window / Tailor shop / Restaurant / Beauty shop	Heat from lights builds up in enclosed windows. Pressing equipment needs ventilation. If food is prepared, exhaust is required. Often vented.
Control systems	Investigate types of controls applicable to a store's needs.
Equipment wiring	Underfloor conduit may be needed to handle remote equipment.
Energy-saving devices	Consider long-life lamps and lighting fixtures as well as devices.
Plumbing	
Gas and water meters	Location of utilities.
Water supply	Availability and location of source.
Piping locations	Check on concealed locations and insulation.
Waste and sewage system	Learn location and size of pipes.
Water treatment system	Determine the capability of the community's system.
Fixtures	Check on water-saving units.
Maintenance room	Place drains, controls, and valves in this area.
Water heater	Large tank or local instantaneous heater at sinks.
Water softening	May be required for municipal water or well water.
Drinking fountains	Public and employee use.
Store equipment	Determine if plumbing hookup is required.
Toilet rooms	Determine number of rooms needed and fixtures for men and women; provide for handicapped.
Tailor shop	Often requires steam piping.
Restaurant	For food-service equipment specifications, coordinate with consultant.
Employee cafeteria	Food and water services, vending machines.
Floor drains	Some wet areas, such as flower shop.
Roof drains	Some buildings have large piping which affects floor layout.
Storm water drainage	For parking and entrance areas.

Table 10-4 **Design and Construction Checklist for New and Remodeled Stores (Continued)**

Area or Service	Considerations
Hose bibbs	For exterior purposes, such as grounds keeping; interior sanitation; and flower and food shops.

Sprinkler System

System, wet or dry	Depends on geographic location.
Fire alarm tie-in	Alarm system design allows for this.
Fire extinguisher	Provide sufficient locations for fire code.
Hose cabinets	Sometimes are built into the wall.
Siamese connection, exterior	Permits water hoses to pump water into building.

Security Systems

Burglar alarm, exterior	Perimeter protection at roof openings, doors, windows.
TV cameras	Building and patron surveillance.
Electronic customer surveillance	Use of detection equipment, usually at entrance.
Glass area	Large glass areas have sensors attached.
Sprinkler alarm	Activated when sprinkler discharges water.
Safe or vault	Fireproof for safekeeping of money.
Door buzzers and remote releases	Control doors and access to protected areas.

Other Items

Furniture	Consider location and type required such as shoe store seating.
Parking lot	Location, maintenance, and size.
Incinerators	Check environmental codes.
Dumpsters	Trash containers, exterior.
Balers	Paper and cardboard can be baled to save space.
Rubbish room	Some large stores and malls require one.
Landscape	Visually enhances interior and exterior spaces.
Maintenance areas	Some stores need a workshop or repair area.
Cutting and patching for remodeling	Walls, ceilings, and floors that have had holes cut in them for mechanical and structural purposes should be detailed to avoid raw look.
Guarantees and warranties	Owner should collect and file contractors' and machinery contracts.

Shopping Centers and Malls

11

Tenant's Criteria: The rules and regulations for designing stores in a shopping center or mall are contained in a printed guide prepared by the landlord called the "tenant's criteria" or the "tenant's handbook." It is the single most important document to guide the lessee, architect, store designer, and contractor through to the completion of the retail facility.

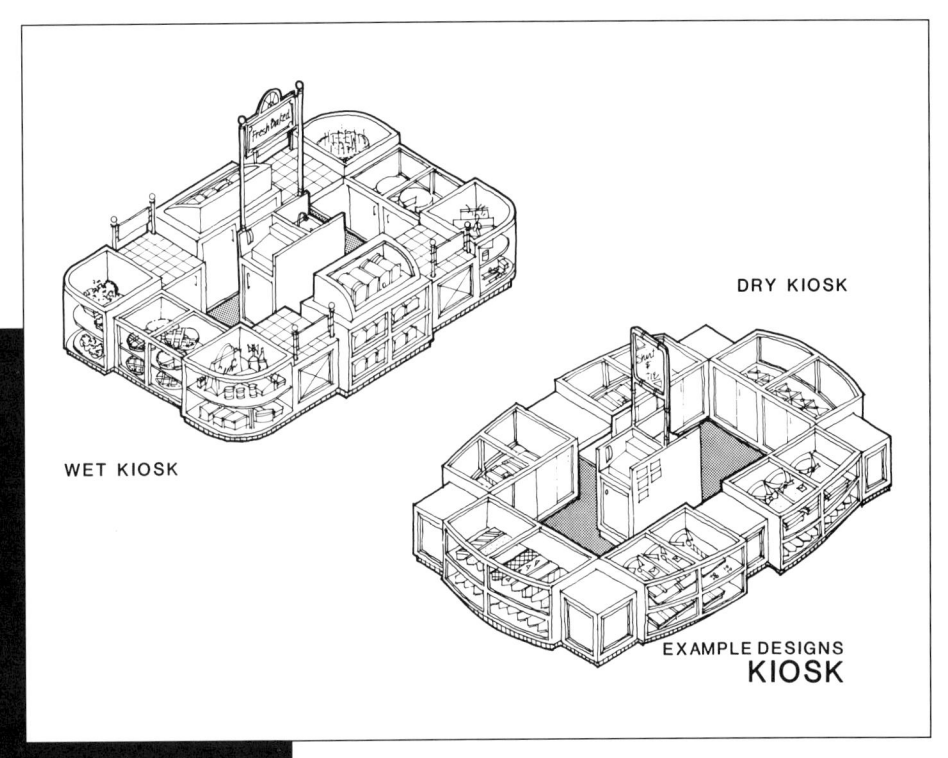

A sample page from the tenant's criteria prepared for The Savannah Mall, Savannah, Ga., developed by David Hocker and Associates, Inc., and R. F. Coffin Enterprises, Inc. Architectural design of the center: Crawford McWilliams Hatcher Architects, Inc., Birmingham, Ala.; Randall Naccari, project architect.

11 Shopping Centers and Malls

1
Replacing visual monotony

From their relatively humble and spontaneous beginnings as the open-air bazaars and marketplaces of past centuries, shopping centers and malls have become both big business and a powerful social force. In just over 60 years–the first suburban centers in the U.S. came on the scene in the late 1920s–shopping centers have followed the population shifts from the city to the suburbs, the exurbs, and back to the city again.

The industry's trade organization, the International Council of Shopping Centers (ICSC), based in New York City, has 26,000 members in 44 countries. Its mission includes "establishing the individual shopping center as a major institution in the community."

Shopping centers come in many sizes and shapes, and fill different market niches: covered malls, open malls, vertical malls, regional malls, urban malls, strip centers, convenience centers, discount malls, factory outlet malls, off-price malls, megamalls, and festival malls. The planning and design of shopping centers is its own sub-discipline, and the reader is encouraged to become familiar with the available literature on the topic, including periodicals.

1
The renovation of Holly Hill Mall, Burlington, N. C., utilizes intermediate archways and a center court structure to reduce the visual monotony of the mall's long corridors. Renovation of the project included 70,000 square feet of interior mall space, plus a 40,000-square-foot J. C. Penney anchor. Developer is JMB Urban Development, Chicago.

Design: Dalton Moran Shook Inc., Charlotte, N.C.; Charles Terry Shook, AIA, principal in charge.

Shopping Center Rental Profile

Table 11-1   **Average Shopping Center Rents**

Specialty Centers and Strip Centers
Annual $ Per Square Foot
(Through October, 1989)

	Specialty Centers	Strip Centers
Atlanta, GA	$ 18.00	$ 12.50
Austin, TX	9.50	9.00
Broward Co., FL	13.50	10.00
Chicago, IL	17.50	11.00
Cleveland, OH	19.00	12.00
Denver, CO	17.00	6.00
Honolulu, HI	87.00	26.50
Houston, TX	12.00	7.50
Los Angeles North, CA	34.50	22.50
Miami, FL	27.50	12.00
Phoenix, AZ	17.00	10.00
Portland, OR	12.00	9.50
San Diego, CA	24.00	18.00
San Francisco, CA	27.00	24.00
Seattle, WA	15.00	13.00
Tucson, AZ	16.00	8.50
Washington, DC	27.00	19.00
West Los Angeles, CA	27.00	31.50

Source: *ICSC Research Quarterly*, April, 1990, pp. 4, 5
©1990 International Council of Shopping Centers, New York City

This chapter presents a representative survey of current shopping center types. The explosion of new suburban shopping centers constructed in the 1960s and 1970s has given way to remodeling and enlarging of existing centers, and the opening of specialty centers and malls.

While the total of Gross Building Area (GBA) increased through the second quarter of 1989 over the previous year by more than 11 percent, the actual number of projects declined by 1.7 percent, according to the ICSC. Developers, required to obtain approvals and permits to satisfy a lengthy list of environmental and construction items, are making the most of each building opportunity.

11 Shopping Centers and Malls

Table 11-2   Most Frequent Anchors in Strip Centers and Open Malls - 1988

By Size Range: Percent of Centers

Centers 50,000–99,000 sq. ft.	Supermarkets	53%	Supermarkets include: Winn Dixie, Food Lion, Publix. Drugstores include: Revco, Walgreen, Phar-Mor, Pay Less. Discount department stores include: Wal-Mart, K mart, Ames, Bradlees, Target.
	Drugstores	37	
	Eating and drinking places	20	
Centers 100,000–199,000 sq. ft.	Supermarkets	62%	
	Drugstores	37	
	Discount department stores	32	
	Apparel stores	16	
	Home improvement stores	11	
Centers 200,000-399,000 sq. ft.	Supermarkets	53%	
	Discount department stores	45	
	Apparel stores	19	
	Home improvement stores	17	
Centers over 400,000 sq. ft.	Discount department stores	50%	
	Apparel stores	50	
	Supermarkets	33	
	Wholesale clubs	33	

Source: *ICSC Research Quarterly*, October 1989, p. 1.
©1989 International Council of Shopping Centers, New York City

From Milan to Minnesota

Milan's Galleria Vittorio Emanuel II, built between 1865 and 1867, is still one of the world's best examples of a commercial space that is grand, urban, and social. Its monumental entrance dominates the north side of the city's hub, the Piazza del Duomo. Inside, the Galleria is an impressive and much-copied example of a mixed-use structure; the four-story-high arcade of shops, cafes, and offices is covered by a glass barrel vault and a beautiful 160-foot-high glass cupola.

In the U.S. at this time, stylish shopping was epitomized by what was known as Ladies Mile in New York City. Along this stretch of Sixth Avenue from Fourteenth Street to Twenty–third Street were the most elegant purveyors of merchandise to the booming city's wealthiest shoppers. Merchants such as Arnold Constable, B. Altman, Lord & Taylor and others occupied veritable palaces of retailing. Ornate stone structures were built in the best Beaux-Arts and Palladian designs that architects could create.

In the mid-1890s, department store tycoons John Wanamaker and Marshall Field adapted the galleria concept and erected massive mercantile establishments built around great marble central courts. These stores became

2
Grand, urban, and social

Milan's Galleria Vittorio Emanuele II, constructed between 1865 and 1867, is a still-elegant forerunner of many of today's enclosed malls. The glass barrel-vault roof lets natural light into the interior, a four-story-high simulation of a typical Milanese streetscape.

11 Shopping Centers and Malls

3
Suburban Square, a 60-year-old shopping center

3

First opened in the late 1920s, Suburban Square in Ardmore, Pa., outside of Philadelphia on the upper-income Main Line, has maintained its image and target customer while expanding its retail base over the years. Its first anchor store, a Strawbridge & Clothier branch, is still an important tenant. Suburban Square remains an open center, with fountains, mature trees, and well-tended landscaping creating a distinctive ambience.

dominant retail forces in their cities for decades. Now, the shifting demographics of downtown Philadelphia has led to the downsizing of Wanamakers. Marshall Fields, Chicago, has invested $100 million to renovate its two million-square-foot flagship State Street store.

In the late 1920s, the first two shopping centers to bring central business district names to the suburbs were opened: Country Club Plaza in Kansas City, and Suburban Square Shopping Center in Ardmore on Philadelphia's exclusive Main Line. Strawbridge & Clothier was the first department store to open a branch store in 1930, and was Suburban Square's original anchor. Now a 73-store center, its mood of quiet tradition, residential scale, and handsome landscaping have contributed to this center's continued success.

144

4, 5 & 6
As big as 48 city blocks

The enclosed mall shopping center genre took form in the early 1950s with Northland in the Detroit area. It was followed by Southland, and Cherry Hill Center to serve southern New Jersey. These centers were characterized by a "dumbbell" configuration: two anchor stores at each end connected by a long corridor lined with shops.

Centers with skylight roofs and second and third levels began to appear in the early 1970s; Woodfield Mall, near Chicago, is an early example. Mall interiors began to replicate a streetscape, and owners approved pop-out store fronts rather than the strict flush front specifications they had previously insisted upon.

The mid- and late 1970s was the era of the "festival malls," the high profile urban centers developed by The Rouse Company which often revitalized whole downtown districts by adaptive reuse of quality existing structures, augmented by new construction. Boston's Faneuil Hall, Harborplace in Baltimore, and South Street Seaport in New York City were initial successes, followed by the mixed-use St. Louis Union Station. The average number of annual visitors to these centers is from 10 to 18 million.

High-style urban centers arrived in the late 1970s. Water Tower Place in Chicago epitomized a contemporary super-sleek vertical mall. Georgetown Park in Washington, D.C. is classical and romantic, evokatively Victorian.

Shopping and entertainment combine on an unprecedented scale at the West Edmonton Mall, Edmonton Alberta, Canada. "Mega" in every sense of the word, the two-story West Edmonton Mall is the equivalent of 115 football fields. It offers parking for 20,000 cars, has 11 anchor stores, 800 shops and services, a car dealership, a National Hockey League-size skating rink, an indoor 560,000-square-foot Fantasyland, and several submarines which cruise the 400-foot-long lake of the Deep Sea Adventure.

Not to be outdone by their neighbors to the north, a joint venture of Melvin Simon & Associates of Indianapolis and Triple Five Corporation Ltd., Edmonton,

4

West Edmonton Mall, Edmonton, Alberta, Canada, is actually a 5.2 million-square-foot super-megamall, with over 800 shops and services, 11 anchor stores, a car dealership, and hundreds of amusements. Main attractions are the World Waterpark, Dolphin Lagoon, Fantasyland Amusement Park, Ice Palace, the Santa Maria ship, Pebble Beach Miniature Golf Course, and Sea Life Caverns. West Edmonton Mall opened in in three phases from 1981 to 1985. Total cost was $1.1 billion.

Design: Maurice Sunderland Architects, Inc., Toronto; Brian Dennis, principal in charge.

11 **Shopping Centers and Malls**

5

6

146

Alberta is developing the mammoth Mall of America in Bloomington, Minnesota, in the Twin Cities area. The first phase of the 4.2 million square foot undertaking is scheduled to open in the fall of 1992. It will have four major department stores, four junior department stores, more than 400 specialty stores, plus restaurants, nightclubs, 18 theaters, and a walk-thru aquarium. Another draw is a 300,000 sq. ft. Knott's Camp Snoopy.

Franklin Mills, an off-price discount megamall that now occupies the former Liberty Bell Racetrack in northeast Philadelphia, boasts a sprawling entertainment center, driving and putting ranges, and bowling alleys.

The Tenant's Bible
Retail stores that lease space in shopping centers and malls will be guided by a document known as the "tenant's criteria" or the "tenant's handbook." It is prepared by the center's management to inform and assist the tenant, architect, store designer, and contractor with the owner's criteria for the store's construction.

The handbook contains information for the architect and the designer, and specifies the landlord's obligations, the tenant's construction obligations, and the contractor's requirements. It covers the submittals of designs to the landlord, including:

- construction drawings
- floor plans
- sections
- store front design
- materials and color selection
- sign and graphics program
- type of windows and door closures
- reflected ceiling plan
- plumbing drawings
- mechanical drawings for HVAC
- electrical plans
- sprinkler system drawings

The landlord will review and approve these drawings before or during the construction bidding period. Plans, specifications, and construction for a tenant's demised space will conform to all codes and criteria that are applicable to the site location.

In addition to the basic codes–building, electrical, plumbing, and mechanical–requirements to satisfy fire safety and handicapped codes must be met. For centers with food courts, the local health department codes should be consulted prior to design.

The design professional should ascertain from the client that the space is properly insured in compliance to the standards established by the landlord.

HVAC
The landlord will often provide full information on the technical aspects of the center's system. The store designer retained by the lessee retailer will then follow the basic rules established for the engineering design requirements. (See Chapter 9, Systems.)

Some owners will provide the tenant with air conditioning, or provide just chilled or hot water. The tenant is then responsible for air-handling equipment, duct work, and control wiring.

The landlord can charge the tenant an amount based on a scale that is shown in the lease. If the landlord is realizing a profit on this charge, the tenant should understand this at the outset.

Tenants must have their air conditioning and air handling equipment carefully calculated and documented. "Borrowing" any of the air conditioning in public walkways and corridors is prohibited by center management.

Plumbing
Tenants' access to piping, valves, and sanitary facilities must be detailed for the landlord's review. Depending on the size of the store, tenants may be required to provide their own toilet facilities. Toilets for the handicapped are now almost universally required. Designers should consult the national handicapped code, American National Standards Institute.

11 Shopping Centers and Malls

Typical pages from Tenant Manual produced for The Savannah Mall, Savannah, Ga.

Developer: David Hocker & Associates, Inc., Owensboro, Ky., and R. F. Coffin Enterprises, Inc., Cleveland, Ohio.

Design: Crawford McWilliams Hatcher Architects, Inc., Birmingham, Ala., Randall Naccari, project architect.

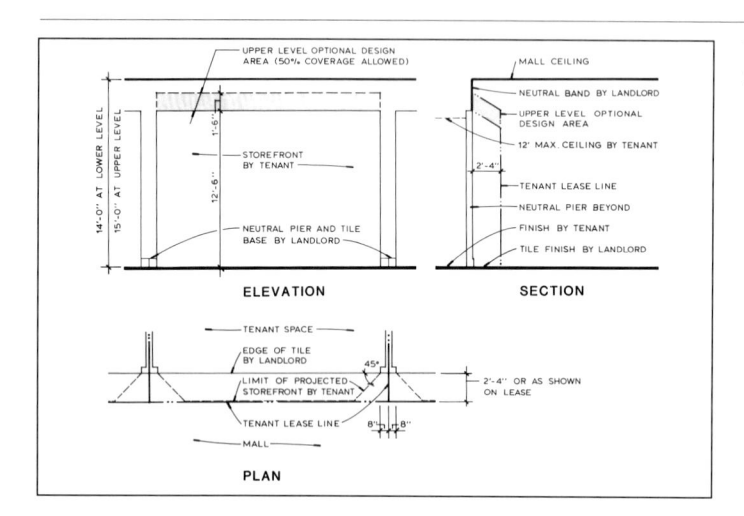

Tenant Storefront Details
2'-4" Projection

Tenant Storefronts
Example Designs

Tenant Storefronts
Example Designs

148

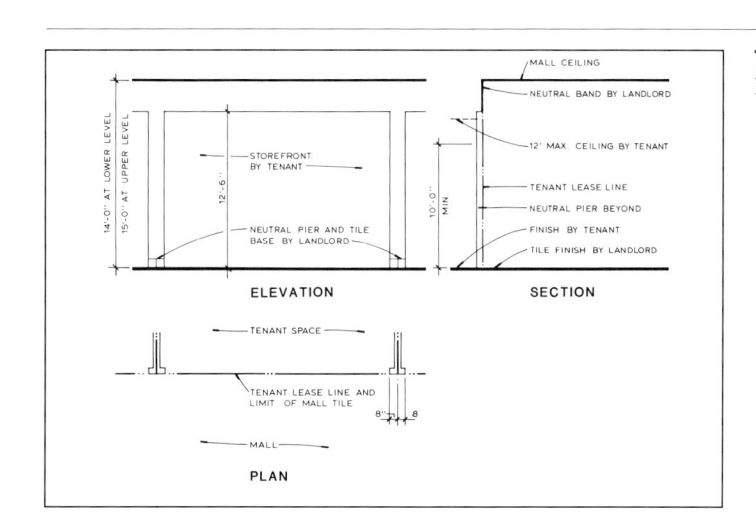

Tenant Storefront Details
Non-projected fronts

Tenant Storefronts
Example Designs

Tenant Storefronts
Example Designs

149

Shopping Centers and Malls

Sprinklers are another required element in the planning for the store's plumbing system. Flush, concealed heads that do not detract from the design of the store's ceiling are now available.

The cost of sprinklers is often offset by savings in fire insurance. Fire extinguishing hoses are hooked up to the standard pipe system. Fire extinguishers are required for hand manual operation throughout the store and number and locations are specified by local building or fire officials.

Food Courts

Food courts have become a popular attraction for enclosed malls. They are a natural extension of the shopping center-as-social-node philosophy, and are successful profit areas for landlords.

If you have been retained to design the food court, assemble all the landlord's specifications as well as those of the local health department before the design process begins. Specifying acceptable exhaust fans, hoods, power supply, and scrubable materials in both the food preparation and the dining areas are the designer's responsibility.

Storefronts

Storefront design is a major landlord concern. Approval is not an overnight procedure; it could take several weeks or even months, depending on the hierarchical structure of the landlord's organization.

Landlords have relaxed their previous strict insistance on flat store facades. The tenant's criteria guidebook will often illustrate the types of pop-out, greenhouse, or projecting storefronts that are permissible for the center.

The designer should also check into requirements for:

▶ a 6" or 12" tile base to protect glass storefronts against damage by cleaning machines

▶ the extension of public walkway flooring material into the store's entryway

▶ control by the landlord of materials used three to six feet inside the store

Sign Bands

Along with storefronts, sign bands receive much attention from the landlord, as described in the tenant's criteria book. Local building codes must also be considered; if the project is an historic restoration, the exterior sign design may also be scrutinized by a local review committee.

Most centers ban moving or rotating signs; signs made of paper or cardboard; and signs which emit noise.

The materials palette for non-illuminated mall signs includes:

▶ etched glass

▶ silkscreened canvas

▶ wrought iron

▶ chrome, brass, or copper

▶ carved wood

▶ stained glass

▶ ceramic tile

▶ plastic laminate

▶ marble, granite, or slate

Electrical and Signing

A 220-volt (or higher) transformer or generator is provided by the landlord. The tenant provides a space on a back room wall for equipment such as meter sockets and panels required by local codes.

The designer should confirm that service is being brought to the tenant's demised premises.

The consulting electrical engineer can advise the designer on applicable energy codes. These codes specify the allowable watts/square foot the store can use for lighting, and the amount of energy that equipment can consume. Energy codes in California, New York, and Massachusetts permit different maximums varying from 2 1/2 watts to 4 watts per square foot for lighting purposes with other provisions for task or display lighting.

Study the lease exhibit for fixtures that are banned, and other lighting limitations:

▶ exposed fixtures, such as 2'x 4' fluorescent fixtures

▶ glare from the store onto the mall

▶ hours of operation for illuminated signs

7
Bi-level shopping center to revive town center in Hastings, U. K.

7

Priory Meadow, a new 420,000-square-foot shopping center, will provide the community of Hastings, located in England's South East region, with a revitalized commercial center across from its gothic Town Hall. A traditional Clock Tower will face the new Town Square. The articulated bays of the Queens Parade facade shown here establish a rhythm carried around the elevations. Rusticated limestone pilasters frame the recessed stucco panels around display windows.

*Design:
Clark Harris Tribble Li (New York) /Covell Matthews Wheatley (London); Richard Tao, principal in charge, and Gregory Cranford, AIA, project designer.*

11 Shopping Centers and Malls

8
Rink is focal point of family-oriented mall

8

A new olympic-size ice skating rink and an extensive food court strengthened the position of Northcross Mall as the premier family entertainment mall in Austin, Tex. The renovation of the 60-shop, 319,000-square-foot mall, originally opened in 1975, was a total upgrade, including lighting, signs, landscaping, flooring, color palette, and exterior facade. White neon column capitals provide a festive touch. Neon was also used to identify food concessions, and tops the gazebo shop (right).

Design: Hambrecht Terrell International, New York, Daniel J. Barteluce, AIA, principal in charge.

9
80-foot-high mast supports tensile fabric roof

10
Plan of Park City Center showing central court as its hub

Construction Considerations

Penetration through the center's roof is controlled by the landlord. Openings for a tenant's air conditioning and air handling equipment may have to be performed by the landlord's roofing contractor because of roof warranty clauses.

Before work on the project commences, meet with the general contractor and review these points:

- contractor's procedures to perform work in accordance with the standards established by the building supervisor

- temporary power supply

- demolition procedures for a remodeling job

- provisions for cleanup and trash removal

- access to the site for delivery of materials

- tool and materials storage

- procedure for inspection of the finished store and acceptance by the landlord

9

10

Renovation of the 20,000-square-foot court at Park City Center, Lancaster, Pa. produced a nontraditional roof design, a tensile fabric roof supported by a 80-foot-high mast. The octagonal space, 160 feet across, is filled with natural light during the day, adding to the park-like setting. At night, the skylight atop the mast becomes an attracting beacon for the regional mall. The asymmetrical placement of the mast assists pedestrian orientation within the space.

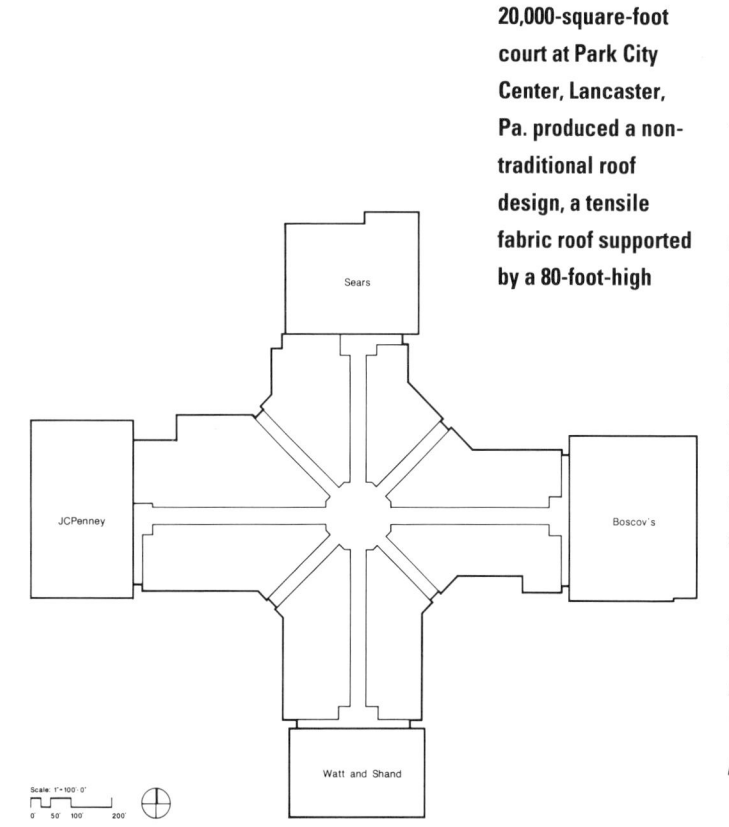

Design: Cope Linder Associates, Philadelphia; Steven W. Henkelman, AIA, principal in charge.

153

11 Shopping Centers and Malls

11 & 12
Predesigned structural steel provides for future needs

To achieve optimum flexibility at the Atrium at Chestnut Hill (Mass.), and to work within a floor-to-floor height of 13'6", and ceiling height of 10', the structural steel for the 800,000-square-foot, $60 million center was predesigned with unreinforced penetrations in many beams to allow for the passage of ducts and pipes for future tenants.

Design: Jung/Brannen Associates, Inc., Architects, Boston; Yu Sing Jung, FAIA, principal in charge; Weidlinger Associates, Consulting Engineers, Cambridge, Mass; Minhaj Kirmani, PE, principal in charge.

11

12

Trends in Merchandising Facilities

12

- **Specialty strip centers**
- **Retail in mixed-use developments**
- **Government-sponsored projects**

- **Megamalls**
- **Major store renovations and expansion**
- **Hypermarkets**
- **Food courts**
- **Manufacturer's chain units within department stores**

- **Specialty chains**
- **Minimalist design**
- **Airport shops**
- **Museum shops**
- **Food store design**

1

An all-Gap stores specialty strip center, Wisconsin Avenue, Chevy Chase, Maryland.

Design: Charles E. Broudy & Associates

12 Trends in Merchandising Facilities

2
100 new stores for downtwon Phoenix

2

Retail in mixed-use developments

The first phase of Arizona Center in downtown Phoenix, opened late fall, 1990, contains The Shops at Arizona Center, a 100-store specialty retail center. The other two major components in this phase are a 322,000- sq.-ft. office building, and The Gardens at Arizona Center, a three-acre, multi-level landscaped urban plaza. The $515 million, 18.5-acre project will cover eight city blocks when completed and will include 1.9 million square feet of office space, a 600-room hotel, parking for 5,400 vehicles, a total of 450,000 square feet of retail store space, and the plaza. Rouse-Phoenix Development Corp., a subsidiary of The Rouse Company, Columbia, Maryland, is the developer.

156

3
Retail core at Chevy Chase Pavilion

3

Retail in mixed-use developments

Washington D.C.'s Chevy Chase Pavilion, located at the intersection of Western Avenue, Wisconsin Avenue, and Military Road, has a 170,000-square-foot glass-topped three-level central atrium court devoted to retail. Office space occupies 230,000 square feet, and a 190-room, 160,000-square-foot Embassy Suites Hotel completes the project, developed by The Donohoe Companies.

*Design:
Clark Tribble Harris & Li Architects, Washington, D.C.; Christopher M. Knight, AIA, principal in charge.*

12 Trends in Merchandising Facilities

4
Burnham's Beaux-Arts masterpiece is brought back to life

4

Government-sponsored projects

Daniel H. Burnham's glorious Union Station in Washington, D.C. is a tribute to railroading's golden era. Modeled after Rome's Diocletian Baths and the Arch of Constantine and formally opened in 1907, its white marble facade has grand ionic columns and allegorical sculpture. When rail traffic dropped in the 1960s and 1970s, Union Station was threatened with demolition.

In 1981, Congress passed the Union Station Redevelopment Act, and two years later the Union Station Redevelopment Corporation was created to assist the Secretary of Transportation in revitalizing the crumbling monumental structure.

A $160 million public/private partnership has successfully brought Union Station back to life as a transportation hub, shopping center, and entertainment complex. Amtrak funding of approximately $70 million restored the building and train concourse; the District of Columbia contributed $40 million for a five-level, 1,300-car garage; and $50 million was invested in improvements for retail use by Union Station Venture, a consortium made up of La Salle Partners, Chicago, Williams Jackson Ewing, Baltimore, and Benjamin Thompson & Associates, Cambridge, Mass.

The shopping complex includes 135 stores. In the East Hall, the light fixtures, marble floors, and scagliola columns and pillars were restored to Burnham's original design. The internally-lit, brass-trimmed mahogany display cases are movable, and can be reconfigured to suit each tenant. They can also be removed when the hall is used for public events.

*Design:
Public and retail spaces: Benjamin Thompson & Associates, Inc., Cambridge, Mass.; Benjamin Thompson and Philip Loheed, principals in charge. Station restoration: Harry Weese & Associates, Washington, D.C.; Stanley N. Allan, principal in charge; Karl J. Landesz, project manager.*

158

5
*4.2 million square feet
of enclosed retail space*

5

Megamalls

More than one-half of the Mall of America's 4.2 million square feet is for retail stores, including four major anchors: Macy's (275,000 sq. ft.), Nordstrom's (250,000 sq. ft.), Bloomingdale's (240,000 sq. ft.), and Sears (190,000 sq. ft.). Constructed on a 78-acre site formerly occuped by Met Stadium in Bloomington, Minn., in the metropolitan Minneapolis-St. Paul area, the $600 million project includes a $70 million, 300,000-square-foot enclosed family entertainment area, Knott's Camp Snoopy. Parking for 12,750 cars will occupy seven levels in two parking decks and four surface lots. Mall of America is a joint venture partnership of affiliates of Melvin Simon & Associates, Inc., Indianapolis, and Triple Five Corp., Ltd., Edmonton, Canada.

*Design:
The Jerde Partnership, Inc., Los Angeles; John Jerde, principal in charge.*

159

12 Trends in Merchandising Facilities

6 & 7
Redefining Neiman-Marcus

Major store renovations and expansion

Neiman-Marcus's chain-wide program of full renovations for existing stores and expansion into new markets will polish its image for unique and au courant merchandise carried in elegant store surroundings. Major remodeling projects include Atlanta (see page 125), Houston, Minneapolis, and Phoenix. The new 90,000 square-foot facility illustrated here opened in the fall of 1990 in the Cherry Creek Mall, Denver. A prime merchandising objective is more

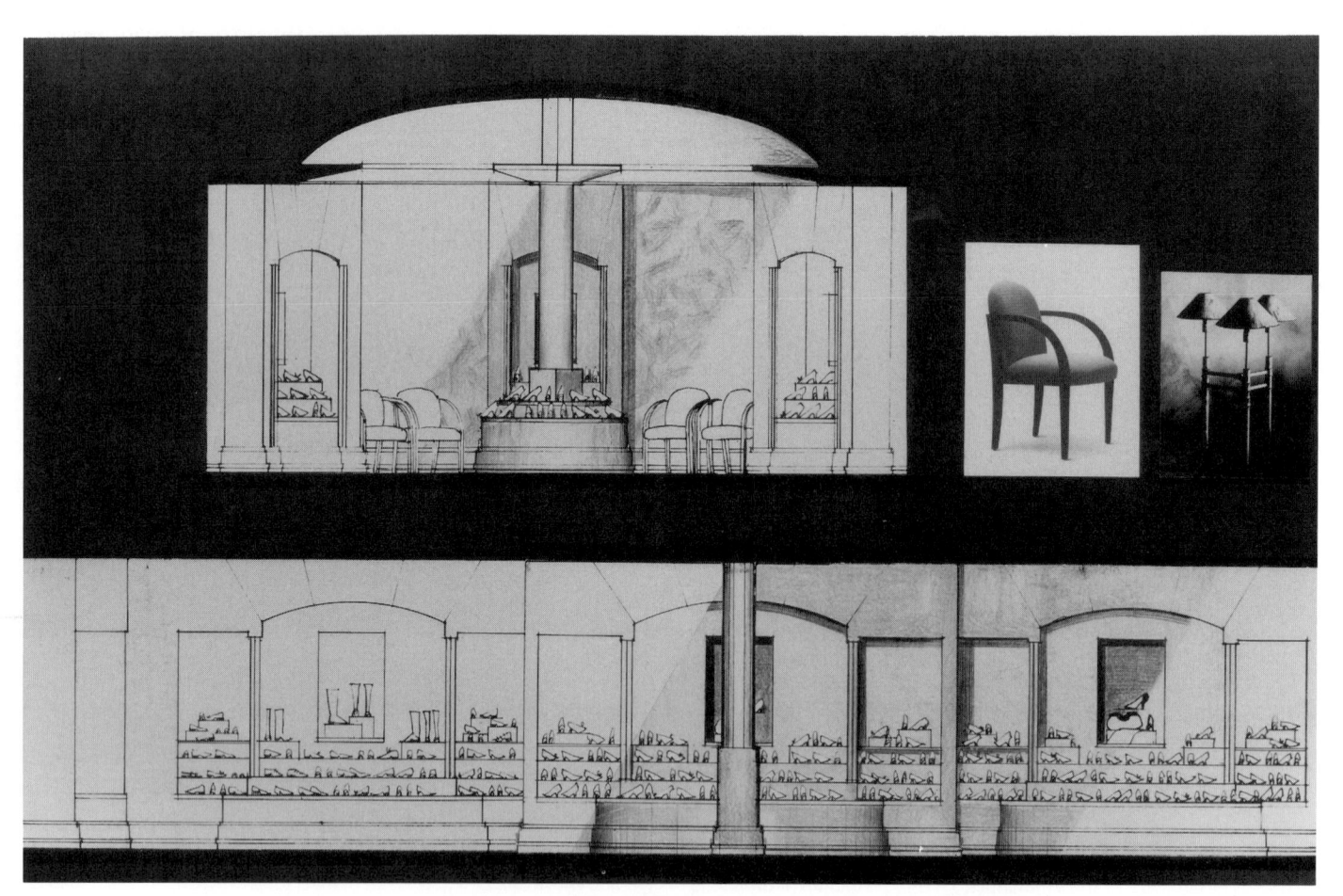

6

160

flexibility in the store's design to accommodate merchandise selections that expand and contract seasonally on the sales floor without relocating walls. This technique will keep the store looking fresh and exciting, targeted to the Neiman-Marcus fashion-oriented, repeat customer.

Design: Robert Young Associates, Inc., Dallas, Tex; Thomas Herndon, ISP, principal in charge.

12 Trends in Merchandising Facilities

8 *Defining retail space in acres*

8

Hypermarkets

Hypermarkets, a dominant factor in French retailing for almost two decades, came onto the U.S. scene in the late 1980s. Store size is measured in acres: Carrefours, located in Philadelphia, is the largest U.S. hypermarket at 330,000 square feet, equivalent to 7.5 acres. It carries 64,000 different products, from radishes to refrigerators. Angled neon tubes suspended from a metal space frame grid ceiling help shoppers identify major service areas at a distance. Other hypermarket operators are Bigg's, American Fare, and Hypermart, U.S.A.

9
Total mall renovation adds an airy, open dining space

Food courts

Green Acres Mall, Valley Stream, New York, originally opened in 1956, underwent a total renovation of 400,000 square feet and a two-level expansion that added 300,000 square feet of selling space, and a food court located beneath a skylight roof. Two design themes used throughout the mall—outlining of multi-level ceilings with Tivoli-type lights, and reflective surfaces—are continued here. Interior landscaping and colorful ceiling-hung banners add to the ambience.

Design: GSGSB, New York; Michael G. Bobick, AIA, partner in charge.

9

● ● ● ● ● ● ● ● ● ●
⑫ Trends in Merchandising Facilities

10 & 11
Image and advertising at DKNY boutiques

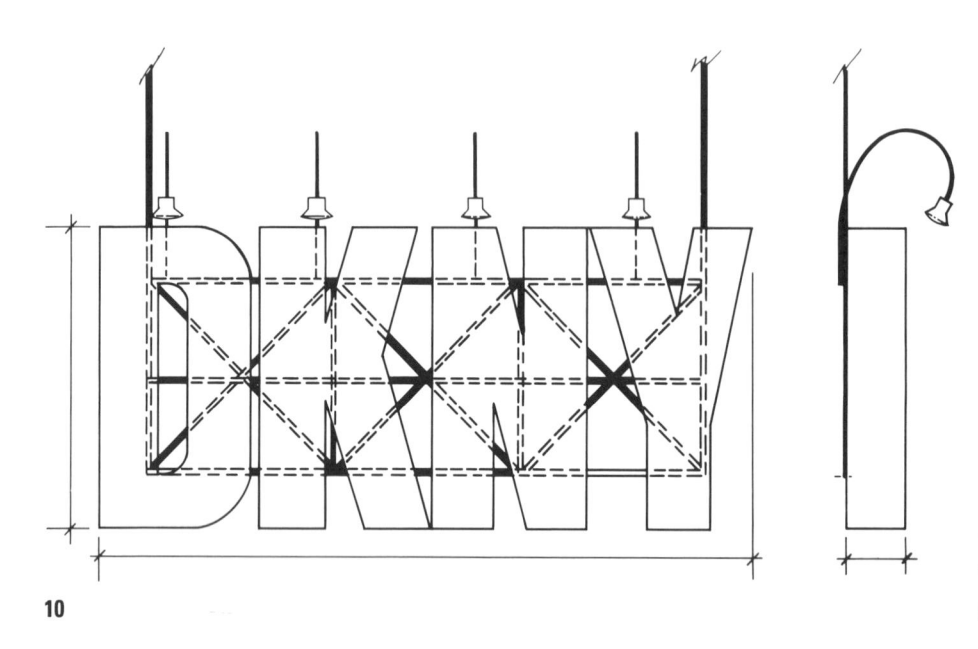

10

Manufacturer's chain units within department stores

DKNY is one of the biggest successes on Seventh Avenue. The casual clothing line is generally half the price of items in the regular Donna Karen collection. In its first two years, DKNY grossed close to $100 million and its boutiques were operating in approximately 400 stores. Design for the shops-within-a-store was created by the firm's advertising agency which presents a microcosm of New York images as a unifying theme. According to the designer, Peter Arnell, "The image of the company houses itself in the retail space so that there is no break in the communication between the advertising the customer sees and the boutique where she shops."

Design: Arnell/Bickford Associates, New York; Peter Arnell, partner in charge.

11

12
Remodeled Duty Free Shoppers draws two million shoppers/yr.

12

Specialty chains

Downtown Waikiki's Duty Free Shoppers renovated 100,000-square-foot outlet is the chain's largest and tallies the highest $/sq. ft. The three-level store has a multi-layered granite facade with an elaborate entranceway. An indoor/outdoor food court is located on the roof. The company estimates an annual two million visitors to the store which is three times larger than the original facility.

Design: Hambrecht Terrell International, New York; Daniel J. Barteluce, AIA, principal in charge.

12 Trends in Merchandising Facilities

13
Hong Kong stores have playground features

Minimalist design

While Hong Kong's two Kinderkind shops are whimisical interpretations of the current minimalist school of applied design, they offer their young customers places to climb and turn somersaults while parents concentrate on items to be tried on. The merchandising theory behind this type of visually spare store design is to not overburden the customer with too many choices.

Typically, one example of the simple and sporty clothing styles carried is displayed. A low-placed television set is built into the deep blue divider wall.

*Design:
Tsao & McKown Architects, New York;
Calvin Tsao, and Zack McKown, AIA, principals in charge.*

13

14
Shopping en route

Airport shops

Bloomie's Express occupies an 1,800-square-foot space at New York's Kennedy International Airport. Neon sign is ruby red, underscored with white. Red is also used as an accent ceiling-line border and on the base of the central display fixture, and around the entire store. Checkerboard-patterned floor is grey and white.

Design: Fitzpatrick Design Group, Inc., New York; Jay Fitzpatrick, principal in charge.

12 **Trends in Merchandising Facilities**

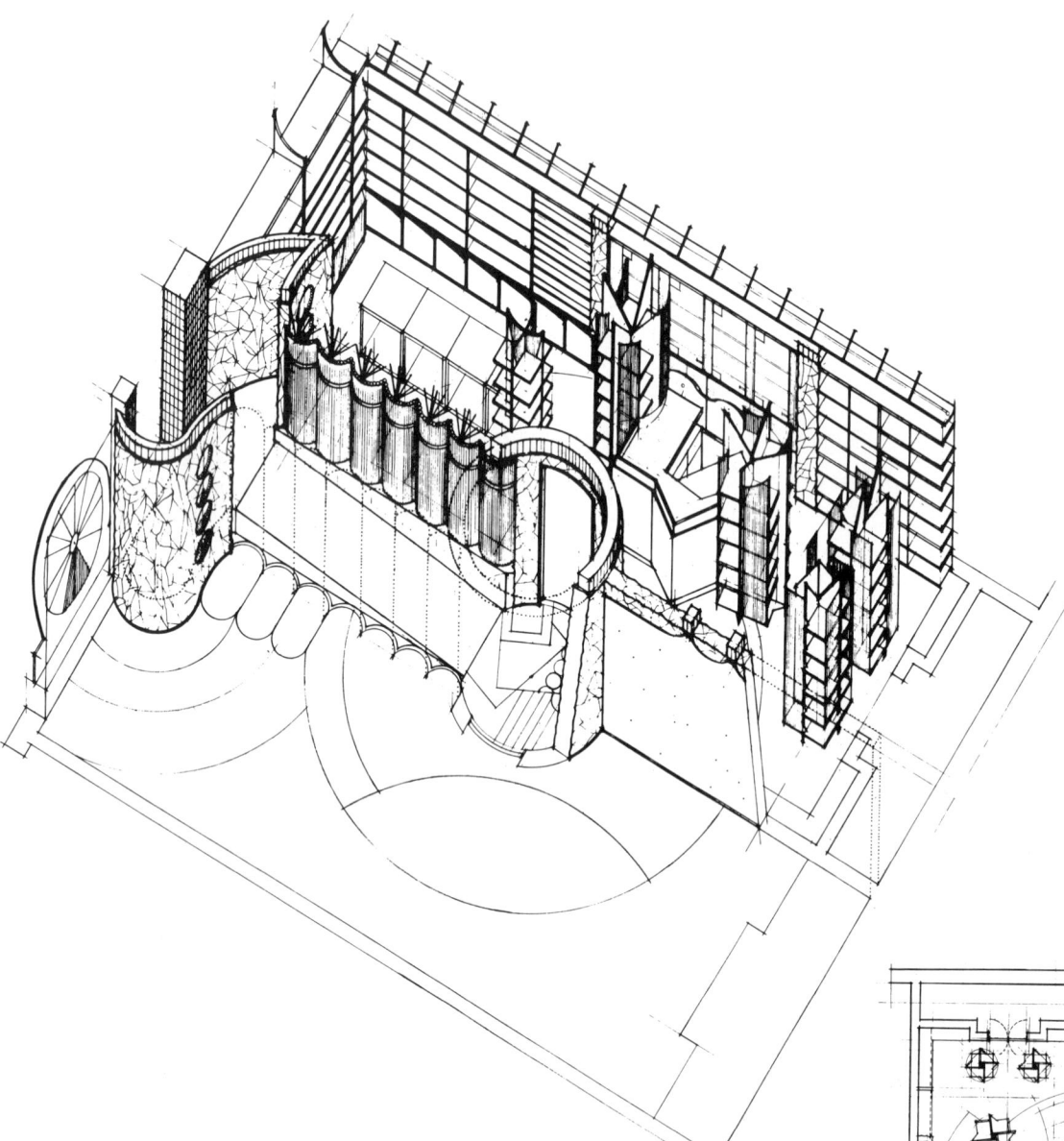

16 *Axonometric*

15 *Plan*

Museum shops

The 1,800-square-foot retail space for the Contemporary Arts Center, Cincinnati, is in itself a work of applied art. It communicates experimentation, individualism, and free expression, replicating the process behind the items shown at the Center itself and carried in the shop.

The interior is a seemingly spontaneous mix of colors, materials, forms, and textures. Based on the designer's concept of organic

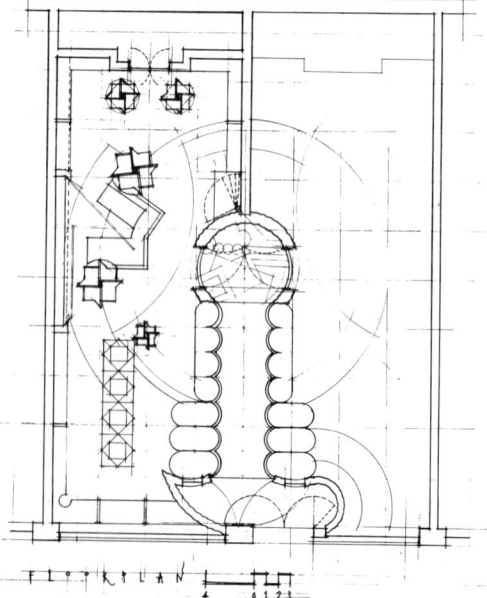

15

16

168

17
An "organic" bookstore and artware gallery

architecture, it has a circular plan. The bookstore is separated from the gallery by a ramped corridor. Curves and pinwheel patterns fabricated from plastic laminate and other inexpensive materials abound. Discs are suspended from the ceiling, acrylic tubes support shelving, and angles and curves play against each other throughout.

*Design:
Terry Brown Architect, Cincinnati;
Terry Brown, partner in charge.*

17

12 Trends in Merchandising Facilities

18 *A user-friendly supermarket*

18

Food store design

In the highly-competitive California food market, Lucky Stores determined that an updated design could increase their market share and provide a competitve edge. The design concentrated on feature areas of the stores—bakery, deli, frozen food, fruit and vegetable departments—as well as the checkouts. A warm, friendly environment was achieved through architectural detailing and graphics. The design program was implemented for a retrofit of existing stores as well as a template for new construction.

Design: WalkerGroup/CNI, New York; Kenneth H. Walker, AIA, partner in charge.

The Future of Retailing

13

- **Gap Stores Amplify the Merchandising Message**
  by Millard S. Drexler, The Gap, Inc.

- **The Winners and the Losers**
  by Harris Gordon, Deloitte & Touche

- **Sheppard Line Subway to Be Glitzy Malls**
  by Christopher Hume, The Toronto Star

- **Bergdorf's Magic Formula Crosses Fifth Avenue**
  by Ira Neimark, Bergdorf Goodman

- **Pea In the Pod Pampers Customers With Style**
  by Dana and Marcello Rosen, Pea In the Pod

- **Revlon Breaks the 25-Inch Barrier**
  by Hernando Sanchez, Revlon, Inc.

- **The Keeper of the Image**
  by Cynthia Cohen Turk, MARKETPLACE 2000

- **The Rouse Company: Dimensions in Competitive Positioning**
  by Larry Wolf and Susan Haight, The Rouse Company

Gap Stores Amplify the Merchandising Message

Millard S. Drexler
President
The Gap, Inc.
San Francisco,
California

One of the things that attracted me to The Gap in 1983 was the fact that its name was well-known throughout America because of its heavy emphasis on advertising and its excellent real estate. I also liked the fact that The Gap was in the casual wear business. But what I felt The Gap needed to address then–and what I still feel about most shopping experiences–is that the customer wants to see merchandise in an environment that's simple, easy to shop, and has a strong point of view.

For example, back in 1983 the dominant categories in the The Gap were jeans, which the company was founded on, and sweats. It was critical, not only to our image but to our success, that the customer get an immediate, visual sense of what the store stood for. The best way to do that was through color. We took our sweats program, which was then running in five fairly dull colors, and did it in 21 great colors arranged along the entire back wall of the stores. Then we took the jeans business–which was moving on sales of rigid unwashed Levis and Gap jeans in those days–and introduced washed and stone-washed jeans, and

Design:
Charles E. Broudy &
Associates

turned it into a fashion business. Both changes were simple, strong, and easy for the customer to see.

Today, The Gap's philosophy is to have an easy, simple-to-shop, very pointed assortment of clothing with color as an emphasis. When the customers walk into the store, they can clearly see what we stand for. Our total focus is developing, designing, producing, and selling casual-wear clothes. We *truly* specialize. While a department store can have 150 buyers, The Gap might have 10 or 12 key merchandisers running the whole company. Our *entire* effort in the company goes toward making a four-, five-, or eight-thousand square foot space work for the customer. We run a business with a single, narrowly focused mind-set, as opposed to a general merchandising organization dealing with multiple categories of goods.

Larger Gaps

Six or seven years ago, our average store size was 4,000 square feet, but recently we've jumped in size to 6,000- and 8,000-square-foot stores. As we became dominant in more categories, we found we simply weren't able to present them all properly in the same 4,000 square feet. We needed a larger store environment not because we wanted more assortment, but to properly address the merchandise we had.

"It's a chain-wide challenge to present a clean, uncluttered, simple cachet creatively."
— Millard S. (Mickey) Drexler.

Jeans are a perfect example. They've fallen year after year as a percent of the company's business, and part of the reason is that we haven't been able to house, stock, and present jeans well enough. The appropriateness of large stores is obvious, and we've decided to proceed with their development.

Store displays at the Gap are minimal and relatively uncomplicated. It's a chain-wide challenge to present that clean, uncluttered, simple cachet creatively . Since we have new merchandise coming in every few weeks, our display technique is always evolving.

Integrated design

The design of the store is as critical an element as the presentation of the goods. Both are actually part of the same process. Our company strives to maintain a single image, incorporating the way the store is designed; advertising; how the merchandise is assorted and colored; how our sales people treat the customers; and even the way we run our back office. All convey a singular attitude: satisfying the customer. None of our merchandising concepts are add-ons. The Gap stores are clean, simple, uncluttered, and tastefully designed. Our merchandise is clean, simple, and uncluttered. Our advertising is also clean, simple, and uncluttered.

In the nineties, the successful retailer is going to have to become more sensitive to the customer's needs and wants. Customers aren't shopping for the fun of it anymore, but to fulfill clothing needs, just as they have to fulfill food and housing needs. The days of doing business just because the merchant opens the doors are clearly over. Competition is forcing all of us to be a lot better in terms of what we have to sell and how we do it. Specialty retailing means sensitivity retailing– being sensitive to the quality, price, and assortment of the product.

Finally, working closely with our architect is very important to our management goals. Our company was fortunate to be able to build a relationship with our architect, Charles E. Broudy & Associates, and we consider them as a critical part of the process that drives the entire business.

The Winners and the Losers

*Harris Gordon
Partner, TRADE/
Retail Unit
Deloitte & Touche
Boston,
Massachusetts*

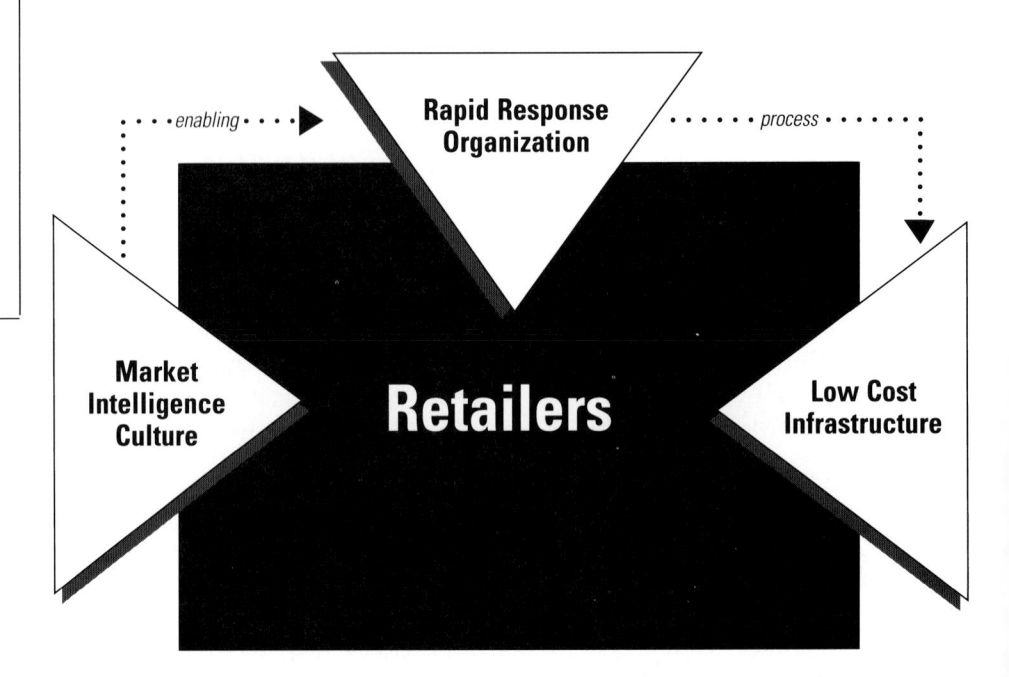

There are three strategic concepts that will separate the winning retailers from the losing ones. The winners will: install a marketing intelligence culture; set up a rapid response organization; and plan for a low-cost interest structure.

Installing a marketing intelligence culture

Retailers have grown apart from their customers. There was a period when retailers served their customers in a way that encouraged two-way communication. But now we are missing customer feedback. With catalog sales, customers might call in for items that are out of stock or not available, and the salespeople can record that. But there is no way to capture passive demand in current retail: customers drift in and out of stores, and retailers have no idea what they are looking for. They don't really know what customers find, what they don't find, why they buy, or why they don't buy. Store management can't just demand that their buyers be on the floor every day; *management needs to install an intelligent system that will provide ongoing feedback in a consistant way.* Today there are market research methods that do customer tracking: they can analyze the intent of customers before they enter the store, and, after they leave, they can find out where they went in the store, and what they bought. Once the retailer puts such a mechanism in place, customers need only be invited to participate.

Rapid response
Retailers must know what their competitors are doing, as well as what their customers want. A steady flow of merchandise into the store depends on a time-based response to the marketplace and a store strategy focused on low-cost and scale. The Limited has an incredible rapid-response organization. With a merchandise testing program already in place, they can bring their merchandise to certain select stores which are statistically representative of the chain, test it out, and then have the appropriate amount shipped to them within 60 days.

Low-cost structure
Stores should be easy to maintain and easy to change. The Gap is a good illustration of flexibility. They realize that if they pay too much attention to a particular moment in style, they will become out of fashion immediately. So they make a strong, clean first statement and manage to remain fashionable for quite a while. The Limited does the same thing. It has lab stores in Columbus, Ohio where it comes up with concepts, and then it determines how to roll out those concepts across the country so that they are flexible and affordable enough to be put into malls.

Repositioning for a Tasteful Age
As the population grows older, I think there will be a greater focus on taste and quality rather than on fashion and fad. People will not buy what they bought when they were young, and they will buy less. It is a growing trend to purchase 'investment clothing;" it goes along with aging. Simultaneously, stores are going to have to heighten their level of sensory excitement in order to separate themselves from the pack, and will devote more attention to self-expression.

Malls face the same problems that retailers face: how to stand out in the crowd, and how to reposition themselves for the changing population. Instead of focusing on teenagers, they will have to attract an older population, and to do this they will be forced to abandon some of the glitz and present their merchandise in a different way. They might offer adult classes on the premises, play classical music, and so on. In the process, these malls will lose the attraction that they had to teenagers. It is the older population that has the greater disposable income.

I'm not saying that everyone needs to reposition themselves to an older market, because there is always room for an end-game play. Contempo Casuals has stayed with the younger crowd and has done really well with it. McCrorys bought up all the five and dimes in America and is staying with it. J.C. Penney moved from resembling Sears five or ten years ago, and today it looks like a four-star department store. All of these stores have repositioned themselves well for the future.

Mail Order Catalogs: The ATMs of Retail

The era of explosive growth in the retail industry is behind us. What we have at the moment is a mature industry with various players consolidating and fighting for turf. For one retailer to grow, another one has to lose sales.

The volume generated by mail order catalogs has affected the whole retail industry. Now that they represent between eight to ten percent of all sales, receipts from the sales floor no longer have to be a store's bread and water. Fifteen years down the road, mail order sales may represent 15-25 percent of retail transactions. Just as ATMs revolutionized the banking industry, direct delivery to the customer will revolutionize the retail industry.

What this means is that a shoe store will no longer have to provide its entire range of men's shoes in every store, but just a basic range. It can hold its backup merchandise at a fulfillment center, where customers may place an order, and then have the merchandise delivered to their homes in a day or two.

Sheppard Line Subway Stations to be Glitzy Malls

by Christopher Hume

If planners get their way, Metro's future subway will be a place where commuters spend money as well as time.

Preliminary designs for the proposed Sheppard Ave. subway line foresee a series of stations that are full-blown malls. Forget the conventional notion of holes in the ground with platforms, stairs and ticket booths. As envisioned, these stops will be destinations in their own right.

Shoppers in Motion

A designer's idea for a subway station on the proposed Sheppard subway line shows a mall with a shiny marble floor and steel columns.

It's not that Toronto Transit Commission officials have suddenly woken up to reality. The change in philosophy comes as a result of private-sector involvement in the massive $2 billion scheme to eventually run a subway along Sheppard Ave. from the Allen expressway to Scarborough Town Centre.

In return for putting up 25 per cent of construction costs, investors want to create money-making opportunities for themselves. This translates into shops, restaurants, cinemas, dry cleaners, and so on.

The idea isn't novel. After all, the old Eglinton station originally had a dreary little mall with a coffee shop and assorted stores where travellers could wait more or less comfortably for their bus.

But compared with what the Sheppard line could look like, Eglinton merely hinted at the retail possibilities inherent in mass transit.

"We feel subway stations represent a tremendous opportunity to increase revenue recovery and are a tremendous opportunity to create attractive additions to our community," said Paul Stagl, vice-president of Arendscor, a North York development firm that is a member of Solutions Through Partnership, the private consortium that wants to help build the subway.

The consortium's task force has commissioned Thomas Consultants and the International Design Group to plan the stations.

"The scheme is not wholly profit-driven," Stagl said. "We want them to be a more pleasing and esthetic place for people to be."

This shouldn't be hard to accomplish. The first stations built in the early 1950s under Yonge St. belong to the public washroom style of architecture. Originally finished in shiny Vitrolite tiles, they were engineered rather than designed. Efficiency was the intention. Even the art-enhanced Spadina subway line offered little more than decorated walls.

That will all change with the Sheppard line. Each station–12 are envisioned–will be an underground complex that's part community centre, part shopping concourse. They will be situated at major intersections with entrances located at all four corners.

The first level below ground will contain parking as well as kiss-and-ride drop off spots. The real action, however, happens two floors beneath the street, where there'll be a large retail area lighted through a series of skylights.

In contrast to the underground city downtown, for instance, these are intended to be open and shopper-friendly. By creating space for stores and advertising, organizers estimate they can raise $100 million annually.

But it's unlikely the results will be a radical departure from the type of mall architecture with which Metro abounds.

Reprinted with permission. *The Toronto Star,* Monday, May 21, 1990, page A2.

Bergdorf's Magic Formula Crosses Fifth Avenue

*Ira Neimark
Chairman and Chief Executive Officer
Bergdorf Goodman
New York, New York*

Bergdorf Goodman's new Men's Store is now occupying a 40,000-square-foot, three-level space that we expect will produce sales of $1,000 per square foot. The Men's Store is a mirror image of the original Bergdorf's across Fifth Avenue in standards of merchandising, and the special quality of the store environment–elegant, luxurious, and comfortable.

Bergdorf's customers entering the Men's Store for the first time won't have to say, "Where am I?" They'll know they are in Bergdorf's. We've even duplicated the 58th Street rotunda. In the Men's Store, it contains men's neckwear.

When we remodeled the main store in 1983-4 and installed escalators, the total usable square footage grew to 140,000 square feet. The men's departments on the first and second floors increased from 8,000 square feet to 15,000 square feet. The main and second levels of the store are producing over $2,000 per square foot; men's apparel and accessories are a strong $1,000 per square foot. As a rule, the average department store does about $250 per square foot; a good performance is $350; and an outstanding figure is $500; $700 per square foot is exceptional. Our productivity is considered one of the highest in the country. We analyze gross margins/per sq. foot very carefully; it's what pays the bills.

Close supervision

In 1988, F.A.O. Schwarz moved from 745 Fifth Avenue, directly across the street from our only store at 58th Street and Fifth Avenue, where they had been located for over 50 years, to the nearby General Motors Building. It was clear that taking over the F.A.O. Schwarz space would be a natural extension of the Bergdorf style to men's clothing and accessories. "Style" refers to more than fashion; it is also management style. Our management team is involved on a daily basis with both merchandising and service. If Bergdorf's were to expand successfully, it would have to be under our own direct supervision. And this was the opportunity.

Bergdorf's, which was founded in 1901, has been at this location since 1928. It was once the site of the Vanderbilt mansion, and the current store was created from seven small commercial buildings. The new Men's Store is located in a landmark structure that what was originally the known as the Squibb Building. The architects for the Men's Store, Bridges & Lavin, have designed the exterior with details that echo the main store, again to give that feeling of familiarity. We believe that men who previously

Architecture: Bridges & Lavin, Architects, AIA, New York; Don Lavin, AIA, Partner in charge.

> *"There should be no question in the minds of our customers about where they are."*
> — Ira Neimark

would not be attracted to a men's department in a women's apparel store will be more inclined to shop in what they perceive is a store devoted to men's wear.

Location and lifestyle

Our location is key. We have 10 important hotels in a 10-block radius, including The Plaza, the Parker Meridien, the Regency, the Sherry Netherland, and the Pierre. This area includes some of the city's top office buildings–the GM Building, AT&T, IBM, and Trump Tower.

Our women's store is geared to customers who stay at the best hotels when they travel, vacation at the best resorts, dine at the best restaurants, are members of the best clubs. This market is entitled to a store that understands its lifestyle. The Men's Store will cater to the same type of customer. The Turnbull & Asser shop duplicates the Germyn Street shop in London. The Charvet customer will feel that he is in their Place Vendôme store in Paris. At Bergdorf's, they will feel comfortable. It is very clear that we relate to their standards. The store's design and the merchandise quickly communicate this very essential message in a club-like atmosphere.

Pea in the Pod Pampers Customers with Style

Dana Rosen, Chief Executive Officer, Marcello Rosen, President, Pea in the Pod Dallas, Texas

DR: Pea in the Pod evolved out of personal experience. I have been involved in fashion most of my life, and I could not believe how little was available to the woman after she became pregnant. It was either polyester with lace down to the wrist or bows up to the neck! There was *nothing* available for the woman who had any sense of style. So when I looked at baby boomer statistics, I knew there was an excellent opportunity for me in retail maternity. Nobody else in the industry was offering a quality fashion presentation.

The philosophy of the store is to provide pregnant women with the quality and style of clothing they are normally accustomed to wearing. We have a private labeling operation, designed in part by leading U.S. designers, as well as in-house designers. We stress service, because if there's any time a woman needs pampering, it's when she's pregnant. What we're here to do is to give that woman a comfortable atmosphere that she can identify with, and where people can identify with her. Our staff receives the latest medical information about pregnancy, and offers tips to our customers during this period. And our assortment of clothing covers every aspect of her lifestyle–from the boardroom to the carpool to Las Vegas for a vacation. We're not only a fashion organization; we're a service organization.

For the architecture and design of our stores, I wanted to have the sparkle, ease, and light of one's own home. Light to me is attention. When the attention is placed properly on the clothing, it too becomes visible and bright. I wanted the architecture not to interfere with the clothing, but to create a feeling of comfort in an understated way, so that the customers would not even be aware of why they felt comfortable.

MR: The purpose of the design was to create architectural touches that were consistent with our customers' own personal environment and socio-economical level and are an appropriate backdrop to the clothing.

Dressing room psychology

DR: Our fitting rooms are extra-spacious. The purpose of typical smaller dressing rooms with the curtains at the entrance is to get as many customers in and out as possible. Our objective at Pea in the Pod is to keep customers in the dressing rooms as long as possible. We do entire wardrobing for them, and that takes time, energy, and attention. We're not interested in the amount of sales per hour; we're interested in each individual person. So we bring the entire store into that large dressing room.

MR: We do not allow a woman to carry her own clothing, but carry it for her. We open doors for her, bring her clothes to the car, and sometimes even bring the car to the door. Our sales people are educated and understanding, and they act graciously, which is important at a time when a woman is very emotional. We are very fortunate to be dealing with the creation of life; and so we try to create not only a close, endearing relationship with the customer, but a whole environment for her.

Investment maternity wear
DR: The woman who shops at Pea in the Pod can purchase investment dressing that will be appropriate before, during, and after her pregnancy. I've had women who have shopped with us from one pregnancy all the way through to the next, and never stopped shopping. And my staff and I always wear the clothing we sell. We simply accessorize it and have it altered in the appropriate spots. We do top-to-bottom dressing, from the garments and the accessories to the hosiery. We look great, and we make our customers look and feel that way!

MR: When selecting locations for our stores, we basically look for fashion malls. We want a location where the customer that is accustomed to high fashion shops before and after maternity; Nordstorm, Neiman Marcus, and Laura Ashley, for example, represent a certain market. Age is also a factor of our demographics. Since the average bearing age has been rising steadily–from 18-30 years ago, to 24-45 today–most of our customers have a higher buying capacity. They want the better quality and style of clothing that wasn't available before.

A dual-channel industry
DR: We see the future of retailing going in two directions: the strong niche specialty retailing, and the off-ramp, discount, lean-and-mean atmosphere with very few amenities. The discounters get the product in the stores and move it out: their theatrics are huge stacks of merchandise and very low prices. The other retailing channel is the specialty business, where the customer develops a relationship with the retailer, who is often located in a convenient mall. With mall space becoming more expensive, the ultimate challenge to retailers and designers is to offer as much merchandise in as small a space–and with as understandable a presentation–as possible.

MR: Products are going to get more narrow in focus. Time is now a major commodity; customers want to see all the lines that exist in a particular area at once. If a shop does not have what a customer is looking for, she can assume she will not be able to find it. This will give specialty retailers an advantage over department stores.

179

Revlon Breaks the 25-inch Barrier

● *Hernando Sanchez*
Vice President
Marketing &
Merchandising
Creative &
Communications
Group
Revlon Inc.
New York, New York

"The Revlon counter is not a piece of furniture; it is a living environment. We are moving away from the 'corral,' the look of the impenetrable boxy counters enclosing the Beauty Advisors. Rather, we are opening up the counters into islands so that consumers can move through and around them, where the shopper will not have 25 inches of solid counter separating her from the Revlon Beauty Advisor."

Hernando Sanchez spends more than 60 percent of his time traveling worldwide, meeting with international merchandising heads of the Revlon cosmetics empire, which includes such brands as Revlon, Ultima, Marcella Borghese, Almay, Max Factor, and now Jeanne Gatineau. He is implementing three important merchandising concepts to bring Revlon and its beauty products closer to the user: the design of its department store spaces; the introduction of Revlon Universal Merchandising units (RUMs), open stock units for mass merchandising; and "Color Try-Ons," a system of cosmetic mini-samplers dispensed in rolls from slick modular units.

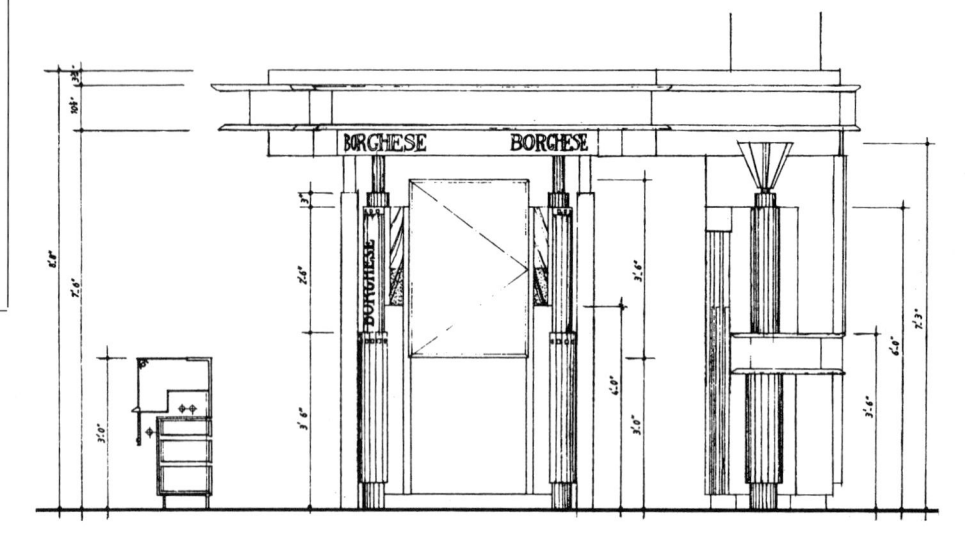

Mr. Sanchez considers each dramatically-shaped product to be a jewel, and gives them Tiffany-window treatment. Dramatically backlit headers, called "glorifiers," display the products mounted at an undulated angle that implies energy and rhythm. Angled counter-top lipstick merchandisers carry the theme within the shopper's reach.

Open-plan beauty for the world's department stores

Simpson's in Toronto, Myer Department Stores in Australia, the Revlon Color Studio in Bloomindale's, IPSFA in Venezuela, and J. C. Penney units in Plaza Las Americas Shopping Center, San Juan, Puerto Rico, and Rockaway, New Jersey, among other stores, are now serving Revlon customers from new departmental plans that transformed the previous hard-edge square layout into a graceful figure 8. Within the same 80 square foot space (Revlon's average "footprint" or "real estate" allotted to them on the selling floor), Mr. Sanchez and his design team created product islands, barrier-free stations where the customer perceives privacy and the personalized attention of the Beauty Advisor.

"Even the new counter design is like a jewelry boutique," Mr. Sanchez proudly points out.

For years, Mr. Sanchez has championed the concept of putting Revlon's Beauty Advisors out in the open where they can walk around and achieve the important one-to-one relationship that is so important to building and maintaining brand loyalty, a fast-disappearing aspect of consumer shopping patterns. Has less counter space meant more sales? "The response has been excellent," Mr. Sanchez reported. "Volume has increased significantly in stores where the new departmental configuration has been installed."

RUMs and Color Tester Rolls

In 1989, the first Revlon Universal Merchandising Units (RUMs) were installed in Australia and South Africa. Mr. Sanchez and his design team have given a new visual image to the typical open stock merchandiser with a new concave shape and undulating shelf design. Since drug stores and mass merchandising outlets account for up to 75 percent of Revlon's volume in Anglo Saxon countries, the potential payoff in higher sales per unit is sizable. The Basic RUM is 12 feet wide by 7 feet 8 inches high; an optional Treatment Lab add-on which includes a curved mini-counter extends the RUM by another two-and-one-half feet. The "Color Boutique" glorifier also utilizes the undulating band of stylized lipstick tubes, in counterpoint to the merchandise below.

Mr. Sanchez is very enthusiastic about the Color Try-Ons program which began a national roll-out in mid-1989. Rolls of 450 sealed "microchips" dispense single applications of Revlon products, including foundation, eyecolor, powder, eyeshadow, lipstick, and nail color for the customer to sample in the store or take home for comparison before making her selection.

Color tester housing consists of injection molded components which can be assembled into two, three, and four-tier displays. The main four-tier display has a clear crystal styrene cover which rolls back to reveal 12 different rolls of product applications. All units are designed to use on the counter or to hang.

International cosmetic customer profiles

Customers everywhere, Mr. Sanchez indicates, look for service and excitement. Worldwide, there are four basic marketing channels and customer types that Revlon point-of-sale experts aim for when devising promotional and store design strategies.

Revlon's new departmental design and fixturing programs support the company's emphasis on strengthening its customer relationships. "We must make a meaningful statement about who we are." — Hernando Sanchez.

Orient: Japan is currently Revlon's second largest market, and Mr. Sanchez predicts that in five to ten years it will be equal to or surpass total U.S. volume. Revlon products sold in Japan carry retail prices that are two to three times higher than the same products sold elsewhere. Skin treatment products are top sellers, accounting for approximately 65 percent of total volume, with fragrances and cosmetics responsible for the balance. Japanese merchants, Mr. Sanchez notes, are open to experiment with new display techniques.

Anglo-Saxon: This category includes the U.S., U.K., Canada, Australia, and South Africa. Major channels of distribution are department stores, boutiques, perfumeries, and pharmacies, which, outside of the U.S., are indepedendently owned. Revlon considers its department store presence for image rather than high profit. Even with sales per square foot in the $3,000 range, its 80 square-foot-slice of department store real estate still struggles to generate profit after clearing expenses, which could include up to 10 salespeople earning $30,000 per year. An estimated 60 to 80 percent of Revlon's sales is generated by pharmacies.

Europe: Perfumeries dominate the retail marketplace on the continent, followed by department stores. Most perfumeries are small, privately-owned establishments; an exception, according to Mr. Sanchez, is the German-based Douglas group of stores.

South America: "A big mix" is the way Mr. Sanchez describes the South American market. Merchants have been enthusiastic in their initial response to the new open plan departmental layout and display elements that glamourize the products at the point-of-sale.

Revlon's new departmental design and fixturing programs support the company's emphasis on strenghtening its customer relationships. "Our departments and displays must make a meaningful statement about who we are," he stresses. "Our objective is to make one or two strong statements that customers can read, and remember."

The Keeper of the Image

*Cynthia Cohen Turk
President
MARKETPLACE
2000
Coral Gables,
Florida*

The first generation of the automatic replenishment system occured in the early 1980s. Retailers were primarily interested in implementing systems and ordering. I addressed such questions from retail clients as, "How can I control my inventory?" "How do I order?" "How do I reach a 'stock keeping unit' level inventory?" "What kind of 'point of sale' equipment do I have?"

But after the drastic drop-off of Christmas sales in 1987 and the wave of bankruptcies in 1988 and 1989, retailing changed measureably. Department stores were consolidating; regional specialty stores were gobbled up by national specialty stores; and the marketplace became dominated by larger companies. The whole environment grew intensely competitive.

A new breed of buyers

Chains expanded and centralization decreased. Retailers who previously spent their time trying to standardize were forced to realize that to be a national chain, they could no longer make all their stores look the same. For example, you can't sell the turquoise slacks in Boston that you do in Palm Beach! Being a national retailer means using the staff–centrally or decentrally–to buy for specific markets, and simultaneoulsy maintaining a system of control over inventory.

Now, in the 1990s, there is more concern with what consumers want and what environments they shop in. I work on the store's marketing, design, and buying strategies so that every aspect of its business will eventually be geared toward one specific position in the marketplace. The color of a store's logo, the shape of its shopping bags, the style of the light fixtures, the carpeting or tile on the floor, and even the wrapping paper can influence the type of consumer the retailer attracts.

Micro-marketing

To create an effective market position, a retailer may either want to add to or remove components of the existing consumer base. "Micro-marketing" is based not on the old horizontal or vertical lines of age, sex, or income, but on more finite aspects of the consumer's behavior and lifestyle. An entire market can be created around an affinity for a certain style, such as "country." Laura Ashley represents affinity: its market cannot be segmented by age, demographics, economics, or geography. Its customers simply like little flowered prints.

Retailers frequently say, "I know who shops my store." But they don't know *enough*. Do they know why some people reject their stores? Do they know the shoppers that might be interested but never make it to the door? Just knowing who made the transaction yesterday isn't enough. *Merchants can no longer take for granted that if one person doesn't come, somebody else will. There is too much competition. The consumer is being bombarded by other alternatives.*

Every store has to consider itself a destination store now–even the small stores, even the stores in malls. There is competition with other aisles in the mall, other wings, and stores near other anchors. A mall often had two anchors: if customers walked from one end to to the other, they went by every specialty store along the way. Now malls have four or five department stores and a movie theater! And there are malls where the parking space is so segmented that customers cannot even see all the anchors from the outside. They may go to just one section of the mall and never see the other stores!

Retailers should also be aware of their environments. A home-center store, an apparel store, and an office products store each needs an appropriate environment. A record store may do very well if it is close to a movie theater. Or it may do better with a limited format, that is, when the store keeps open a specialized set of hours and occupies a smaller square footage–in the basement, or in the first floor of an office building complex. It is often convenient to edit the inventory to fit a smaller square footage in a different environment, or appeal to only one segment of your customer base. The merchant can develop mini-versions of the overall concept, depending on the location. If a record store is located downtown in a working environment, don't put in selections for 14-year-olds. Instead, feature classical music or Broadway shows.

The "keeper of the image"

I always encourage retailers to have a consistent image. Good image management starts within the organization. *Put one person in charge!*

In a traditional retail organization, too many perple have decision-making power over the image presented. This results in a fragmented and contradictory image which can put the buyer and the seller out of step. I had a retail client in Texas who found out that his customer was really a size 14 polyester dress-buyer, while his ads in the newspaper promoted slacks shown on thin models who looked like juniors. Later, I was working with a specialty apparel chain and discovered that the image generated to their mail-order customers was completely different from the image seen by customers who walked in the store. There were other incongruities, from the store layout, to the demeanor and dress of the salespeople.

They changed their operation to insure that every new store design, every promotional campaign, every catalog, and every private label product was consistent with the image they wanted to portray. Structurally, the "keeper of the image" in a retail organization is not another position that needs to be added. It only requires a changing of the titles of the existing senior managment and some reshuffling of their responsibilities. For a moderate-sized specialty chain (100 stores), the COO might take the responsibility. Or the director of marketing and advertising might become the director of image. It all depends upon the size and organization of the chain. It is not uncommon for people who started as catalogers to branch out into store management. Sometimes, their image remains centered around the catalog, and their store becomes a three-dimensional articulation of what the catalog was.

Otherwise, because the different areas within a retail organization have different functional responsibilities, each person will come up with his own interpretation. They all start out wth the same, "Here's the targeted customer," but their interpretations will be different. The result can be in-store promotional campaigns that are different from the mail-order catalog. The overall theme can become confused, too: there is, first of all, the image of the store; within that, different seasonal themes; as well as design themes for private-label lines.

Everything should be focused on appealing to the targeted customer, including the store's ambience. To sell some types of products, the salespeople should be upbeat and the store should have visible energy. In other stores, the atmosphere should be sedate and quiet. In the past, this need for consistency was taken for granted, and only gut merchants understood it instinctually. One of the problems in the 1990s is that we don't have as many gut merchants; they've all been trained in the same school. We have to put back more personal touches in retailing. Customers want to feel good about making their purchase. *This is why enhancing the personality of the store is so important and why the industry has to get back to selling at retail.*

The 1990s: The age of good design
There has been too much visual boredom. Malls have become boring. Too many were built that looked the same and all individuality of geography and region was lost. If I went to a mall in Chicago, Texas, New York, Florida, or California, I'd see the same anchors and the same specialty stores. And if I were standing in the middle of a mall, center court, I would have no idea where I was. The Limited was always in the same location, Sears was always in the same location and so on.

Now, there's competition among the malls. And so, finally, developers have begun to regionalize and attempt to differentiate them from one another. We're still only in the second and third generation of malls; they are really a phenomenon of the last 20 years. But we're going through a period in which the older ones have to be refurbished in order to compete with the new. Many malls that are 10 years old still consider themselves "The New Mall," when in fact they are shabby and old-format. Smart retailers have gone from a seven- or eight-year remodelling cycle up to a five-year cycle. They are also building stores that are more modular, so that they can change their image yearly or seasonally, refresh their look, and provide something interesting to the customer.

Macy's is experimenting with this; Burdine's in Florida has done some interesting things; The Limited is fresh and is starting to be daring. Benetton has been daring with its advertising campaign, but not with its stores. In the past, retailers have been afraid to be daring, but stores in the 1990s are going to gave to be visually exciting to draw traffic.

Good design does not have to cost a lot of money, but it has to be creative and innovative. We're just on the verge of major changes in the retail environment for the nineties.

183

The Rouse Company: Dimensions in Competitive Positioning

Larry M. Wolf,
Director of Retail Leasing
Susan Haight,
Vice President
The Rouse Company
Columbia, Maryland

The Rouse Company leases space in shopping centers to specialty retailers of all sizes, large chains like The Limited, on down to mom-and-pop stores. When the Campeau Corporation first bought the Federated Department store group in 1988, our tenants expressed their concerns and anxieties to us about the negative effects that this move could have on the industry, but business proceeded as usual. Chains and independents that were doing well then have continued to flourish; those that are experiencing difficulty now were having trouble then.

We did experience an increase in requests for protection in case we lost a department store, and the center's sales declined. Yet, most of the retailers we work with feel that the worst is behind us. Department store retailing will be put back into the hands of the merchants instead of developers.

Lately, we have had a number of manufacturers contact us to explore the idea of opening specialty stores. For example, the Liz Claiborne organization has opened its own stores. They may not have pursued this idea if they had not been apprehensive about the future of department stores as a primary outlet for their goods. We advise manufacturers to be sure that they understand the difference between selling their merchandise in a department store and a specialty store.

On the other hand, major department store chains have gone into the specialty store format, stores of between 3,000 and 4,000 squre feet that have a definite customer focus. Macy's has Aeropostal and Fantasies, and J.C. Penney has In Detail and Amanda Fielding. They are, in effect, asking themselves the question: Are there ways for us to grow the business other than in a department store format?

The performance of strong, flexible chains like The Limited and The Gap has been exceptional, given the very rough retail climate of the past few years. By carefully segmenting themselves, they have succeeded in attracting more customers.

Aid to independents

There is no doubt that the small independent operator is disappearing from the retail scene. The Rouse Company is still committed to finding small merchants and giving them an opportunity to make it in the big leagues. Where possible, we structure their deals differently from the chains. They may get a higher cash allowance, or a lower initial rent.

We also find consultants who can work with these independents to strengthen their competitive position. Sometimes store owners will need help with their display program, or they might need to balance their merchandise mix.

Store design turnover

Store design has become a major aspect in the total merchandising picture. A few years back, we used to make a deal for a 12-year lease with chains like Brooks Fashion or The Limited, and we could be almost certain that the same store would look virtually the same for the next 12 years. Now, what we contract for today will almost certainly look different in 12 months. That's how rapidly we find that retailers are addressing the store design issue.

Renovations and acquisitions

Renovations are a high priority with The Rouse Company– renovations of shopping centers by restoring, updating, upgrading, and re-merchandising them. Our most recent renovations have been Faneuil Hall in Boston, and Willowbrook Mall, Woodbridge Mall, and Cherry Hill Mall, all in New Jersey.

In addition to remodeling our centers, The Rouse Company is acquiring existing centers. We are looking primarily at regional centers, but we have considered some community centers, especially if we can expand them by adding new stores. We have a successful track record in taking over and significantly improving the performance of existing centers, and we plan to be more aggressive in identifying and acquiring them. Sites to build new centers is limited, and therefore development is more difficult. We believe that acquisitions represent an opportunity for growth.

The 200,000-square-foot Underground Atlanta, June, 1989

14 Retail Graphic Standards

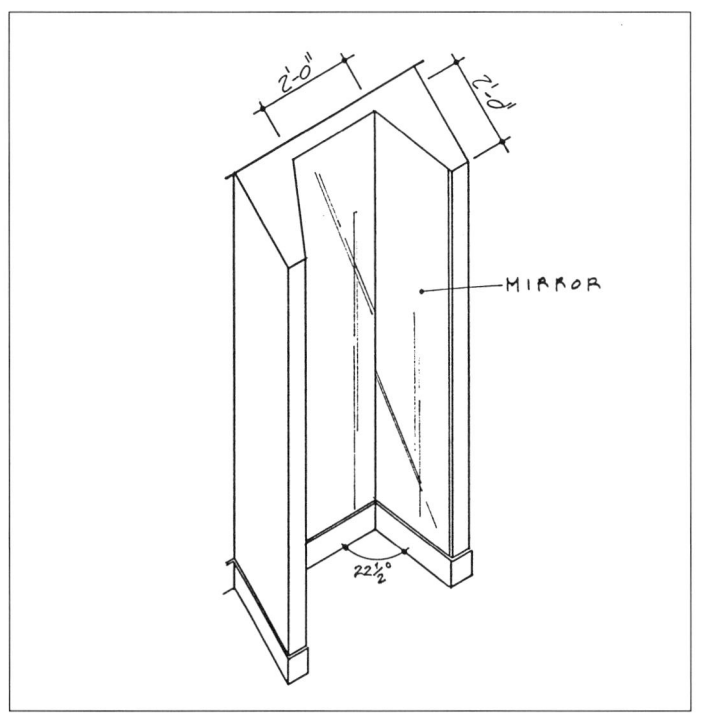

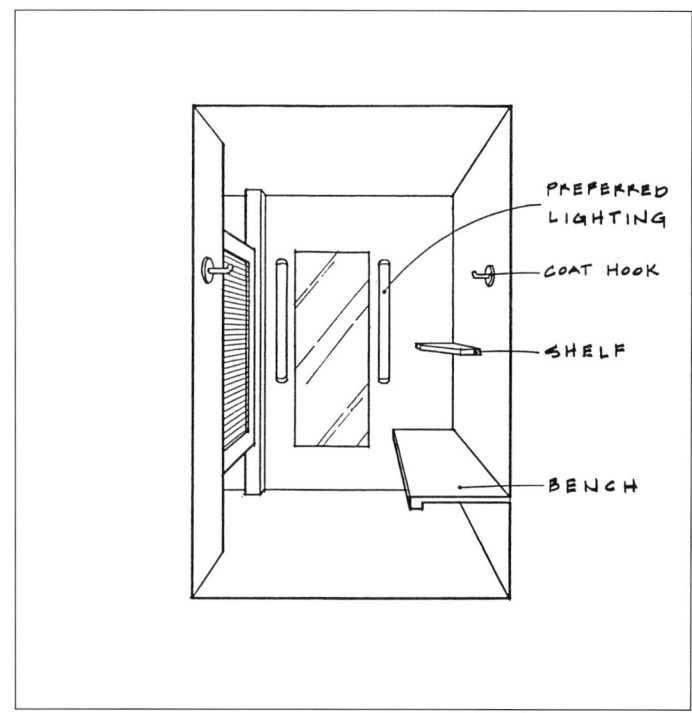

3-way mirror.

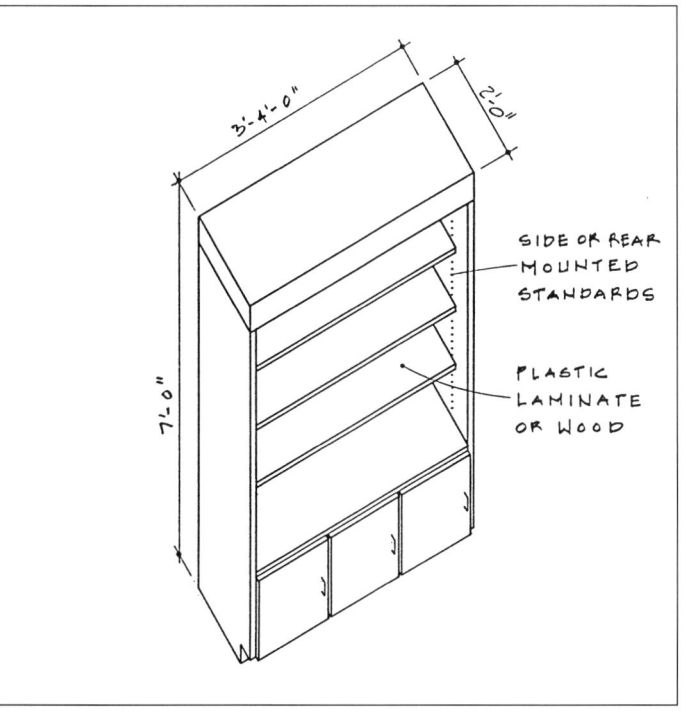

Fitting room.

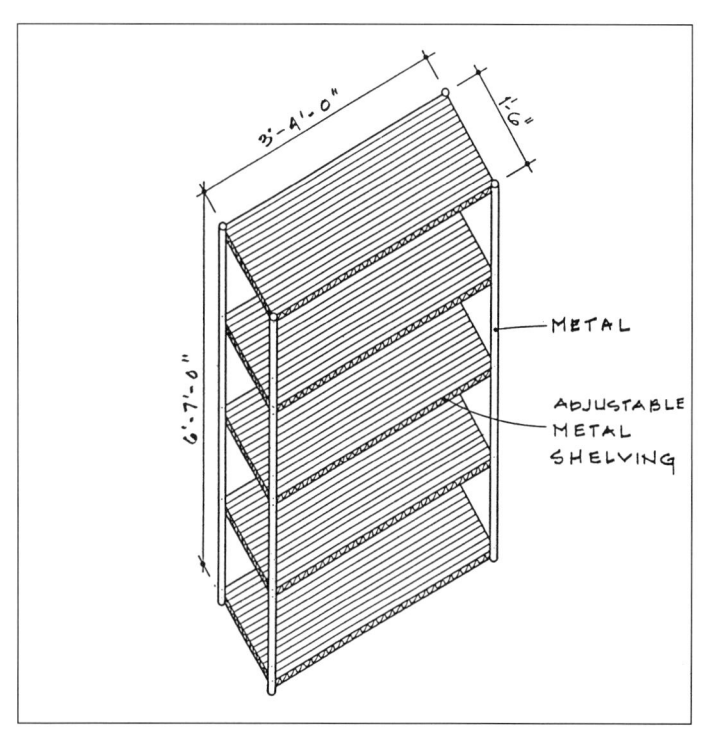

Case with shelving and base cabinets.

Storage display shelving (for food, hardware).

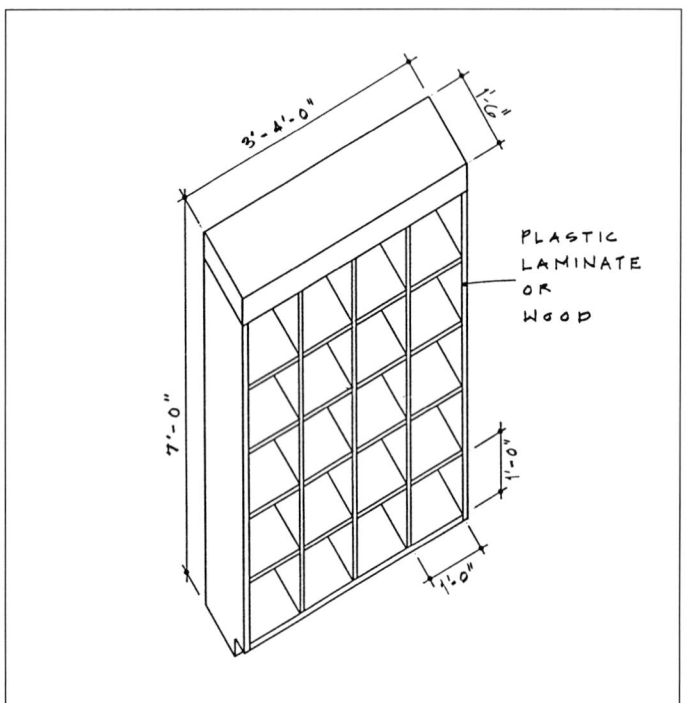

14 Retail Graphic Standards

Cubby case (for shirts, gloves, towels).

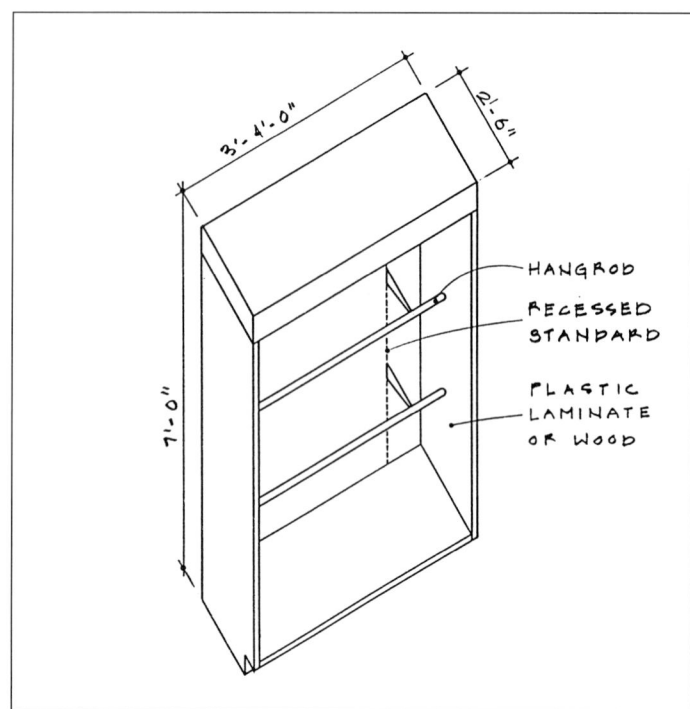

Case with hangrods.

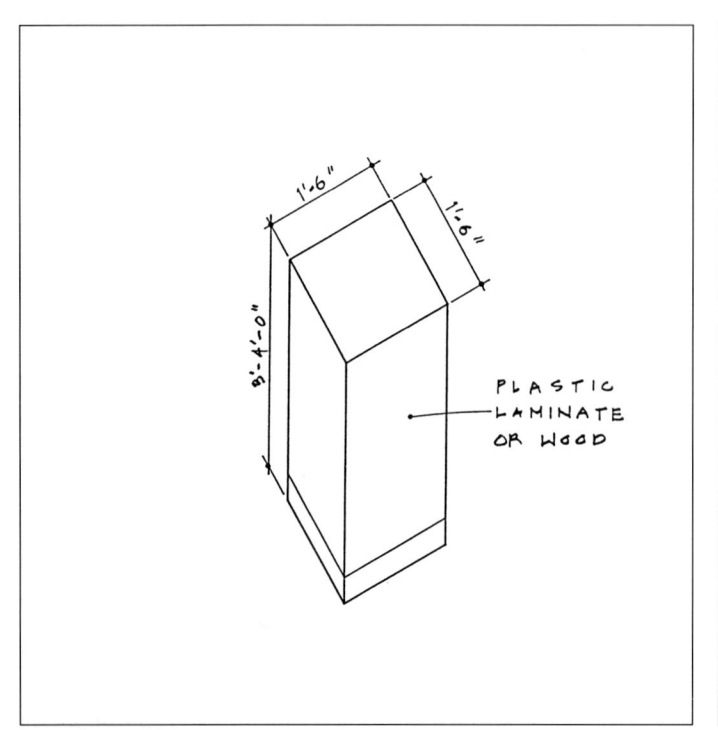

Display pedestal.

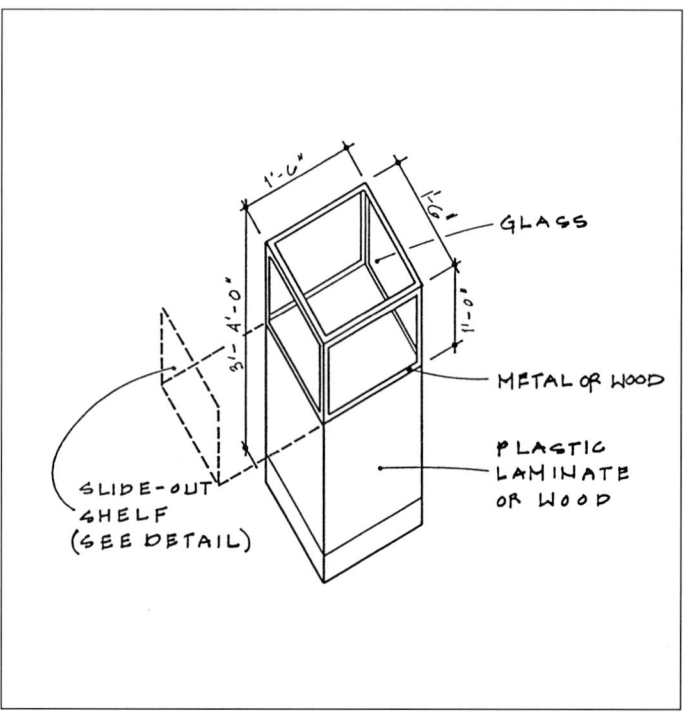

Display pedestal with case.

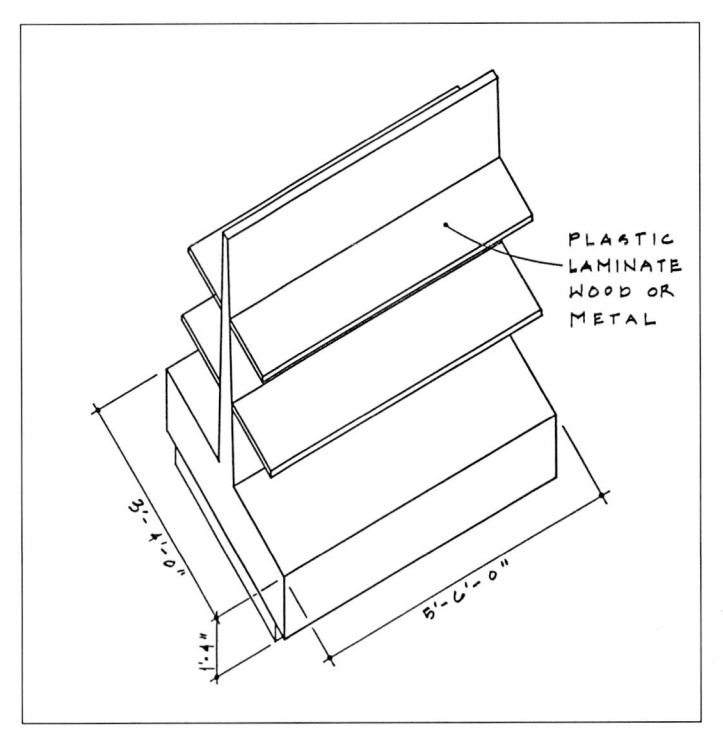

Gondola (for food, gifts, hardware, etc).

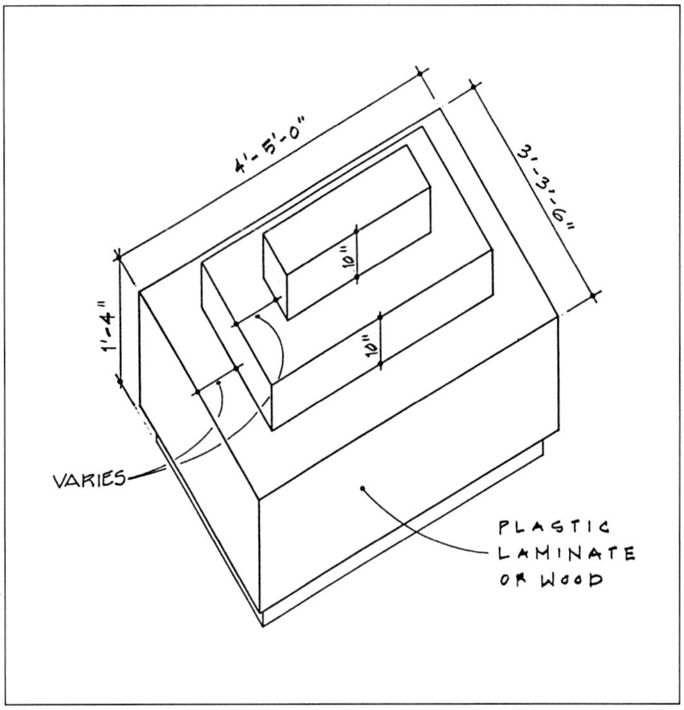

Pyramid display platform.

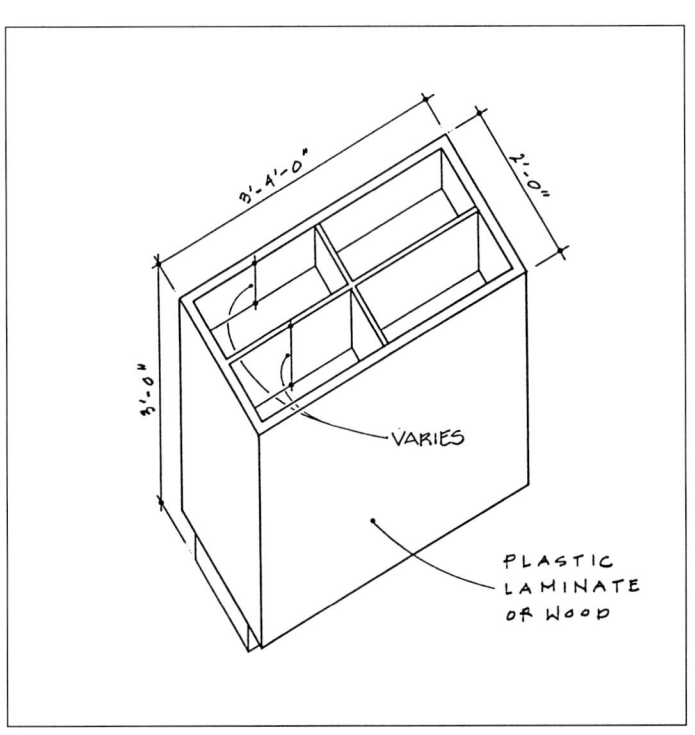

Display bin (for records, tapes, CDs).

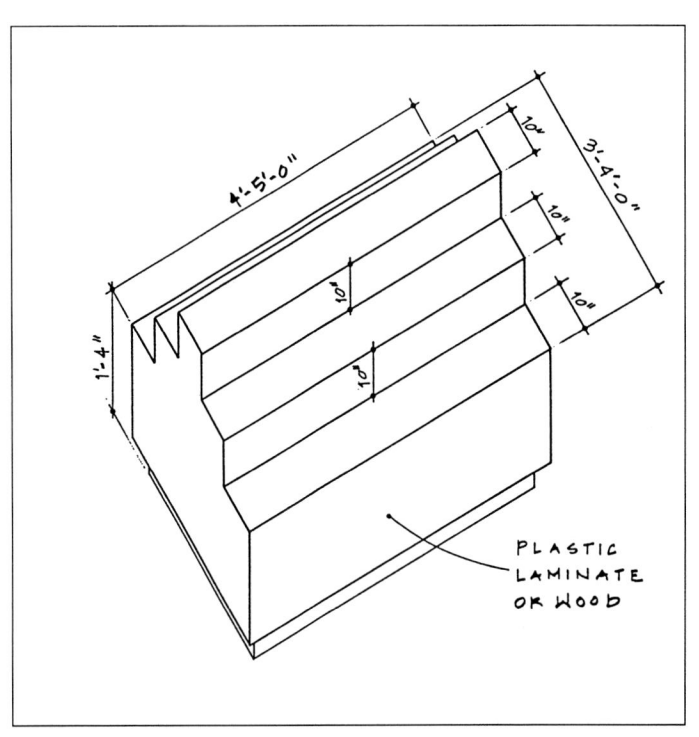

Stepped gondola (for gifts, clothing).

14 Retail Graphic Standards

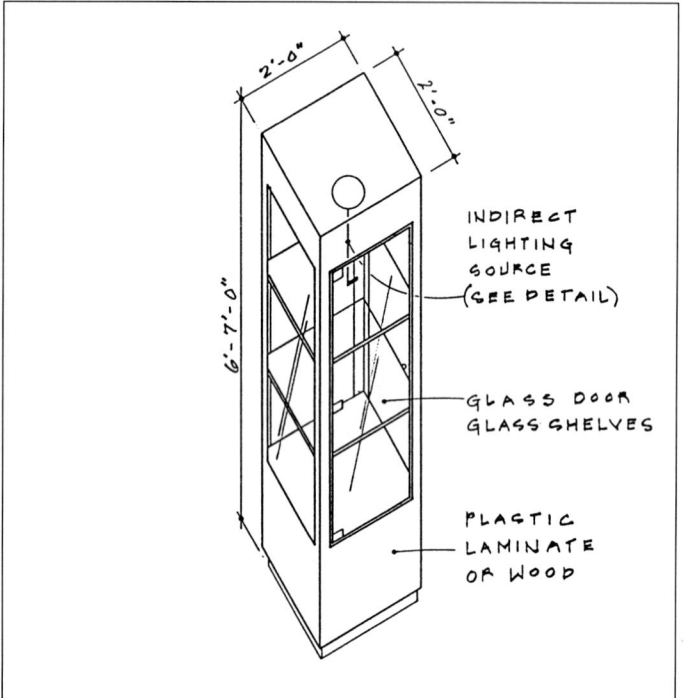

Tower display for art, museums, gift shops (#1).

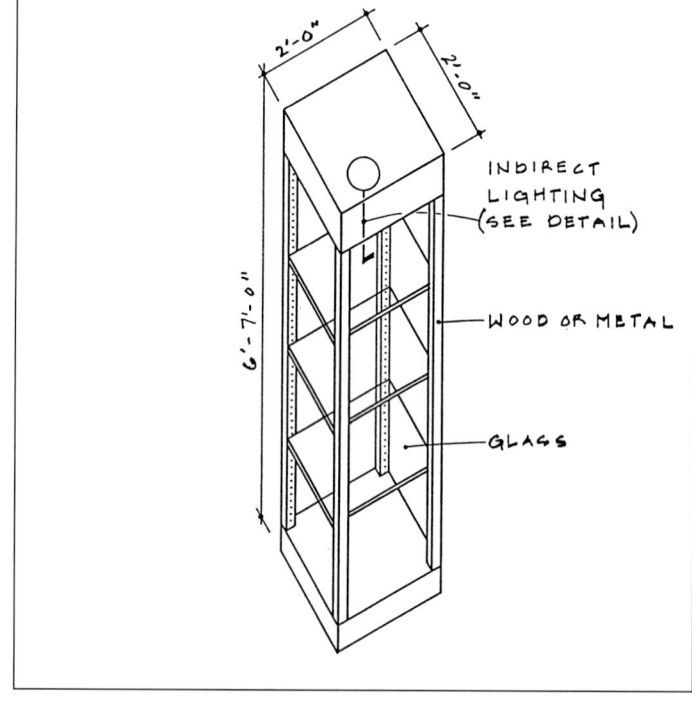

Labels: 2'-0", 2'-0", 6'-7'-0", INDIRECT LIGHTING SOURCE (SEE DETAIL), GLASS DOOR GLASS SHELVES, PLASTIC LAMINATE OR WOOD

Tower display for art, museums, gift shops (#2).

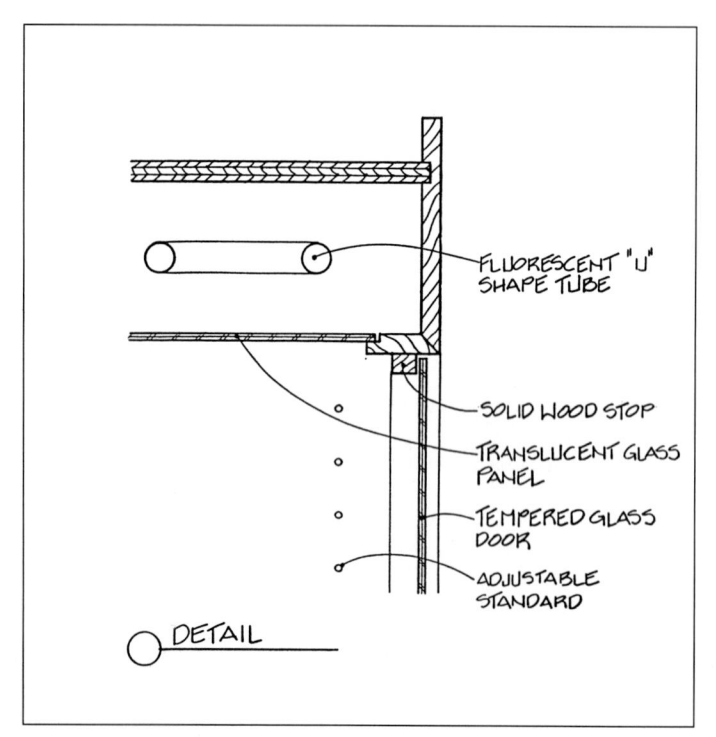

Labels: 2'-0", 2'-0", 6'-7'-0", INDIRECT LIGHTING (SEE DETAIL), WOOD OR METAL, GLASS

Tower display lighting.

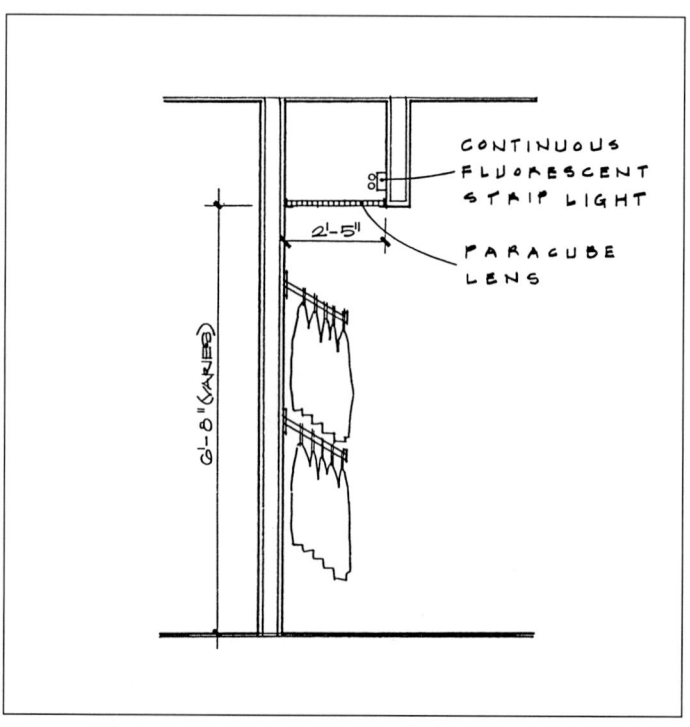

Labels: FLUORESCENT "U" SHAPE TUBE, SOLID WOOD STOP, TRANSLUCENT GLASS PANEL, TEMPERED GLASS DOOR, ADJUSTABLE STANDARD, DETAIL

Valence lighting.

Labels: CONTINUOUS FLUORESCENT STRIP LIGHT, PARACUBE LENS, 2'-5", 6'-8" (VARIES)

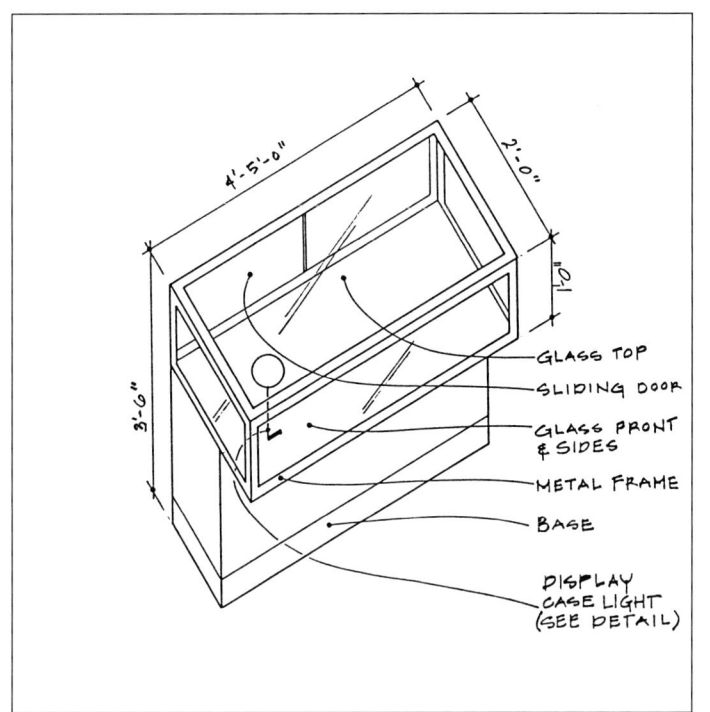

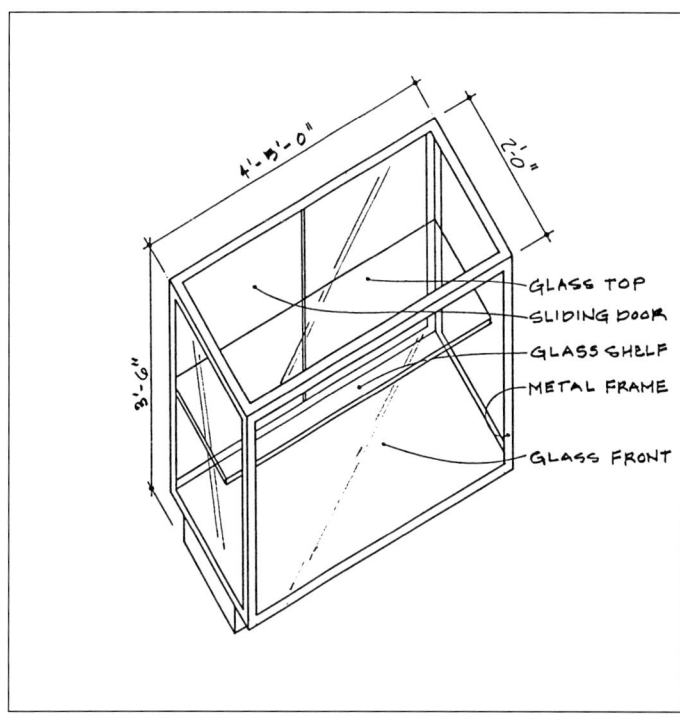

Display case.

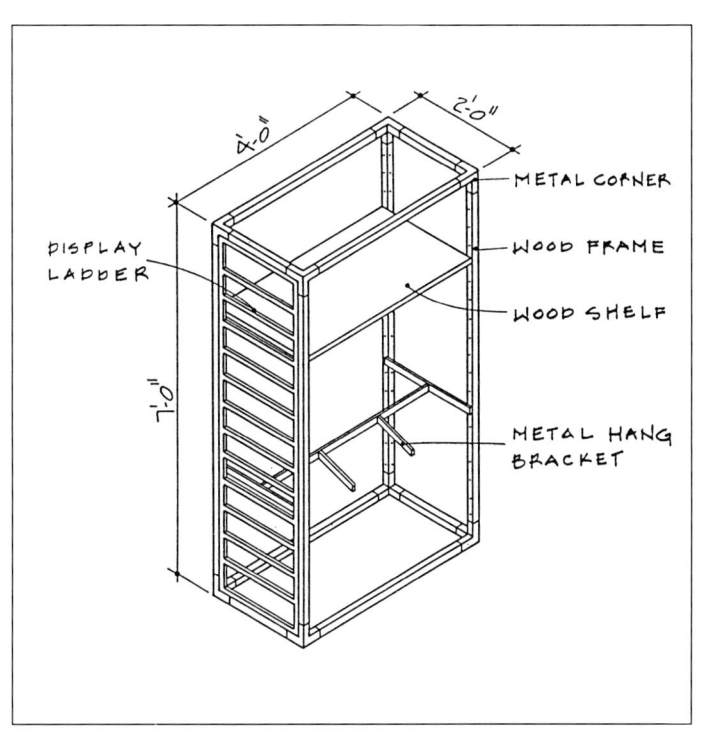

Display case with glass.

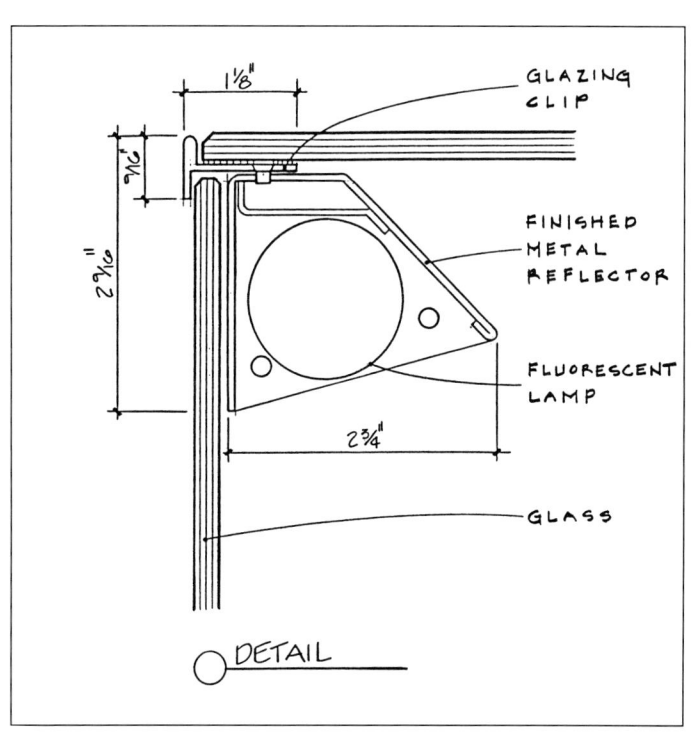

Display case for clothing.

Display case lighting.

189

14 Retail Graphic Standards

4-way stand with fixed and adjustable arms.

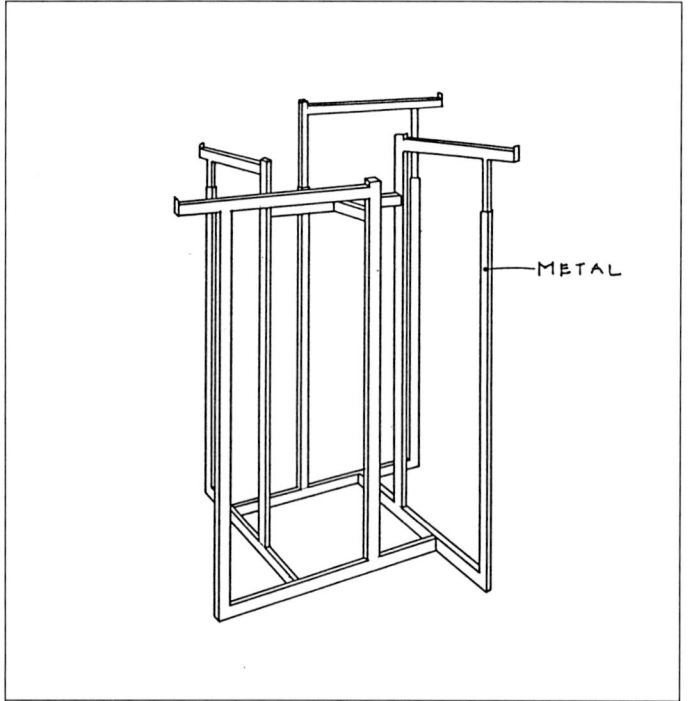

4-way stand with fixed and adjustable arms.

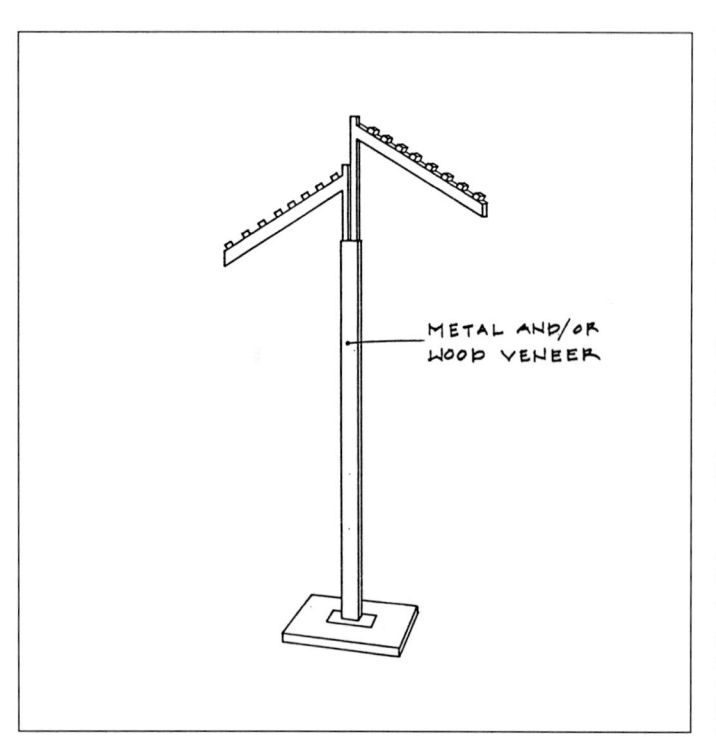

T-stand with adjustable arms.

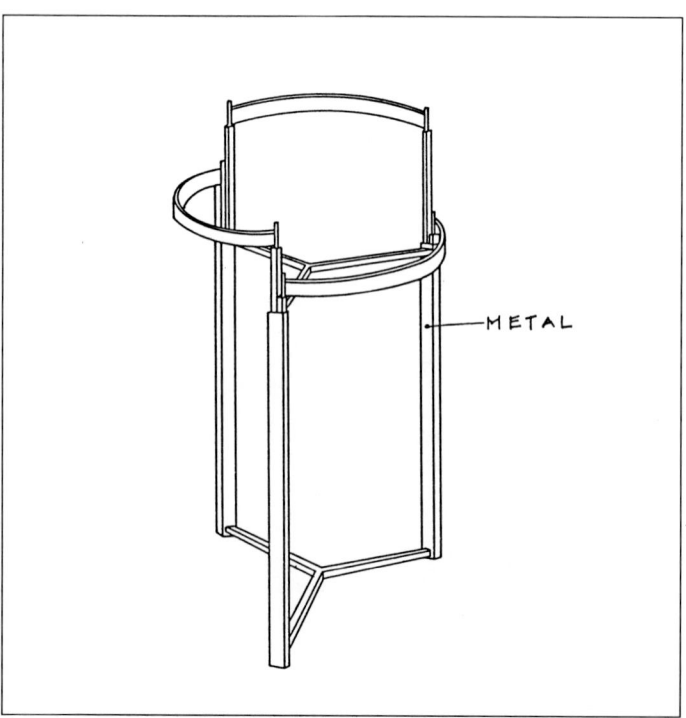

Circular 3-way stand, adjustable arms.

190

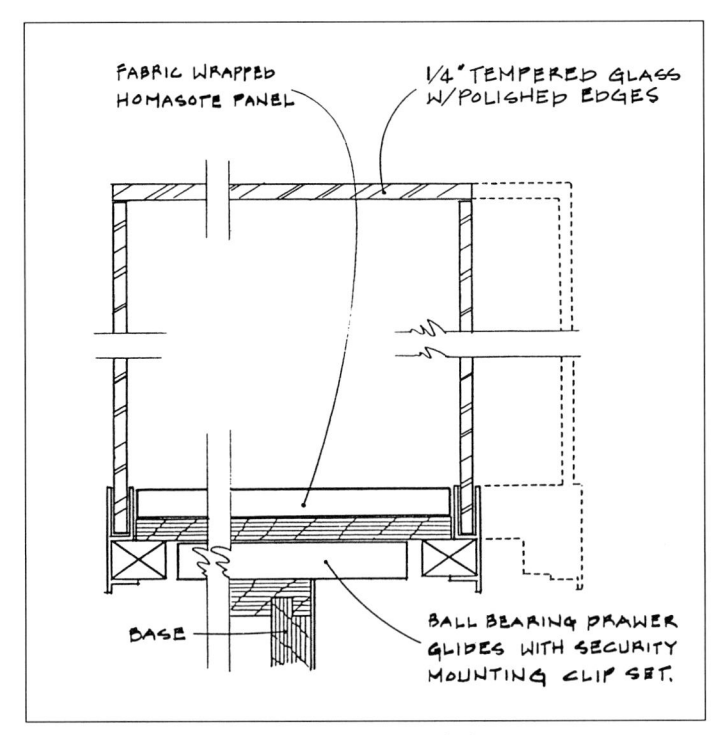

Detail, display pedestal with slide-out shelf (#1).

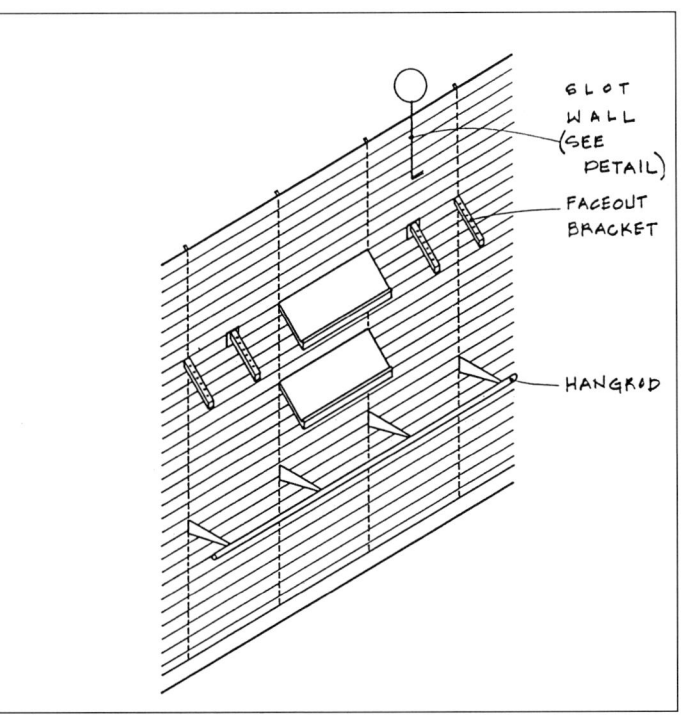

Detail, display pedestal with slide-out shelf (#2).

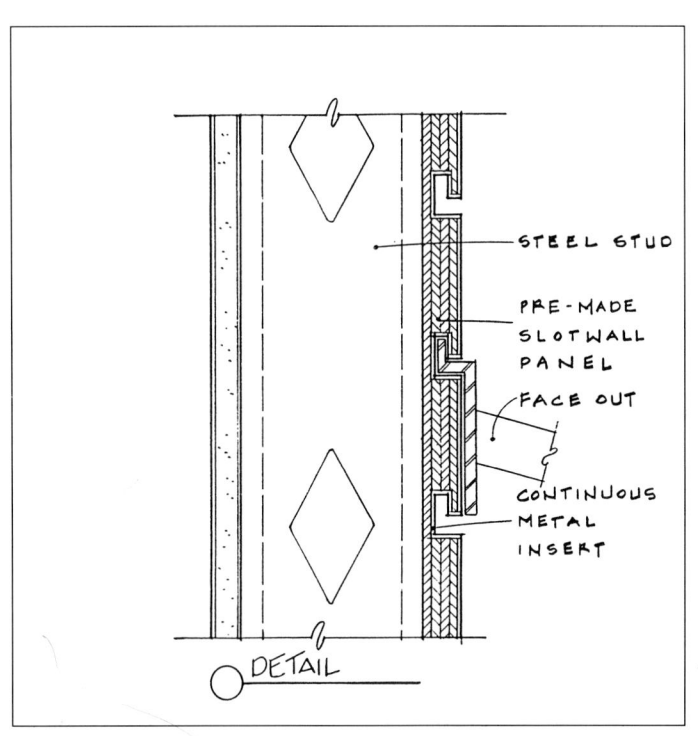

Slotwall with hardware.

Slotwall detail.

191

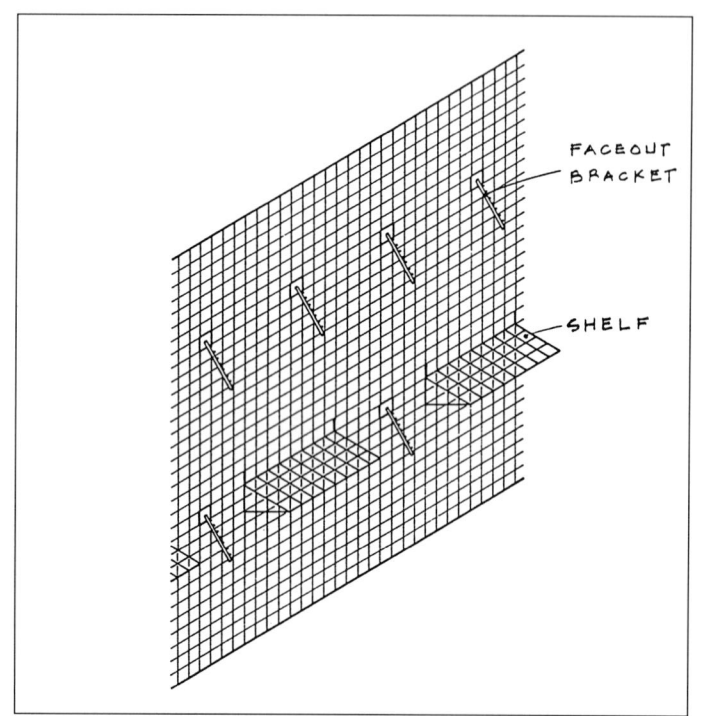

14 Retail Graphic Standards

Metal grid display wall with hardware.

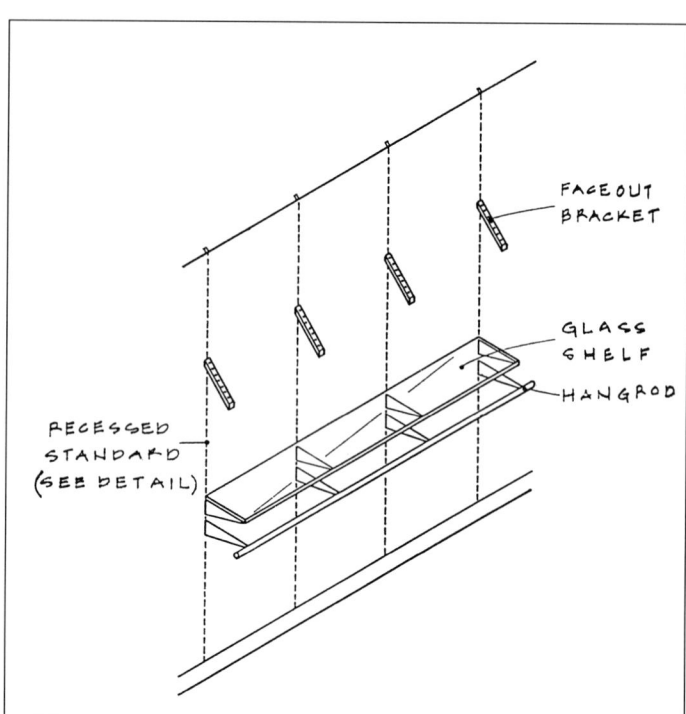

Recessed standards with hardware.

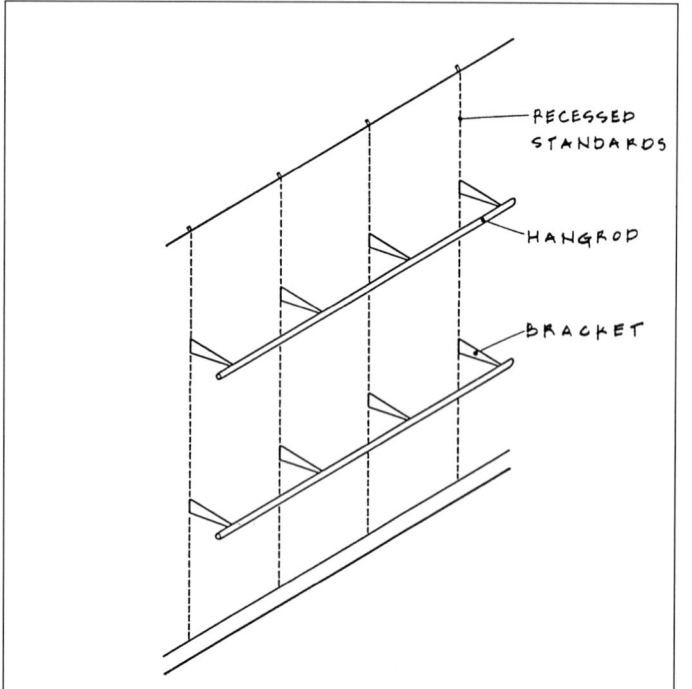

Detail, recessed standards with hardware.

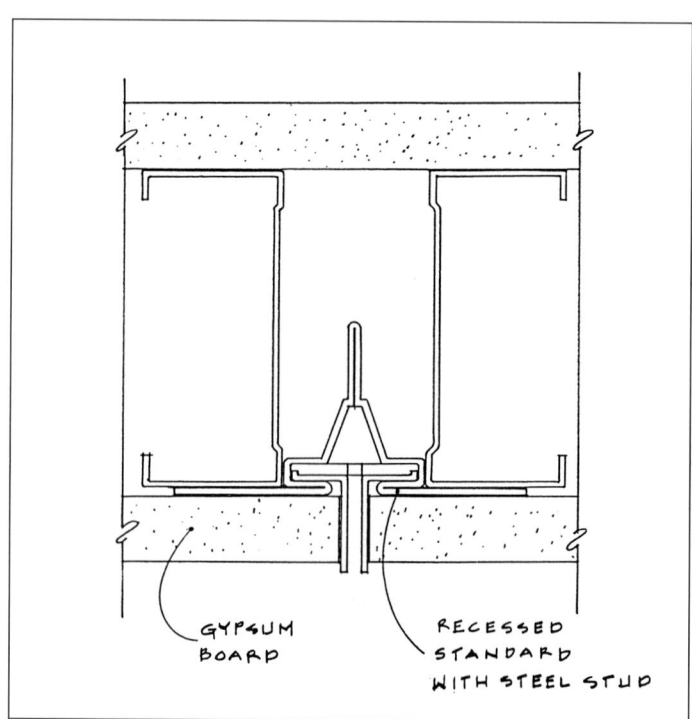

Detail, recessed standard.

Photo Credits

	Page	Photo	Photographer
Chapter 2	13	3	Elliot Fine
	14		R.Byron
	18	6	Elliot Fine
	19	7	Courtesy, The Gap, Inc
	20	8	Norman McGrath
	21	9	Courtesy, The Gap, Inc.
Chapter 3	26	2	Craig Jackson
	27	4	Wade Zimmerman
	28	7	Michael Datok
	29	9	Robert Miller
	31	11	Matt Wargo
	32	13	Lewis Tanner
	33	15	David Franzen
	34	17	Paul Gobeil
	35	20	Michael Malone
	36	22	John Vaughan
Chapter 4	37		Hedrich-Blessing
	39	1	Matt Wargo
	41	3	Rick Alexander and Associates (Tim Buchanon)
	42	4	Courtesy: Carson Pirie Scott Audio/Visual Dept.
	47	11	Mark Ross
	49		Courtesy, The Gap, Inc.
Chapter 5	51		Scott Francis
	52	1	Matt Wargo
	56	2	John Hall
	64	4	George Cott
Chapter 6	66	1	Alan Schindler
	67	2	Courtesy, Jon Greenberg & Associates
	68	3	Barbara Eliot Martin
	68	4	Barbara Eliot Martin
	69	5	Mark Ross
	70	6	Stanley Kao (NODA Inc.)
	71	8	Dave Whitcomb/RTKL
	76	10	Feature Four
	77	11	Maxwell MacKenzie
	78	12	John Hall
	79	13	Hedrich-Blessing/Jim Hedrich
	80	14	Gil Amiaga
Chapter 7	81	1, 2	R. Greg Hursley, Inc. (Courtesy of Communication Arts, Inc.)
	82	3	John Wadsworth
	82	5	William E. Mathis (Courtesy of Communication Arts, Inc.)
	85	7, 8	David Hundley/ Gerstman + Meyers, nc.
	86	9	Warren Jagger
	87	11	Bill Hodges
	88	12	R. Greg Hursley/Communication Arts, Inc.
	89	13	David Hundley/Gerstman + Meyers, Inc.
	92		Matt Wargo (Bailey BAnks & Biddle)
	93		Jeremy Preston (Royal Arcade)
	94	14	Architectural Illustrator: Andrew Hickes

193

Photo Credits

Chapter 8	95	1	Hernando Sanchez
	97	2	Scott Sutton/Sutton Photographic
	98	3	Franzen Photography
	99	5	Sadin Photography Group
	101	7	Masoe Abe
	102	8	Craig Jackson
	103	9	Scott Sutton/Sutton Photographic
	104	11	Joseph Weishar
	105	12	Stanley Kao/NODA, Inc.
	106	13	Scott Sutton/Sutton Photographic
Chapter 10	126	3	William E. Mathis
	127	4	Richard Anderson
	128	7	Robert Pisano
	131	8	Courtesy, GSGSB
Chapter 11	140	1	Tim Buchman/Rick Alexander and Associates
	143	2	John Stapleton
	144	3	John Mainka
	145, 146	4, 5, 6	Irving Weisdorf Postcard Factory, Inc.
	151	7	Rendering: Howard Associates
	152	8	Greg Hursley
	153	9	Rendering: Richard Meyer
	154	11	Ali Amuzgar
	154	12	James G. Shanley
Chapter 12	155	3	Rendering: Art Associates
	158	4	Steve Rosenthal
	163	9	Courtesy, GSGSB
	165	12	Architecural Illustrator: Andrew Hickes
	166	13	Keron Studios
	167	14	John Wadsworth
	169	17	Carson Hirschfeld
	170	18	Scott Francis
Chapter 13	184		Courtesy, The Rouse Company
Back Cover			Saks Fifth Avenue, John Hall; Boyd's, Charles E. Broudy; Strawbridge & Clothier, Matt Wargo; The Gap, Courtesy, The Gap, Inc.

194

Bibliography

Barr, Vilma and Tom Harack: "Scribner's—The Next Generation," *Retail Store Image*, Jan./Feb. 1989, pp. 24-26.

Baxter, Lynn: "Architecture and architectural graphics: missing each other at the shows," *Identity*, Summer, 1989, p. 6.

Beck, Paul E.: "Security: Finding the Right Mix," *Consulting/Specifying Engineer*, March 1990, pp. 47-60.

Berg, Eric N.: "K Mart Gambling on Renovation," *The New York Times*, March 7, 1990, p. D-1.

Fernández, Kay Harwell: "Distinctive Design enhances the Shopping Experience," *National Mall Monitor*, March, 1987, pp. 46-48.

Illuminating Engineering Society of North America: *Recommended Practice for Lighting Merchandising Areas*, New York, 1986, pp. 17, 18, 47.

International Council of Shopping Centers: "Average Shopping Center Rents," *ICSC Research Quarterly*, April, 1990, pp. 4-5; "Most Frequent Anchors in Strip Centers and Open Malls," 1988, October, 1989, p. 1.

Kornblum, Annette: "Some Customers are Always Wrong," *The New York Times Magazine*, June 10, 1990, pp. 19, 56-63.

"Lighting Costs Cut: It's All Done With Mirrors," *Chain Store Age Executive*, July, 1989, pp. 63-64.

McCain, Mark: "Seducing Customers in Highly Competitive Markets," *The New York Times*, May 7, 1989, Section 10, p. 17.

National Research Bureau: "Glossary," *Shopping Center Directory*.

Ramirez, Anthony: "Will American Shoppers Think Bigger Is Really Better?" *The New York Times*, April 1, 1990, p. 11, Section F.

Schinnerer, Victor O. & Co., Inc.: "Preserving the Record," *Guidelines for Improving Practice*, Chevy Chase, Md., Vol. VI, No. 8, pp. 1-4.

Segal, Gordon: "Crate & Barrel: Success Develops From a Unique Idea," *International Trends in Retailing*, Fall, 1986, p. 32.

Glossary

Accessibility. The ease or difficulty with which the customer reaches a given store by automobile, public transportation, or walking.

Additional markons. Upward revisions of original selling prices.

Anchors. The retail outlets in a shopping center which have the largest amount of square footage and are fundamental to the center's positioning strategy.

Attraction. The pulling force exerted by a shopping center or business district, based on merchandise availability, price advantage, physical comforts, and convenience.

Back of the house. Stockrooms; non-selling area.

Ballast. A device that modifies incoming voltage and current to provide the circuit conditions necessary to start and operate electric discharge lamps.

Book inventory. The retail value of the inventory, presumed to be correct until physical inventory is taken.

Breadth of selection. The offering of a variety of different merchandise lines in one store or shopping center.

Cashwrap. A counter that houses cash register and wrapping facilities.

Central business district (CBD). The commercial area of a city, historically of high land value; high concentration of retail and service business offices; occassional hotels and theaters; and heavy traffic flow.

Circulation plan. A plan showing expected customer movement throughout the sales areas. It is the basis for the location of fixtures, displays, sales counters, cashwrap desks, and other facilities.

Community center. A shopping center that has a wider range of facilities for the sale of soft lines (apparel) and hardlines (hardware, appliances, etc.) than a neighborhood center. Anchors are a supermarket plus a junior department store, variety store, or discount department store.

Contrast. The relationship between the brightness of an object and its immediate background.

Convenience goods. Merchandise that is consumed daily and purchased frequently, such as food and drugs.

Convenience goods shopping center. A shopping area that usually contains between 30,000 and 75,000 square feet of gross area and occupies between four and eight acres of land. The principal tenants are a supermarket and a drugstore.

Convenience goods stores. Food stores, eating and drinking places, and drug and proprietary stores.

Convenience services. A category which includes personal service facilities, such as barber shops, beauty shops, shoe repair shops, and dry cleaning shops. Like convenience goods, these services are used very frequently.

Cumulative services. The sales advantage that results when two or more compatible retail facilities are clustered together at one location rather than being widely separated.

Curtain wall. A wall that "hangs" on a structural frame. In the store interior, it may be installed above the wall cases to give it a "built-in" effect.

Depth of selection. A variety of different styles, sizes, and prices in any one given merchandise line.

Diffuser. A device commonly put on the bottom or sides of a luminaire to redirect or spread the light from a source, used to control the brightness of the source and the direction of light emitted by the luminaire.

Discount. A center in which a discount store is the major tenant in the development with additional retail space consisting of smaller retail tenants and/or a supermarket. This type of center usually draws a lower socio-economic group than an off-price center.

Disposable income. The proportion of a consumer's income that remains after expenditures for food, clothing, and shelter.

Dollar sales per square foot of sales area. The result of dividing annual sales of an area, department, or store by the number of square feet occupied by the specific area.

Double hang. Two hang rods, one over the other.

Economizer. A system of controls and duct work that permits "free" cooling of a building with outside air when the outside temperature and humidity are suitable.

Energy management system. An integrated group of products that regulate energy usage in a building. Options include load control, an environmental control system, or a combination of the two.

Environmental control system. An integrated group of products that control the building's heating, cooling, and ventilation equipment.

Exposure (or visibility). The ability of potential customers to see and recognize a store.

Face-out. A sloping hangrod that permits a waterfall effect for display of apparel, handbags, etc.

Factory outlet. Manufacturer's factory outlets, once located at the factory site, can today be found in malls or shopping centers, and often sell first-quality, current-season merchandise.

Fashion outlet. A center consisting of manufacturer's retail outlet facilities where goods are sold directly to the public in stores owned and operated by the manufacturers.

Fashion-oriented. A center comprised of apparel shops, boutiques, and hand-craft shops carrying selected merchandise, usually of high quality and high price.

Festival/entertainment. A center consisting primarily of food, specialty retailers, and entertainment facilities.

Fixed expenses. Expenses that do not fluctuate significantly despite changes in sales, service, or manufacturing activity, and normally include rent, taxes, salaries, depreciation, etc.

Fixture density. The ratio of the area occupied by the sales fixtures to the total area of the sales space. It should not exceed 50 percent of the total sales area.

Fixtures, sales. The cases and displays used for merchandise presentation and storage.

Fixtures, stock. Mass-produced display units.

Footcandle. The basic measure used to indicate level of illumination. One footcandle is equal to one unit of light flux (one lumen) distributed evenly over a 1-square-foot surface area.

Full-line department or discount store. A unit which offers a complete selection of soft goods, housewares, domestics, drugs, shoes, hardware, paints, auto supplies, sporting goods, toys, furniture, and appliances.

General merchandise stores. Retail stores that sell a number of merchandise lines, such as department stores, discount department stores, and variety stores.

Gondola. A freestanding shelving unit.

Gross leasable area. The total area designated for tenant occupancy and exclusive use, including basements, mezzanines, and upper floors; or the total area on which a tenant pays rent.

Gross margin. The amount of revenue to cover fixed costs and yield a profit after all variable costs have been deducted, determined by finding the difference between the net cost of the goods (after cash discount) and the net sales (after all price changes, workroom costs, and inventory shortages have been subtracted).

Gross margin percentage. A figure calculated by dividing the dollars of gross margin by net sales for the period.

Hardware. Shelving and hang rod metal fixturing components.

HID. High-intensity discharge lighting, including mercury-vapor, metal halide, and high-pressure sodium light sources. Low-pressure sodium lamps are often included in the HID category.

Household composition. The number, sex, and age of the people in a household.

HVAC. Heating, ventilating, and air conditioning.

Initial markon. The spread between invoice cost (plus transportation, before discount) and initial retail selling price.

Kilowatt. A measure of electric current and voltage equal to 1000 W.

Lamp. A light source, commonly called a "bulb" or "tube."

Lens. A glass or plastic shield that covers the bottom and/or sides of a luminaire to control the direction and brightness of the light.

Limited-line department or discount store. A unit which concentrates on a complete selection of soft goods, house-wares, drugs, and shoes.

Louver. A series of baffles arranged in a geometric pattern, used to shield a lamp from view at certain angles to avoid glare.

Luminaire. A complete lighting fixture including one or more lamps and a means for connection to a power source. Many luminaires also include one or more ballasts and elements to position and protect lamps and distribute their light.

Magnet. The store in a shopping center or district that is the prime attractive force drawing customers to the center or district.

Major retail center (MRC). A concentration of at least one general merchandise store with a minimum of 100,000 square feet of floor space.

Major shopping district. A shopping area that contains one or more major magnets or large department store units.

Mall shops. Stores in a regional shopping center other than the major department stores, typically located between two anchor stores.

Markdowns. Downward revisions of selling prices.

Market penetration. The amount of personal consumption expenditures which a retail operation or complex captures in a specific market area. Also called "share of the market."

Market positioning strategy. A marketing strategy that promotes an "image" of the store or shopping center to its patrons.

Merchandise mix. The types of merchandise offered for sale in a retail facility.

Merchandise planning. An analysis of merchandising records and achievements, leading to attainment of higher merchandising goals.

Mezzanine (or balcony). An area that equals less than 50 percent of the first floor and is above and open to that floor. Before completing plans, the local and state building codes relating to exits, ceiling height, and other conditions should be checked.

Minor shopping district. A shopping district which combines a minor magnet–a junior department store, a large apparel store, or specialty shoppers' goods facilities–with convenience goods facilities.

Mixed-use development. A large-scale real estate project with: three or more revenue-producing uses which are mutually supporting and developed as a unit (retail, office, residential, hotel/motel, recreation); functional and physical integration of project components, including pedestrian connections; and development in conformance with a coherent plan.

Multiple packing. Items bought packaged in units of two's or three's, such as sheets and pillowcases.

Neighborhood center. A shopping area that provides for the sale of convenience goods (foods, drugs, sundries) and personal services (laundry, barbering, shoe repair) for the day-to-day needs of the immediate neighborhood. It is often built around a supermarket, which is the principal tenant.

Net income. Income before income taxes, determined by deducting from net sales or net revenue all the expenses for the year or the accounting period under study.

Net selling area. The area devoted to retail sales, not including storage, mechanical, or office space.

Off-price. A center consisting of retail stores that offer brand name goods found in conventional stores at 20 percent to 70 percent below manufacturers' suggested prices. Off-price store merchandise is generally of higher quality than discount store goods.

Open-to-buy. The value of merchandise, at retail, that can be added to inventory at a given time without exceeding planned figures.

Operating profit. The amount remaining after expenses are subtracted from gross margin.

Overcounter selling. The presentation of merchandise to a shopper by a salesperson stationed behind a showcase or counter.

Pedestrian circulation. The pattern of pedestrian movements between shopping facilities.

Primary market population. The population residing in a retail center's primary trade area, the geographic area responsible for 60 to 70 percent of the center's traffic.

Primary shoppers' goods. Merchandise with a cost, rate of depletion, and frequency of purchase in-between that of convenience goods and secondary shoppers' goods. Apparel, shoes, and books, are examples.

Productivity. Annual sales per square foot of gross leasable area.

R-factor. Resistance of an insulating material to heat flow. The higher the R-factor, or R-value, the more efficient the insulator.

Reflector. A device used to redirect the light from a lamp or luminaire by the process of reflection.

Regional center. Provides shopping goods, general merchandise, apparel, furniture and home furnishings in full depth and variety. It is often built around one full-line department store with a minimum GLA of 100,000 square feet. A typical regional center has a GLA of 400,000 square feet, and can contain more than 1 million square feet.

Rounders. Circular hanging racks.

Glossary

Secondary shoppers' goods. Big-ticket items, including furniture, major appliances, and automobiles. Because of their cost and long life, these goods are purchased less frequently than primary shoppers' goods. Consumers typically travel greater distances to shop for secondary goods than for other types of goods.

Self-service. Merchandise that is on open display for shopper selection without sales help.

Set appeal. The attractiveness of articles sold in sets, such as dinnerware.

Shopping center. A group of architecturally-unified commercial establishments planned, developed, owned, and managed as an operating unit, and providing on-site parking.

Shopping district. A shopping area of varied composition. Business districts are known as "unplanned centers," and new shopping centers are normally referred to as "planned developments."

Standard metropolitan statistical area (SMSA). Metropolitan areas defined by the Federal Government for purposes of data reporting and allocations of certain Federal grants.

Standards and brackets. Adjustable metal hardware that supports shelving and hang rods.

Stock overage. A condition in which the physical inventory of a store or a department is higher than the book inventory.

Stock shortage. A condition in which the physical inventory of a store or department yields a lower retail figure than the book value.

Stock turn (*See* Turnover).

Strip center. A line of stores often identified by an outdoor canopy.

Super-regional center. A shopping area that provides an extensive variety of comparison goods, services and recreational facilities. It is built around at least three major department stores no less than 100,000 square feet each and contains about 750,000 square feet of GLA.

Theme/specialty. Shopping centers with features that distinguish them from other centers: architecturally unified shops; restaurant and entertainment facilities; strong tourist appeal; or tenants that offer unusual merchandise.

Time-of-day. A calendar clock pre-programmed to turn designated equipment on and off at specific times.

Trade area. The geographic region from which the continuing patronage of a shopping area or store is obtained.

Trading up. Shifting a portion of the merchandising emphasis from lower-price lines to the top of the scale.

Turnover. The number of stock turns achieved in a year. The more frequently merchandise is sold, replaced and sold again, the more profitable the merchandising operation will be.

Valance. A horizontal band that shields lights which are directed on merchandise; or, a sign band above products.

Variable expenses. Expenses, or costs, which vary in total in direct proportion to production or sales volume. Raw materials, cost of merchandise, piecework labor, and sales commissions are examples.

Index

AM Partners Inc., 33, 98
Abraham & Straus (A & S), 70, 71, 92
Accessory Place, 97
Adams, James, 128
Addis and Dey's, 68
Advertising (*see* Promotion)
Airport shops, 167
Ala Moana Shopping Center, 33
Alcott & Andrews, 69
Allan, Stanley N., 158
Anchor stores, 142
Ann Taylor, 18, 50, 75
Antonio Parriego, 93
Architectural retail, 88
Architecture Group, The, 17
Architectural Woodwork Institute, 59
Arizona Center, 156
Armstrong, Elizabeth, 34
Arnell, Peter, 164
Arnell/Bickford Associates, 164
Artlines, 33
Atrium Shop, 82
Atrium at Chestnut Hill, The, 154
Awnings (*see* Entranceways)
Bailey Banks & Biddle, 92
Banana Republic, 44, 85
Banners, 92
Barneys New York, 12
Barteluce, Daniel J., AIA, 152, 165
Bayside Marketplace, 81
B. Dalton Bookseller, 82
Benetton, 185
Bennet, Anne E., ASID, 78
Bennet-Wallace, 78
Bergdorf Goodman, 16, 179
Beltrami, 44
Beverly Center, 50
Bloomingdale's, 16, 51, 159
    Bloomie's Express, 167
Blum, Leslie Design, Inc., 83
Bobick, Michael G., AIA, 131
Boyd's, 9, back cover
Bridges, Robert J., 80
Bridges & Lavin Architects, AIA, 16, 80, 177
Bridgewater Commons, 39, 88
Brown, Terry, 169
Bucarian, 93
Burdine's, 185
Carpenter, Earl E., 125
Carrefours, 162
Carson Pirie Scott & Co, 42
Caruso, Ingrid, 28
Cashwrap station, 103, 112
Ceilings:
    lighting, 69
    materials and finishes, 63
    renovating, 126-7
    types, 55
Chains:
    specialty, 165, 175
    units within department stores, 164
Cherry Creek Mall, 160
Chevy Chase Pavillion, 157
Clark Harris Tribble & Li Architects, 151, 157
Cline Bettridge Bernstein Lighting Design, Inc., 70, 71

Coach Leatherwear, 29
Coffee Grinder, The, 27
Coffin, R. F. Enterprises, Inc., 139
Color, basic store program, 51-64
    in displays, 106
    in light, 72, 74
    psychology, 57
    as selling aid, 58-59
Comme des Garçons/Shirt, 46
Communication Arts Incorporated, 81, 88
Construction manager, 130
Construction, 119-138
    checklist, 133-136
    costs, 120
    do's and don'ts, 129
    insurance-approved security, 118
    legal considerations for, 129-136
    schedule, 121-124
    of shopping centers and tenant stores, 147-154
Contempo Casuals, 177
Contemporary Arts Center, 168-169
Contract, 129-32
    for shopping centers, 153
    (*See also* Tenant Manual)
Cope Linder Associates, 153
Cove lighting, 66, 68, 70
Covell Matthews Wheatley, 151
Crabtree & Evelyn, Toronto, 76
Cranford, Gregory, AIA, 151
Crate & Barrel, 11
Crawford McWilliams Hatcher Architects, Inc., 139
Cross Gates Mall, 13
Cross Keys Village Shopping Center, 127
Crosson, Michael, 106
Customer profile, 4, 176, 181, 185
D'Oria, Marian, 99
DFW Consulting Group, Inc., 108-110
DKNY, 164
Dalton Moran Shook Architecture Inc., 41, 140
Dalton, Terry E., AIA, 41Deane, T., 39
Deloitte and Touche, 174
Dennis, Brian, 145
Department stores, 40, 186
    chains within, 164
Design & Planning/Interiors, 27
Design consultants, 94, 129-130
Design West, 34
Destination point, 2, 38, 40, 184
Differentiation strategy, 2, 81, 177
Dill, Kevin E., 20
Directional retail, 88
Displays, 12, 95-106, 112
    electronic, 86
    fixtures, 103
    island, 5, 180
    lighting, 68, 69, 72, 78, 79, 180
    manufacturers', 5
    security measures, 117
    visual, 6
    wall, 5
    windows, 78-79
    (*See also* Showcase)
Dole Kids Shop, 98
Donohoe Companies, The, 157
Dorf, Martin E. and Associates, 66

Dressing rooms (*see* Fitting rooms)
Drexler, Millard S., 172-173
Dumas-Hermés, Rena, 20
Duty Free Shoppers, 165
Ebstein, Barbara, FASID, 86
Ed Mitchell's, 104
Eddie Bauer, 128
Elder Craftsmen, The, 78
Electronic article surveillance, (EAS), 7, 117-118
Electronics Boutique, 13
Energy conservation: codes, 67, 150
    lighting, 66, 70, 71, 73, 76, 80
    HVAC systems, 107-111
Entranceways:
    arches, 131, 140
    awnings and canopies, 44-45, 79
    doorways, 45-46
    graphics, 88
    lighting, 79, 80, 86
    vestibules, 46-47, 113, 118
    (*See also* Facades)
Environmental considerations, 41, 119, 120-121
Episode, 36, 99, 113
Equipment:
    marking and pricing, 113
    merchandise transfer, 113
    receiving, 112
    storage, 113
    security, 117-118
Exterior:
    entranceways, 44-46
    lighting, 47
    materials, 42, 43
    programming, 3
    signs, 87, 90-91
    Store Design, 37-50
    windows, 42, 44
Facades, 39, 71, 79, 165 (*See also* Entranceways)
Fashion Centre, The, 82
Faunce Corner Crossing Shopping Center, 18
Finishes, 51-64
    for signs, 87
    types, 60-64
    trade associations, 59
Fiorino, Nella, 76, 101
Fire prevention (*see* Safety concerns)
First Issue, 32
Fisher, Ellen S., 27
Fitting rooms, 116, 182
Fitzpatrick Design Group, 51, 167
Fitzpatrick, Jay, 51, 167
Fixtures:
    construction and design of, 121, 123, 124, 128
    display, 103
Floors:
    functions, 112
    lighting, 66, 68
    materials and finishes, 54, 59-61
    renovating, 126-127
    salesfloor, 104, 124, 180
Fluorescent lighting (*see* Lighting)
Food courts, 150, 163, 165
Food store design, 170
Footcandle level, 71, 72, 76, 79
Franklin Mills, 147

199

Index

GSGSB, 131, 163
Galleria Vittorio Emanuele II, 142, 143
Galleria, The (Tyson's II), 17
Gap, The, 14, 21, 45, 155, 172-173, back cover
Gap Kids, 100
Gardens, The, 67
George, Fred, 18
Gersin, Robert P. Associates, 28
Gerstman + Meyers, Inc., 85, 89
Gerstman, Richard, 85, 89
Gordon Company, The, 37
Gordon, Harris, 174-175
Gosses, Ron D., 106
Government-sponsored projects, 158
Graphics (*see* Signs)
Great Northern Mall, 68
Green Acres Mall, 163
Greenberg, Jon & Associates, Inc., 67, 97, 103, 106, 112
Gross Building Area, 141
Gruber, Thomas S., 39
Hahn Company, The, 88
Hahn Shoes, 17
Haight, Susan, 184
Hambrecht Terrell International, Inc., 82, 99, 152, 165
Hardman, Craig, 128
Hayden, Michael, 89
Hearst Business Comunications, Inc., 59
Hellmuth, Obata & Kassabaum, P.C., 64, 126
Hemisphere, 19, 48-49
Henkelman, Steven W., AIA, 153
Hermés, 20
Herndon, Thomas, ISP, 161
Hess's, Greenbrier Mall, 105
Heuer Law Group, 129
Heuer, Charles R., Esq., AIA, 129-132
Hocker, David & Associates, Inc., 148
Hodges, Bill, 87
Holly Hill Mall, 140
Honeybee, 92
Horton Plaza, 44
Hume, Christopher, 178
Humes, Paul, 128
HVAC system, 107-111, 117, 118, 20, 130, 134, 147
Hypermarkets, 162
Illuminated Engineering Society of North America, 72, 73, 74
Image continuity, 82, 85, 99, 175, 184-185
Impulse purchasing, 6, 112
Insurance (*see* Construction; Contract)
Interior:
 construction, 133
 elements of, 15
 Shaping the Store's, 9-22
 signage, 91
 traffic flow, diagram, 6
International Council of Shopping Centers, (ICSC), 140-142
International Design Group Inc., 76, 92, 93, 101, 176
Investment dressing, 177, 183
Italian Marble Center, 64
J.C. Penney, 140, 177, 186
JMB Urban Development, 140

Jackson, Craig, 26, 102
Jacob, Paul, AIA, 79
Jahn, Helmut, 89
Jerde Partnership, Inc., 150
Jerde, John, 159
Joslin's, 106
Jung, Yu Sing, FAIA, 154
Jung/Brannen Associates, Inc., 154
K-mart Corp., 120
Kagan, Leonard, AIA, 71
Kawakami, Gary K., AIA, 33
Kenzo, 93
King of Prussia Shopping Center, 39
Kirmani, Minhaj, PE, 154
Knight, Christopher, AIA, 157
Knogo Corporation, The, 116, 118
Knott's Camp Snoopy, 147, 159
Kraft Dairy Group, 89
Kroeger Supermarkets, 89
LED signs, 86
Landesz, Karl J., 158
Landmark:
 lighting, 70
 storefront, 82
Laura Ashley, 184
Lavin, Don, AIA, 16, 80
Layouts, basic store, 23-36
 construction, 119, 123, 153
 multiple store, 128
 receiving, 113
 tenant storefront, 148-149
Legal codes, 94, 129-136, 147-150
Lerner New York, 67
Lerner Woman, 103
Lighting, 65-80
 exterior, 40, 44, 47, 79-80
 cove, 66, 68, 69, 70
 colored, 72, 74, 79
 display, 68, 69, 78
 fluorescent, 67, 69, 70, 71, 74, 75, 6, 77, 80
 halogen, 74, 76
 lamp comparison, 65
 landmark, 70
 limitations, 150 mirrors, 68
 nighttime, 79
 planning, 7, 69, 73, 76
 windows, 78-79
Limited, The, 67, 83, 177, 185, 186
Liz Claiborne, Inc., 32, 106, 186
Loheed, Philip, 158
Los Angeles Dodgers Shop, 86
Lucky's Supermarket, 87, 170
MacLachlan, Ron, 76
Macy's, 10, 131, 159, 185, 186
Mail order catalogs, 177, 185
Maintenance, 56
 HVAC, 107-111
 lighting, 80
Mall of America, 147, 159
Malls (*see* Shopping Centers)
Malone, Michael, AIA, 119
Mannequins, 67, 69, 99, 106, 117, 25
MARKETPLACE 2000, 182

Marshall Field's, 99, 116, 144
Materials:
 basic store program, 51-64
 ceiling, 55
 display case, 99
 exterior, 42
 flooring, 54
 security system, 53
 signs, 89-91
 types, 60-64
 trade unions, 59
McCrory's, 177
McKown, Zack, AIA, 166
McMullen Creek Market, 41
Megamalls, 159
Meline, Ken, PE, 108-111
Melvin Simon & Associates, Inc., 71, 145, 159
Merchandise:
 characteristics of, 3
 displays (*see* Displays)
 movement, 112
 preparation, 113
 siting, diagram, 6
 transfers, 113
Message, 16
Minimalist design, 166
Mirrors:
 lighting, 68
 as security measure, 117
Mirviss, Lois, 56, 125, back cover
Mixed-use developments, 156, 157
Motherhood, 83
Museum Shops, 168
Myers, Laurent, AIA, 77
Naccari, Randall, 139
Nakaoka, J.T., AIA, 16
Nan Duskin, 30, 31, 52, 127
Narva, Kenneth D., 94
Nashville Tent & Awning Co., 87
National Association of Display Industries, 64
National Association of Store Fixture Manufacturers, 64
NBBJ/ Retail Concepts, 128
Neiman-Marcus, 125, 160-161
Neimark, Ira, 16, 179
Neon, 68, 71, 88-89, 99, 105, 152, 162, 167
New Orleans Centre, 64
New Vision Studios, Inc., 83, 104
Nisch, Kenneth, 67, 97
Nordstrom, 12, 37, 113, 159
Northcross Mall, 152
Norwood Oliver Design Associates, Inc., 70, 105
Obata, Gyo, FAIA, 126
Oliver, Norwood, 105
Olssen's Books and Records, 77
Owings Mills Town Center, 79
Pavilions Shopping Center, 45
Parking area, 40
 lighting for, 79
Patri, Piero, 37
Pea in the Pod, 119, 178-179
Pfaltzgraff Store, 35, 59

200

Pfeiffer & Miro Associates, 68
Plainview Centre, 94
Plan:
   circular, 169
   curved, 25, 36, 180
   diagonal, 24, 32, 35
   geometric, 32, 34, 251
   pathway, 24, 35
   straight, 24, 26, 27, 29
   varied, 25, 28, 31, 33
   (*See also* Program; Layouts)
Planned Expansion Group, 13, 94
Plumbing, 135, 137
Plymouth Lamston Stores, 97
Point-of-sale:
   displays, 105, 181
   signage, 82-83, 88
Pricing, 5, 113
Priory Meadow, 151
PRO Hardware, 85
Program, 1-8
   checklist, 3–5
   construction, 120-124
   pre-programming, 2
   presentation of, 8
   for support system, 112
   for security system, 116
Promenade, The, 76
Promotion, 82
   through signage, 82-83, 85
Raleigh's, 18
Receiving:
   contruction considerations for, 134
   diagram, 7
   equipment and layout, 112
Rena Dumas Architecture Interieure, 20
Renovation, 12, 124, 126, 185, 186
   projects:
     Bergdorf Goodman, 179
     Holly Hill Mall,140
     Lucky Supermarket, 170
     Nan Duskin, 127
     Neiman-Marcus,125, 160-161
     Park City Center, 153
Revlon Inc., 95, 180-181
Riggings, J., 28
River Chase Galleria, 131
Robert Lee Morris Gallery, 92
Robert Young Associates, Inc., 161
Rosen, Dana and Marcello, 178-179
Rosenblum-Harb Architects, 29
Rouse Company, The, 29, 81, 126, 145, 156, 184
Royal Star Arcade, 93
RTKL Associates, Inc., 39, 71, 77, 79, 92
Rubano Mirviss Associates, 56, 125, back cover
Sackler Gallery Museum
Sanchez, Hernando, 180-181
Shop, 11
Sadow's, 34
Safety concerns, 53, 120
   fire code requirements, 64, 87, 147,150
   fire resistancy, 121
   food and health codes, 147, 150
Safety Zone, The 86
Saks Fifth Avenue, 56, 80, back cover

Sales per square foot, 141, 165, 179, 181
San Francisco Centre, 37, 113
Samuel Pebys, 101
Sanders, D.F., 26, 102
Savannah Mall, The, 139
Schinnerer, Victor O. & Co., 124, 129
Scribner's Bookstore, 82
Sears, Roebuck & Co., 120, 159
Seasonal considerations: program, 5
   for storefront, 42
Security system, 107, 116-118
   diagram, 7
   electronic article surveillance (EAS), 7, 117-118
   equipment, 117-118
   glass, 117
   lighting, 80, 116
   planning objectives, 116
   signage, 86
   visual surveillance, 116
Segal, Gordon, 11
Service:
   customer, 114, 112, 182
   self-, 12, 116
   types, 4
Shealy, Lewis C., 116
Sheppard Line subway, 178
Shook, Charles Terry, AIA, 140
Shop & Display Equipment Association, 64
Shopping Centers, 139-154, 177
   anchors, 142, 184
   construction, 153
   food courts, 150, 163
   hypermarkets, 162
   rents, 141
   tenant's criteria, 139, 147-150
Short Hills Mall, 32
Showcases, 112
   lighting of, 68, 72
   modular, 158
   renovating, 124-5
   security measures for, 116
Signage, 5, 40, 50, 170
   characteristics, 90-91
   consultants, 94
   Do's and Don'ts, 87
   electronic, 85, 89, 94, 150
   fabrication, 89
   international, 92
   lighting, 79-80
   ordinances and codes, 94, 150
   point-of-sale, 82-83, 88, 91
   for security, 86
   Signs and Graphics, 81-91
Silverstein Properties, Inc., 71
Site, 38
   contracting, 129-130, 147
   merchandising, 6
   programming, 4
   selection, 38, 40
Skylights, 68, 153, 163
Smithsonian Institution, 11
Solutions Through Partnership, 178
South Street Seaport Mall, 29
Southcenter Mall, 128

Space:
   diagrams, 6,7
   preparation, 113
   problematic, 77, 113
   programming, 4
   sculptural, 100, 169
   storage, 112
   support (*see* Support system)
Specialty stores, 141, 156, 165, 183, 86 (*See also* Chains)
Stairways, 75, 100, 113
Stagl, Paul, 178
Storage:
   remote, 5
   diagram, 7
   equipment, 113
   space, 112
Stockroom (*see* Storage)
Storefront:
   construction, 133
   differentiation, 81
   materials, 39, 42
   regulations, 150
   tenant designs, 148-149
   texture, 79
   (*See also* Entranceways, Exterior)
Strawbridge & Clothier, 39, 144
Strip centers, 94, 141, 142
Suburban Square, 144
Sunderland, Maurice, Architects, Inc., 145
Support system, 112-115
   basic functions of, 112
   for building operations, 115
   for customer services, 114
   for staff, 114
   for storage, 5, 7
Syska & Hennessy, 71
Systems, 107-118
   HVAC, 108-111
   security, 116-118
   support, 112-115
Takahashi, Brian T., AIA, 98
Tao, Richard, 151
Tenant Manual, 139, 147-149, 150
Terry Brown Architect, 169
Thomas Consultants, 178
Thompson, Benjamin & Associates, Inc., 158
Timex Store, 86
Topaz, 66
Toronto Star, The, 178
Trade associations, 59, 63
Tri-County Mall, 28
Triple Five Corporation, Ltd., 145, 159
Trumbull Shopping Park, 86
Trump Tower, 44
Tsao & McKown Architects, 166
Tsao, Calvin, 166
Turk, Cynthia Cohen, 182-183
Tyson's II, The Galleria, 17
Union Station:
   St. Louis, 82, 126, 145
   Washington D.C., 158
Vestibules (*see* Entranceways)

Index

Vidi, Vici, 47
Vincent, Sammy L., AIA, 17
Vinick Associates, Inc., 11, 86
Vinick, Bernard S., FASID, 11
Visual merchandizing, 104-106
Walker Group/CNI, 16, 170
Walker, Kenneth H., AIA, 16, 170
Wallace, Gordon T.H., 78
Wall:
   displays, 5
   lighting, 66, 68
   materials and finishes, 56, 59-63
   renovating, 126-127
Weese, Harry and Associates, 158
Weidlinger Associates, 16, 154
Weishar, Joseph, 83, 104
Wendel, Till, AIA, 64
West Edmonton Mall, 145-146
Whisler-Patri, 20, 37, 113
Willowbrook Mall, 66
Windows, 42
   display, 44, 78
   etched glass, 88
   graphics, 88
   lighting, 72, 78-79
   security glass, 117
Wolf, Larry, M., 184
Wood:
   ceilings, 126
   finishes, 59, 60, 62-64
   fixtures, 101
   floors, 54-56, 125, 126
   walls, 126
Young, Robert Associates, Inc., 18, 161
Zeckendorf Companies, 71
Zolatone, 56

About the Authors

Vilma Barr is an author and editor of books on design, a contributor to design publications and communications consultant to design firms. Ms. Barr and co-author Charles E. Broudy collaborated on the first edition of *Designing to Sell* (1986) and have led seminars in store planning and design for Drexel University, the International Council of Shopping Centers, and the National Retail Merchants Association.

    She received a B.S. in Business Administration from Drexel University, and an S.M. from the Massachusetts Institute of Technology. Ms. Barr has held editorial management positions with several leading design organizations, and is currently Director of Communications for CUH2A, a Princeton, N.J. architectural/engineering/interior design firm. She is also a consultant to Business/Professional Editorial Services, Inc., New York, and is writing a new book, *The Best of Neon*.

    Professional memberships include the American Society of Interior Designers (press), and the Society for Marketing Professional Services.

Charles E. Broudy, FAIA, heads Charles E. Broudy & Associates, P.C., an architectural and planning firm specializing in merchandising facilities, with offices in Philadelphia and Dallas. His firm has created over 1,500 specialty shops, department stores, chain units, shopping centers, art galleries, museum shops, and showrooms in the U.S. and overseas, and has won several awards for its designs.

    Mr. Broudy's client list includes Ann Taylor, The Gap, Nan Duskin, Hart Schaffner & Marx, Johnston & Murphy, Boyd's in Philadelphia, and museum stores for The Carnegie, Pittsburgh, The Smithsonian Institution, Washington, D.C., and the John F. Kennedy Library, Boston.

    He has served as a seminar leader with Ms. Barr for the ICSC, NRMA, and Drexel University, and for *Architectural Record*. Mr. Boudy organized and taught a course for professionals on "Shopping Center and Retail Store Design" at the Harvard University Graduate School of Design. A graduate of Drexel University, he is a member and past president of the Philadelphia Chapter of the American Institute of Architects.